DATE DUE

The Recollections of Philander Prescott

The Recollections of
Philander Prescott
Frontiersman of the Old Northwest
1819–1862

Edited by

DONALD DEAN PARKER

UNIVERSITY OF NEBRASKA PRESS · LINCOLN

Publishers on the Plains

UNP

MANUFACTURED IN THE UNITED STATES OF AMERICA

To my wife, Florence Myrtle Patterson Parker
and my parents,
Albert George Parker, 1863–1937
and
Jessie Bewley Parker, 1867–1944

Introduction

In the history of the United States that tenuous line of advance settlement known as the frontier has played a particularly decisive role in shaping the nation. The American frontiersman, perhaps because of the unique challenges he faced, has captured the imagination of generations. Yet although the warrior, the explorer, the missionary, have been idealized and romanticized in legend and lore, it was the "common man," the man who sought neither fame nor fortune nor the glory of God but simply a day-to-day livelihood, who typified the spirit of the frontier.

The Northwest Territory and the lands immediately beyond the Mississippi River represented in 1819 the farthest reaches of the frontier; it was a vast area only sparsely populated by Indians, fur traders, and a small number of United States troops. The region encompassing the present states of Wisconsin, Minnesota, and Iowa, and the northern portion of Illinois had been known to white explorers since the 1650's, when the French traders Radisson and Groseilliers made two journeys into the "upper country" to investigate the possibilities for a remunerative fur trade. They were followed in 1673 by Father Jacques Marquette and Louis Jolliet, who reached the mouth of the Wisconsin River and discovered the great Mississippi. Six years later, in 1679, Daniel Greysolon, Sieur du Lhut, planted the banner of France in the principal village of the Sioux tribe near Mille Lacs; and the next year Father Louis Hennepin's party explored the upper Mississippi country and discovered and named the Falls of St. Anthony.

From 1682, when Robert Cavalier de La Salle claimed, in the name of the King of France, the territory drained by the Mississippi and its tributaries, to the outbreak of the French and Indian War in 1754, French supremacy in the region remained virtually unchallenged. In 1763, with the signing of the Treaty of Paris ending the war, possession of the area passed to England. Although the British established a number of forts there, conditions in the Old Northwest remained essentially the same: except for the French-Canadian and British fur traders, the area was practically devoid of white habitation.

In the Treaty of Paris of 1783, at the end of the American Revolution, England ceded to the United States all her lands east of the Mississippi and north to the Great Lakes; the British, however, continued to incite Indian depredations against frontier settlements. In 1794, at the Battle of Fallen Timbers, near the British Fort Miami, "Mad Anthony" Wayne's army soundly defeated an Indian force which had been led to expect assistance from the British, who instead allowed them to suffer defeat. With the surrender of British posts in the Northwest Territory the same year and the conclusion of the Treaty of Greenville with the chiefs of the major Indian tribes the next year, the way was opened for white settlement of the country.

The Louisiana Purchase in 1803 added vast lands west of the Mississippi to the frontier. Two years later, in 1805, Lieutenant Zebulon Montgomery Pike led an expedition to the mouths of the Minnesota and St. Croix rivers and became the first official to assert United States authority over the area. Nevertheless, the British still exerted a major influence in the upper Mississippi region, from Prairie du Chien northward; during the War of 1812 they re-established forts in the Northwest and induced the Indians to side with them. Under the terms of the Treaty of Ghent in 1814, Great Britain renounced all claim to trade south of the Canadian border, and soon thereafter the last British garrison on the upper Mississippi evacuated Prairie du Chien. In 1816 Congress passed an act excluding foreigners from participating in the fur trade, except in subordinate capacities under American supervisors.

The United States government, eager to enforce the provisions of this act and to ensure the loyalty of the Indians, established Fort Howard at Green Bay and Fort Crawford at Prairie du Chien the same year, 1816. Green Bay and Prairie du Chien were still the only white settlements on the upper Mississippi in 1819, when Lieutenant Colonel Henry Leavenworth began construction of a small military post, called Camp New Hope, just below the confluence of the

Minnesota and Mississippi rivers. A year later the troops were moved across the Mississippi to Camp Cold Water, located beside a large spring just north of the mouth of the Minnesota. That same year Colonel Josiah Snelling succeeded Leavenworth and immediately began work on a permanent post, Fort St. Anthony, on the bluffs overlooking both rivers. In 1825 the name was changed to Fort Snelling, but the general area of the fort was known as St. Peter's. Mendota, a fur-trade headquarters, soon grew up just below the fort, on the south bank of the Mississippi.

One of the major duties of the garrison was to keep peace among the warring Indian factions—the Mdewakantons, Wahpekutes, Sissetons, and Wahpetons, all comprising the Santee division of the Sioux, or Dakotas, numbering about 3,800; the Winnebagos, also a Siouan tribe; the Chippewas, an Algonquian tribe about eight times as numerous as the Sioux, their hereditary enemies; the Menominees, closely allied to the Chippewas; and the Sauks and Foxes. According to tradition, the Sioux had occupied the upper Mississippi area for several hundred years. As the Iroquois, beginning about the middle of the seventeenth century, had driven the Chippewas from their homes along the St. Lawrence River, the Sioux were gradually pushed westward and southward. Pressed by the steady encroachment of the white man, the tribes were in fierce competition for food and land. Although the Indians had been in contact with white fur traders, many of whom had taken Indian wives, for nearly two centuries, they had largely retained their tribal customs.

The fur trade, which depended heavily on Indian help, was monopolized in the upper Mississippi area of 1819 by the Hudson's Bay Company and the American Fur Company. Under the rules of the trade, each fall the traders extended to the Indians credits in the form of guns, ammunition, traps, and other supplies. In the spring the Indians returned with the pelts they had collected during the winter and repaid their credits. An Indian who failed to pay off his debt in full might be extended further credits for the coming season by the trader to whom he was already indebted, but he was not allowed to work for another trader. Consequently, many Indians were held in virtual bondage by the traders. Rivalry was keen among the fur companies, and the traders often resorted to trickery, even treachery, to outdo their opposition.

With the stationing of troops in the Northwest, there arose a need

for supplying the military communities with various items, both
necessities and luxuries, not furnished by the Army. For each fort
the government appointed an official civilian sutler whose business
it was to supply these items at a reasonable cost. The sutler, usually
an established merchant of some means, held a position of importance: he was often the garrison's only contact with the outside
world.

In 1819, Louis Devotion, a French merchant from Detroit, secured
the sutler's post at Camp New Hope, the forerunner of Fort Snelling.
Working in Devotion's Detroit store as an apprentice was Zachariah
Wright Prescott, and it is his younger brother Philander whose
adventures are recounted in the following pages. Born in 1801 in
Phelps, Ontario County, New York, Philander was the fourth child
of six and the youngest son of Dr. Joel and Lucy Reed Prescott. His
father died in 1811, leaving the family in rather poor circumstances,
so young Prescott probably received no more than a grade-school
education. The year after his mother's death in 1818, Philander,
unable to find work at home, decided to join his brother in Detroit.
There he was employed by Louis Devotion and subsequently went to
Camp New Hope as a sutler's clerk. Thus it was that Philander
Prescott chanced to witness, and to become a part of, the events that
shaped the history of the northwestern frontier for forty-three years,
from 1819 to 1862.

A Note on the Editing
The text follows Prescott's longhand manuscript except for the
division into sentences, paragraphs, and parts or chapters. In several
places, for the sake of clarity, shifts have been made in order to keep
chronological order.

Errors in syntax have been allowed to stand. The spelling, punctuation, and capitalization, although inconsistent and sometimes in-
correct, have been followed with only a few exceptions.

Any words or letters supplied by the editor are enclosed in
brackets. When it was evident that Philander Prescott was confused in
the recording of dates, the editor has endeavored to correct the error.

Prescott wrote a brief autobiography which was published by the
Minnesota Historical Society in 1894. Material from it which does
not duplicate data in the longer manuscript has been incorporated
here in italic type, enclosed in brackets.

Contents

A section of illustrations follows page 82.
Maps follow pages 40, 90, and 160.

The Recollections of
Philander Prescott

An asterisk (*), whether it occurs in the text or in a footnote, indicates that additional information may be found in the supplement at the end of the chapter.

I

1819–1820

Journey to the Northwest

To His Excellency, Governor Alexander Ramsey, Governor of Minnesota:

The object of this work is to give a short history, or reminiscences, of the author's first travels from the State of New York to the Minnesota country.

In the year [1819], April 19th, I left my native place, Phelps town, Ontario County. At this time my brother, Z. W. Prescott, was living at Detroit, Michigan Territory, clerking in the sutler's store for the Troops. My brother wrote me to come to Detroit and assist him in the Store, and accordingly I left home on the above date.

My sisters prepared a large bundle of provisions and the hour for starting came, and many tears fell from the eyes of my beloved sisters. They said they never expected to see me again, and one of them never did have the pleasure of seeing me again, as she died a few years after I left home.

I was young, being in my 18th year, and the project pleased me much of getting to see the great West, but my relatives did not approve of my leaving them, particularly my sisters, as they were alone almost—one brother only, with whom they lived. Our parents were both dead and we were compelled to separate and work for a livelihood.

I finally mustered up courage and extended my hand for a final and affectionate farewell. It was a trying time, but I shouldered my pack and started on foot, and the first day I came to Canandaigua and put up for the night, wearied, and my feet badly blistered from wearing a pair of tight boots.

In the morning I rose much disheartened, and more than once I thought of turning back, but the thought of seeing the great West and the Indians and the Great Lakes inspired me with new courage and I set out again on foot. On the fourth day I arrived at Buffalo but found the ice still in the lake and I had to remain or wait on the steamboat until the first of May. [*Buffalo still showed the devastations of the War, and but a small portion of the city had been rebuilt.*]

I had but little money, so I went down to Black Rock and went to work for my board until the steamer should leave for Detroit. The little sum of money that I had to spend would only feed me through the voyage; therefore I was compelled to live poor and work whenever I could find anything to do.

Here I will relate a little circumstance about a relative of mine, Mr. Nathan Reed. The Bible tells us that when we are in want not to go to a brother for help, for more likely than not you will be refused, but a friend is far better than a relative in this case. Mr. Reed, who was my uncle on my mother's side, refused to loan me a few dollars in money to take me through the journey, although he was well off and had a plenty and to spare; and in this case I found the lesson in Scripture had fallen upon me, but I bore it all and persevered.

On the first day of May, 1819, I embarked on board the steamboat *Walk-in-the-Water*[1] the first steamer that was built on Lake Erie,— in 1818. The steamer did not start until afternoon. There were a large number of passengers on board. Four yoke of oxen were hitched to a long hauser and they, with the engine, took us over the rapids at the foot of Lake Erie. There was a considerable ice still floating in the lake. The weather was fine and calm, and we had a pleasant voyage except for the first night; the ice was still thick and in large pieces, and when the boat would strike one of them, it would startle all the passengers with the crashing noise.

The second night we were all suddenly called to witness a sad incident; that was a man fell over and was drowned. A piece of the railing on the starboard side of the boat and in front of the wheel

[1] *Walk-in-the-Water*, a sidewheel steamer of 340 tons displacement, 150 feet long and with 28-foot beams, was launched at Black Rock on the Niagara River, just below Buffalo, on May 28, 1818. On October 31, 1821, it was caught in a violent storm and was driven ashore on the sandy beach of Point Albino. (Al Mastics, "Walk-in-the-Water," *Inland Seas*, X [Fall 1954], 219.)

was left unfastened, and the man leaned against it and the piece slipped out and the man went with it, and it was supposed the wheel struck him and very likely killed him. The steamer was stopped and a boat was lowered in search of the man, but nothing was found but his hat.

The remainder of the trip nothing of note transpired, but I will assure you we had some sober-looking faces for a day or two after the accident, and no doubt it made many feel how uncertain is life, and that every day we should prepare for the morrow for we know not what a day may bring forth.

As soon as the steamer *Walk-in-the-Water* landed I went to the clerk and told him my situation and had not money enough to pay my passage. He said I ought to have told him before leaving port. I told him my brother was living in town and had means to pay my passage, and that I would go and get the amount. He, the clerk, said my passage was seven dollars for a steerage passage, so I started and found my brother and got money enough to settle my bill and all were satisfied, although I shipped without notifying the clerk or captain.

I had forgot one little circumstance that took place on board; it was a love scrape. A young girl in the steerage passage had been courted by a man passenger in the same cabin, but it appears that the girl's parents were not knowing to the courtship. But the father accidentally caught them in some corner of the ship and immediately took the man to task for courting his daughter without his consent, and finally they got to high words and loud talk, which brought quite a number of passengers, listening to the conversation.

Finally the captain was called upon to settle the difficulty. Firstly, the girl, after going through a series of questions from the father, stated positively that she had not sought an interview with the man, but that he was the aggressor, and that she had done nothing wrong on her part. The man said her testimony was correct, but he had fallen in love with the girl and wanted to marry her, so the girl came off innocent or unhurt and with flying colors; and the man, by making an honest confession as above stated, got off.

The captain, after inquiring into the matter, found that nothing of a criminal nature had been done. He fined the man a treat for as many of the passengers as were standing about. So the man agreed to the captain's decision and went and brought out his bottle and treated all that wanted to drink; but the captain told him that if he was caught troubling the women again he should be compelled to put him on shore. This seemed to have the desired effect, as there was nothing more seen or heard about courting on the boat during the remainder of the trip.

My brother informed me that troops had received orders to move to the West and occupy the forts on the Mississippi at Rock Island and Prairie du Chien, and to build a new fort on the reserve, including the falls of St. Anthony. This reservation was purchased by Lieut. Z. M. Pike in the years 1804 and 1805 from the Mdewakanton Sioux. The troops had already moved and my brother was packing up the last of the goods belonging to the sutler, Mr. Louis Devotion, and making preparations to follow in a few days. So I found employment for a few days assisting to pack goods for the use of the troops.

My brother left about the first of June. A man by the name of [William] Belcher, another clerk, had started with the troops. A few days after, Mr. Devotion, the proprietor, left Detroit for New York to get a new stock of goods for to supply the troops for the winter. I was then left alone with one man, a servant of Mr. Devotion's by the name of Thomas Hogan, an Irishman.

Not having much to do in the store, the most of the goods having been packed and sent off, I had time to study and I used the most of my time at my arithmetic [*and kept the store in order until Mr. Devotion returned*].

Now and then I used to walk about the city,[2] and particularly along the river, and look at the shot holes in the storehouses along the levee that were thrown across from the British side in the time of the last war. And little did I then think of getting acquainted with the Sioux Indians and that I should learn from them that several of them participated in the war on the part of the British, and many a barbarous story they told me about the cruelties of the other tribes and their treatment of the whites, their women, and children.

[2] Detroit at this time was on the west bank of the strait that connects Lake Erie with Lake St. Clair, the town "consisting about two hundred and fifty houses, including public buildings, and has a population of fourteen hundred and fifteen inhabitants, exclusive of the garrison." (Henry R. Schoolcraft, *Narrative Journal of Travels*, ed. Mentor L. Williams [East Lansing: Michigan State College Press, 1953], pp. 49–50.)

I have left my history a little and now continue again and state as [I] was walking out one Sunday to church with our man, or servant as people may choose to call them, the family that I boarded with saw me walking with the hired man, and when I went in to dinner the old lady of the house set at me and gave me a great lecturing for going in company with such a man.

The family's name was Odren,[3] some Old Country French but of the first class of people. The wars had ruined them and they had lost nearly all they had, and they were then keeping a few boarders at five dollars per week to make a poor and scanty living. I did not find out the real cause of the old lady's lecturing me for some days, but the sequel worked out after a while. It was because I went to the Roman Catholic church with our servant that I got a reprimand. The old lady and husband were Protestants; and the old lady said our servant was a deserter from the British, and went on and abused him terribly behind his back. I swallowed the whole patiently and kept it all to myself.

After that I walked alone in the day time but in the evenings I would get into a canoe and take a little sail on the Detroit River, and sometimes go as far as the Canada side and back. The last time I tried to take a sail on the river I got myself and man into a little difficulty about the boat that we were to have. I had asked a gentleman by the name of Dorr[4] for the use of a boat that was lying in front of the commissary store. Mr. Dorr was quartermaster, otherwise contractor, for beef and several other things, and used the government boats whenever he wanted to move his provisions. He told us we could use one of the boats.

So about dark I and our man went down to the wharf to take a boat and, all at once, we were hailed by some person near the commissary store. We looked around and saw a soldier coming towards us. He hallooed as loud as he could and wanted to know what we were doing with the boats. We told him that Mr. Dorr had loaned us one for to take a little sail on the river.

[3] It is possible that this was the family of Peter Audrain (1725–1820), who was born in France and immigrated to the United States after the American Revolution. In 1796 he went to Detroit, where he later held several offices.

[4] Melvin Door, a commission and forwarding merchant, had a wharf at the foot of Cass Street. He went to Detroit about 1816. (Information from the Detroit Public Library.)

"Oh, and by jabers, I will let you know that Mr. Dorr nor your-selves has any right to take any of those boats!" This oath and threat came out in the full Irish brogue; and—"Sirs, you are to stay under guard until I send for an officer." And he took his musket from his shoulder and stood in a threatening posture, so if we moved he could be ready to fire on us. And he commenced hallooing for the sergeant-of-the-guard.

There we were compelled to stand about one hour before the officer of the day could be found and have a hearing of the case. And no doubt our Irish sentinel was quite happy to get a chance to show a little authority over an American. This I know to be a fact from experience, and I have seen others in the power of the Irish soldiers. They not only carry the laws to the utmost extent and are very inso-lent to a Protestant prisoner, and they ought not to be enlisted for soldiers, for they know very little about the use of firearms and, as they are enlisted for five years, it takes them the whole time to learn the use of firearms. There is more drunkenness and disturbances got up by them than by any other nation that helps make up our armies.

After the officer of the day arrived and heard our story he very graciously told us to go about our business but warned us not to give them, the officers, any more trouble. Very likely the officer of the day had been disturbed in some little party of pleasure, which made him a little sour on the occasion; and this ended our boat riding for the season.

During the summer of 1819 a treaty was made with the Indians of Michigan Territory. Governor [Lewis] Cass[5] was one of the com-missioners and purchased a large tract of country at a trifling expense to the Government. After the treaty was made, large delega-tions of [Indians] came frequently into the city of Detroit and they used to have terrible drunken spells in which many were stabbed and several were killed from the effect of strong water. Large numbers still wore British ornaments, guns, and swords, which they used to carry about, brandishing them, through the streets in the wildest kind of frenzy; troops often had to be called on to take them into custody.

[5] Lewis Cass (1782–1866), soldier, diplomat, statesman, was appointed gover-nor of the Territory of Michigan in October, 1813. He negotiated the treaty of 1819 with the Chippewas at Saginaw, Michigan. The ceded territory included the region for many miles around Saginaw Bay.

An election was held to elect a delegate to Congress in the fore part of October or September (I do not now recollect), but I believe that a gentleman by the name of Wing was elected. Here a stratagem of the Irish soldiers was shown forth. Although the officers of the Territory were acquainted with the facts, nothing was said about the deception. The party above named went and borrowed a large quantity of citizens' clothes and [the Irish] dressed up as citizens and went to the polls and voted, then [went] home to their quarters and another party would take the same clothes and dress up and go to the polls and vote; and so they worked until they got in between 200 and 300 votes. Judge Williams, I believe, was the name of the opposing delegate.[6]

One day I was busy at something about the store and I got the hired man to black my shoes for me. Mr. Devotion, the owner or proprietor of the establishment, came accidentally and saw his man at work blacking my shoes, and asked him whose shoes he was blacking. He said, "The young clerk," at which the owner, Mr. D., flew into a passion and forbade the man ever blacking my shoes again. And then he came to me and wanted to know if I had come out there to be waited upon, and swore some, and told me never to employ the man to black my shoes again, and actually insisted on my getting some slush [*refuse grease or fat from the galley of a ship*] to grease my shoes. He did not stop abusing me until I went and cleaned my shoes myself.

At this time money was very scarce in Detroit, and many of the businessmen had, for their convenience and some for cheating, issued those little bills called shinplasters, from six and a quarter cents to one dollar. This was caused on account, mostly, of the suspension of business after the war.

One Rev. Mr. Ishard,[7] a Roman Catholic priest, was building a large stone church at Detroit, and the old gentleman could not make a "raise" of funds, the times being very hard and money scarce.*

[6] The election was held on the first Thursday in September, 1819. Though Austin Eli Wing was not a candidate himself, he was a strong supporter of the winner, William Woodbridge. John R. Williams, associate justice of the county court, obtained the second largest number of votes. (M.G.M., Detroit Public Library.)

[7] Father Gabriel Richard (1767–1832), a Sulpician priest, was born and educated in France. In June, 1798, he went to Detroit and soon became pastor of St. Anne's Church. Later he was vicar-general of the entire region.

So he set to work and issued a large amount of these little shinplasters, and at first redeemed them for a while until he had got some thousands of dollars issued. Then he stopped payment under the following supposition, that a large amount of his bills had been counterfeited. And when people would go to the old gentleman with some of his bills for payment, he would commence examining them and throwing them out, and he would say, "Dat is counterfeit, and dat is counterfeit, and dat is counterfeit," and so on until he would throw out about three-fourths of the amount. The report was that he raised enough to pay for his church and get out of debt by pronouncing his own bills forgeries and not redeeming them.[8]

After Mr. Devotion returned from New York with his supply of goods for the winter's trade, we commenced packing the few old goods and our provisions and getting the new assortment ready for shipment.

In the latter part of September appeared a sloop. *The Hannah*, if I recollect right, was the name, and Captain Belden master and part owner. Mr. Devotion and the captain were three days bartering before they could agree upon a price for the chartering of the sloop. Finally they agreed after three days, and I believe the price was to be seven hundred dollars for the trip from Detroit to Green Bay, as near as I can recollect.

In a few days the sloop was loaded and all was ready for a start. Our master had settled up all his business except one thing; that was his housekeeper, a woman—or lady, as those who choose may call her. This woman had been brought out from New York by Mr. Devotion, and he had kept her several years in an old French family living a short distance from the store.

The great trouble was to get rid of this woman and send her back to New York. That kept him three days, for she was determined to go with him to the West, and many tears she shed, and clung to Mr. Devotion with a great display of love, etc., and no kind of persuasion could induce her to leave him, and the only way he got rid of her was by threats and money, of which no doubt he had to shell out pretty largely to prevent exposure; and they parted.

The sloop sailed for Green Bay [in October] with a light breeze,

---

[8] It is possible that Prescott was just recording the gossip prevalent at the time of his stay in Detroit.

but got becalmed on the shoals or flats in the lake above Detroit
[Lake St. Clair], there being only about seven feet of water on the
bars. The captain did not like to sail until he got a fair wind, fearful
if he beat up he would get aground by running out of the channel.
While lying to, the schooner *Jackson*[9] passed on her way down to
Detroit.

We had a poor lot of provisions both for cabin and sailors, salt
pork and salt beef; and from the looks of the meat I should think the
captain had taken all the fat off to grease the mast and yards and
rigging of the sloop. We had hard bread, and coffee made in an iron
boiler, which made the coffee almost as black as ink and about as
muddy as the old darkey's face that made it. These 4 items was about
all that we had three times a day during the voyage. Whilst we were
working up the river some Indians came along-side with some fine
fish for sale, mostly large black bass, and asked a hard biscuit apiece
for them. The captain said it was too much and would not take any,
so we had to take to our salt bones again.

We got a wind from the southeast, which caused us to move up
stream slowly, and as we passed along some farmers came out to us
with melons for sale, some of the finest I ever saw, and offered them
for 5 and 10 cents apiece. But the captain said they were too dear and
would not purchase any, but Mr. Devotion purchased two or three
and we made out to get a taste of something fresh, which was quite
refreshing after having lived on salt junk for five days.

As the sun rose the wind rose with it, and about ten o'clock in the
morning we came to Fort Gratiot [on the right bank of the Huron
River] at the entrance of Lake Huron. As we sailed along we could
see the white fish and trout when the water was about twenty feet
deep, as the captain informed us.

Fort Gratiot* was a small wooden fort made of hewn logs. It
commanded the entrance of the lake. It is at this fort that the Sioux
warriors became frightened when on their way to join the British
army at Detroit and Sandusky. It appears that a few British troops
and some 300 or 400 Indians had attacked Fort Gratiot and had been
repulsed. The Sioux, in passing at a distance, saw several bodies of
Indians that had been awfully torn by cannonballs and shot, and
some were cut completely in two. The sight alarmed them very much,

[9] This was the *General Jackson*, with Captain Blake in charge.

and they said they took good care to keep a distance from the forts and out of the range of the big guns.[10]

As we came to enter the Lake there is quite a rapid current, but the wind had risen to quite a breeze, so that the old sloop went through the rapid without using a rope. There is quite an eddy on the north side as you go up, and the captain took advantage of the eddy, and as the sloop emerged from it and struck the current coming out of the lake, the vessel almost stopped and the water rolled up around the bows about 4 feet high from the force of the current rushing out of the lake. But she had headway enough to carry her through, and the moment the vessel came into the still water the sailors all gave a shout, and on we sailed into the open lake and away we sailed for Mackinaw.[11]

The wind kept rising. At last some of the yards began to crack. "Hands aloft," the captain cried. Up they scampered as fast as they could. "Take a reef in the topsail," and on we went at fearful speed. "The right aft!" The captain kept up sail until we got opposite Thunder Bay Islands. Here the wind blew so furiously the captain had to fast the topsail and take a reef in the main sail, and in this way we arrived at Mackinaw.

The captain and Mr. Devotion went on shore and up to the fort to report to the commanding officer where they were going and what freighted with, etc., etc. When the captain and Mr. Devotion came on board I got permission with the mate and our man to go and take a look at the fort and town.

We went and took a look at the old fort that had been taken by the British and had been demolished and abandoned. A new one had been built lower down and nearer the water than the old one. The old fort was on the highest peak of the island. It was very difficult getting wood and water, and [the fort] was supposed to be impregnable. And I should have thought so myself from the many ditches and water holes. I would have thought any force that could have been brought in those days could not have taken the place, and I suppose would not have done so if the Americans had not agreed to capitulate, and in this way they got in.

10 Prescott must be confusing this with some other incident. The British evacuated Detroit in September, 1813, before Fort Gratiot was built.

11 Mackinaw, called by the Indians Michilmackinac, meaning the Great Turtle, was a trading center of the West. Trade goods reached there from Montreal in birch bark canoes by way of Niagara Falls.

The whole of the old fort appeared to be entrenched and with a great many cross ones from ten to fifteen feet deep. Some of them were made to contain water for two purposes, probably to prevent troops from crossing and to keep a supply of water handy, as it was very difficult to get water from the lake, the hillside being so very steep. The new fort I did not go inside of it. It being late, we hurried on board our old sloop.

The next morning preparations were made for another sail across Lake Michigan. Some fishermen came alongside and offered some fine trout and white fish, but our captain was too hard for us again and would not pay the customary price. But the owner of the goods, Mr. Devotion, bought a few, and so we had one mess of good fish from the clear waters of the great western lakes.

The fishing is generally carried on by the French and half-breeds with what they call gill-nets. The nets are from 100 to 150 feet in length; the meshes of the net are about four or five inches square. The fish in passing get their heads through and then hang by the gills, and the most of them are alive when taken out, as they generally visit the nets every morning. The water is from 30 to 40 feet deep.

When they fish, small stones are tied to the bottom of the nets, and strips of red cedar wood, about two feet long and about two inches wide in the center and tapering each way, are used. The sticks keep the net spread to its full height, being about four or five feet. There is a stick or a float, as they call it, opposite every stone or sinker, and this keeps all the meshes or squares even with each other.

The Indians also catch a great many fish, and the half-breeds also catch considerable quantities. The trout are caught amongst the white fish, as the trout prey upon the white fish. The white fish must live by suction, I should say, for they have a mouth very much like a sucker. These fish weigh from four to ten pounds each. The wood used by the inhabitants is mostly brought in old vessels from the adjacent islands.

This Island of Mackinaw was noted for several years for a great missionary school where hundreds of half-breeds have been taught a common education. The Island of Mackinaw was also noted as a great rendezvous for all the northern traders. In the months of June and July the place used to be filled with all classes of people—English, Irish, French, and Americans, half-breeds and Indians. And I have often heard them say that the Island of Mackinaw was the greatest place in the north for pleasure.

Now before the sloop got ready to sail I got another raking down about greasing my shoes. My old boss caught the man cleaning my shoes one morning on the vessel. He stopped him and called me and set me to work at the slush-tub again but, by the by, there was but little to be had, for the captain watched the slush-tub pretty closely, and if he found there was enough to pay for the trouble, he would have it all rubbed on the mast and rigging and spars.

After all was ready we sailed out of the Straits of Mackinaw. The first day we got along very well, but the second day there came on a blow from the northwest. The captain tried to beat up against it and sailed out so far north that he came near getting on to some shoals of sand. The wind kept increasing in violence and a great [storm] rose, which made our old tub of a vessel roll and toss at a great rate.

Finally the captain saw he was losing ground and, as it was getting near night and the lake looked frightful with a raging sea, so he bout ship and [sailed] nearly before the wind under close-reef main sail. And in about one hour we were back where we started from, near an island under the lea of which we took shelter. But before daylight the wind calmed down, so that we laid quite easy, although we had rolled and tossed nearly all night from the agitation of the water by the force of the wind and sea. We found 30 fathoms of water not a great distance from the island.

We found some Indians here wind-bound. They brought alongside some fish, but captain as usual would not give a biscuit apiece for them. Here we had an opportunity of seeing the bark canoe ride upon the swells from the lake. Was their strength equal to their buoyancy, the bark canoe would make the greatest lifeboat that could be found. The bark canoe rode the swells like a duck, and not a particle of water appeared to splash over the bow or sides. They are so frail that they are easily broken, but in the North there is no other canoe used.

The canoes carry from two to ten men, and the traders use a great many of them on the small rivers for transporting goods for the Indian trade, also for fishing; and about the Great Lakes the French fishermen use them in winter when fishing. The object of using them in winter is the ice often moves from the shore by the force of the winds, and the people that set their nets under the ice would be carried off and lost if they did not take the precaution to take a canoe along. So if the ice should move they can jump into the canoe and paddle to shore again. The ice sometimes makes out five or six miles from shore, and the fishermen go out and cut holes and let their nets down under the ice, and take fish all winter in this way.

At daybreak the wind had calmed down a little and the captain set sail again and ran out from under the lea of the island and beat up against a head wind until about ten o'clock, when the wind commenced blowing a gale again from the west and tremendous seas commenced rolling. But the captain battled against it all day until near night and found he was making no progress. The clouds looked very stormy and dangerous, so the captain bout ship again and run before the wind again and came very near of being blown on to the point of the island that we had left in the morning. We just missed it and that was all, and run off about a mile southeast and brought up under the lea of a small island with perpendicular sand banks and very deep water.

Here we laid and rolled all night, and I suppose one cause of our sloop's rolling so was the great high mast she had. The wind calmed down a little in the night and we got under way early in the morning. Again the wind commenced veering around to the south and finally got fair.

The mate was at the helm, for the captain had turned in to rest a little, as he had been 3 days and two nights without much rest or sleep. The mate went to the captain and told him the wind was getting fair. The captain ordered the sails set square to the wind, and then the old sloop made water boil again around her bows. The captain rested till about noon, when the mate told him they were off Washington Harbor. The captain got up and ordered them to run in between some islands and went to the helm. The mate went up to the masthead to look out.

By this time we had got in between two islands. The main one on the south was quite large from appearances and did not appear to be half a mile off. In a few minutes we heard rumbling under the bottom of the sloop. The mate cried out, "Rocks," and she jumped over them her whole length. The captain wheeled her out of the wind; then we lay drifting for a few minutes and not touching any more. The mate said he thought we were over and the captain put her before the wind again.

"A lucky escape that," says the captain.

"Yes," says the mate, "I was thinking about a box or a barrel to hang on to, for I expected to see the bottom go out of the old thing in a few moments more!" The captain said he never knew bad luck without some good luck with it.

We got clear of Washington Harbor [12] without any more trouble. Next came Green Bay about two or three o'clock. The bay is very shallow, mostly muddy bottom, and the water was quite roily, so much we could see nothing where there was a foot of water in a bucket. There was a long heavy sea running over the great flat bar of sand and mud.

The black man was at the masthead looking out for breakers, of which there were some near the entrance of the channel that comes out from Fox River. All at once the darky sang out, "Breakers right ahead!"

The captain was at the helm but did not mind the old darky, so kept on his course. The man sang out again, "Breakers ahead! Captain, yo' goin' right on 'em!" and hastened down as fast as he could and ran about the deck almost frantic, calling, "Captain, yo' smash de sloop!" etc.

The captain gave the wheel to the mate and went up to the masthead and then stood watching the breakers, which we could now see from the deck, and all hands stood shivering, expecting we should strike. The mate stuck to the helm and kept on the course right straight for the breakers. Probably some mate would have mutinied and taken his own course, and we would all have been lost, but no, he kept on, and directly he got a signal from the captain, the sloop turned her course and away she slipped between two piles of breakers where the water was dashing over at a frightful rate.

The vessel was now in the channel and the fort [13] was in sight. The captain came down and says, "Old Darky, what do you think?" The old man brought out a very long sigh and said, "Lord-a-massa, I thought we were all los'."

[12] The island and harbor were named in 1816 for the first vessel to enter the harbor. It was one of three ships transporting troops to establish a United States fort at Green Bay. (James H. Lockwood, "Early Times and Events in Wisconsin," *Wisconsin Historical Collections*, II [1855], 103–104.)

[13] Fort Howard, built on the west side of the Fox River by the United States government in 1816.

In a few minutes we were at the fort. The captain called and reported and delivered the mail, etc., when we sailed up the river about a mile to Mr. John Lawe's, where the goods was to be stored.

The captain was in a great hurry, for the season was getting late for sailing and it was dangerous on account of so many northwesters. An old saying is "praise the bridge that carries you safely over." I think Captain Belden navigated and worked us through probably better than many captains would have done in the circumstances, running through so many shoals and adverse winds to encounter, and no damage or loss. I think we can afford to praise the captain.

We took up board at Mr. Lawe's for a few days until the goods were all stored, then Mr. Devotion rented a small house of Mr. Lawe and we kept house by ourselves for some days, as we could not get boats to go up the Fox River. The boats had all been taken away by the traders to transport goods and provisions for the winter trade.

After waiting and hunting several days, they found an old Mackinaw boat, a leaky old thing. Mr. Devotion had it repaired as well as could be done in that place, and had it loaded with goods bound for Prairie du Chien on the Mississippi. It was very difficult to get hands enough to manage the boat. Finally he found two Frenchmen, two half-breeds, and a Menominee Indian,* and we started, loaded down to the water's edge. [*The Fox River was nothing but rapids for about twenty miles. We made slow progress.*]

I had to pass the Indian agent's [14] office, kept by an old Frenchman; the name I have forgotten. This house and four or five others were all that were at Green Bay when I landed there.* We went on one day with our boat and camped at night at the foot of a very strong rapid [near present-day De Pere]. The next morning we tried to get over the rapid with our load, but we could do nothing; our load was too heavy and the water too strong for our force.

So we unloaded half and tried that, and got almost over, but some of the men slipped and the boat got a start backwards or downwards, and away it went down stream, over rocks and rapids. As the boat was starting two men jumped into it and went over the rapids in it and caught on to the shore about half a mile below.

[14] The Indian agent evidently was Colonel John Bowyer, a native of Virginia. He arrived at Green Bay as agent in 1815 and died in office in 1820. ("Narrative of Morgan L. Martin," *Wisconsin Historical Collections*, XI [1888], 393 n.– 394 n.)

They tried again but with no better success, except they kept the boat from drifting so far. We found that we could do nothing as our boat was old and leaky and without hands enough to manage so heavy a load. The Frenchmen got discouraged and said they would not go on if some of the load was not taken out. The boat had commenced leaking very much, so I finally concluded to go back and see Mr. Devotion and tell him how things were.

One of the men went back with me—the man that was employed as guide and steer-man of the boat. I [left] the boat in charge of another Frenchman and started. We got back about ten o'clock in the morning and I went and reported the facts to Mr. Devotion. He did not say much at first and appeared to be studying what to do. After a while he told me to go back and unload the boat and get it turned up so as to have it ready for calking when he should get up there.

When I started he followed me out for some distance from the house and asked me how I came to leave the boat. I said, "We could not get along and there was no use of staying there and doing nothing." "Well," said he, "you could have sent a Frenchman." I said, "They could not speak English." "That was nothing to you," he said, and he commenced cursing me at a great rate. I never heard such abuse from any man before nor since.

I started on my return, my heart full of sorrow and my eyes full of tears. I thought then I would rather be at home, if it was a poor place, than be amongst so much aristocracy as I found amongst the western people. Most of the business was carried on by a few pretended-rich, and they had under them many men that were treated as much like slaves as anything else, and nobody of common caste could associate with these big bugs nor go near them unless his hat was under his arm.

In the evening I arrived at the boat again, tired and hungry. I went to the boat and took a little spirits and gave my pilot and guide some, and got some supper. The Indian we had along saw us when we drank some spirits and asked why I did not give him some, and said if I did not give him some he would go back. I told him the liquor was not for him nor any of the rest of the hands, but that I was very tired and that was the only reason I drank some. He found he could not scare me into his wish. He went to sleep and never troubled me any more on that subject.

In the morning we went to work and upset the boat and com-

menced working the goods around the rapids by hand. The distance
was not long but was rough with rocks. We worked all day and at
night had got nearly all the goods far enough so that we could load
them above the main rapids.

The next day some of the men went hunting but found no game.
In the dusk of the evening a deer came galloping down to the river
from the opposite side and walked into the water and straight across
the rapids. The men saw it and got out their guns and ran up a little
distance. They waited for the deer to come out of the water and shot
it, and we had a great feast that night, roasting and boiling.

In the morning I went to look at the deer meat, wishing to keep
some for my old master, as he was expected that day. I found that the
deer was half gone. I inquired what had become of the venison. They
said they had eat it. In the evening the master arrived in a small boat
with two men and a few goods. His man went to work and cooked
some supper for him, using the venison that I had hard work to
keep a piece for him. In the morning my master got up a little better
natured than he had been a few days before.

The Frenchmen had learned how he had treated me when I went to
report to him our condition, and they said if he went to swearing at
them they would leave and go back. So he had to treat us a little
more civilly, for there were no other hands that he could get. It was
with much difficulty that he got the few that were going with me.

All hands went to work on the boat and got it calked and pitched.
The next day we tried the rapids again with the empty boat and with
hard pulling we got the empty boat up and loaded and started. We
still found it very difficult going along; the water was so very low
that every little rapid we came to we had to unload half the goods
and take the other half away ahead, and then come back and get the
remainder. And so we worked along until we got up to Winnebago
Lake, and I think we had to repair our boat 3 or 4 times in going
about 30 miles. The river was so low and the rocks sharp that
calking would be pulled out of the seams of the boat nearly every
day. Finally our pitch gave out; then we had to use tallow and ashes,
which served very well, as the water had by this time got very cold,
and every morning there was [ice] along the shore of the stream.

On our way we passed an old Frenchman's hut. The men of the
boat said he had lived there a great many years all alone, and all the
companionship he had was a pig; and the hands said the pig used to

eat out of one end of the trough and the old Frenchman would eat out of the other end, and they disputed for the largest share of food.

When we got [to] Winnebago Lake we were over the rapids. We stopped and warmed as the wind was blowing quite fresh and our boat was quite heavy laden. We had to lay to half a day. At the entrance of the lake was an old Winnebago village. The men went to hunting for caches of corn* but found none except a cache or two of potatoes, but they were mostly rotten.

The Winnebagoes* had lived here from [time] immemorial, as the country once abounded with deer and elk, and wild fowl in abundance; and the Winnebago Lake furnished them with great quantities of fish, and with their gardens they lived in plenty. And being at peace with all nations, they lived apparently happy, except when Strong Water got amongst them; then most always some of them got killed, which always kept up family feuds and intestine wars amongst them.

After dark the wind went down and we started. We got about half-way through the lake and the wind commenced to blow, and we had to go ashore again, but the wind did not blow long, so we started again and got through about daylight and landed for breakfast. Winnebago Lake is about nine miles wide where we crossed it.

The men were all sleepy, having been up all night, and laid down and took a nap whilst the breakfast was cooking. The weather was beginning to get cold and ice was making very fast. We rowed and poled and toiled all day and got to Lake Apockway,[15] or Rush Lake, about dark and found the lake frozen over. The pilot said if we did not go through that night we could not get through at all. So we went to work with our poles and axes and everything that we could find about the boat that could break ice, and broke ice, poles and oars and everything else that was breakable—and finally had to give up.

The ice was too strong for us and we turned back about midnight to try to get a landing. When we got back where we commenced breaking the ice at the foot of the lake, we had to leave our boat some distance from the shore, as the ice where we first commenced breaking had frozen so hard again that it would bear a man up.

[15] Lake Apockway, or Puckaway, had various other spellings, including Apockwag and Apuckaway. It was also called Rush Lake or Rice Lake because of the wild rice found there. (Benton H. Wilcox, librarian, State Historical Society of Wisconsin, letter of January 18, 1955.)

So we left the boat about 2:00 o'clock in the night and walked ashore on the ice; almost perished with cold. Our boat men were pretty expert in kindling fires and they soon had one agoing. But it was [a] cold, bleak place and we could not enjoy the fire much, only to keep from freezing.

When daylight came we moved farther into the wood and made a good camp. We got breakfast and went to work to unload the boat. The goods had to be carried and rolled about the 1/8th of a mile to get to the place where we wanted to build a storehouse for the winter, as we supposed. After the boat was unloaded Mr. Devotion kept the hands one week to build a storehouse. There had formerly been a trading house here and part of it was standing yet, which we used for a kitchen or cook room. So we had only a storehouse to build. When this was done in a rough manner, of round logs and a few puncheons for a roof, the boat hands left us and returned home.

About this time our provisions began to get scarce and our master, Mr. Devotion, put us on about half-rations, that is, the hired man and myself. As for himself, he did not work any, therefore did not eat much, but our servant or man did the cooking, and frequently before meal time we used to get a lunch from the kettle, so that when we went to the table we could be as modest about our eating as the master of the house.

Here is the first place that I saw grouse. I was out hunting one day and a flock flew up and some of them lit on trees. I crawled up behind other trees and got a shot with one of these old English chief fowling pieces. I missed my bird; I was so anxious to get one that it excited me so much that I sighted the bird and not the gun. I missed twice but the third time I made out to break one's wing, and got it and started for home.

When I got home Master asked me what I had been firing at so much. I told him some fowls that I did not know what they were. Said he, "It's a grouse." "Well," I said, "Never saw one before; therefore I was anxious to get one and made shoot until I got one." "Well," he said, "it would be good to make a [fricassee], or stew." So he had it cooked to suit himself, and not being any too well supplied at our meals, we found it very good.

About a week after the men left us, Mr. Devotion got news that some of his goods that had been sent forward as far as the

Portage[16] had got wet and were likely to be damaged, so he said I must go and look after them. [*Two long days' walk.*] We had no guide and what to do we did not know.

In a day or two a discharged soldier from the fort came along and said he was going to Prairie du Chien. He said he meant to follow along in sight of the river until he got to the Portage, then he could get in with some teams hauling supplies for the traders. So Mr. Devotion hired him to go with me to the Portage between the Fox and Wisconsin rivers and return with me.

So we got ready and Mr. Devotion told us to go to Mr. Grignon,[17] a trader living a day's march above us on the Fox River, and ask him for a guide to go with us to the Portage and back again. We found the trader's house without much trouble, which was a lucky hit for us in a strange country and winding about amongst the hills and brush. If we had got lost there was no help for us, for we had no provisions and it was cold, and we should have perished in a short time.

But we got in safe and the old trader [Grignon] give us a good warm meal of venison and a good bed of blankets, although it was in one of these lodges all open at the top that the trader was passing the winter, happy by the side of a young Indian woman, apparently neat and clean, of the Menominee tribe. [*He said he had arrived late in the fall, and had no time for building, except a storehouse and a house for his men. . . . I found his tribe had furnished about all the women for the traders' wives, for they* (the Menominees) *are generally good-looking and their first children were as white as many of the white children. The old man said he had been a long time in the trade, and probably would stay there as long as he lived, as it suited him, and he did not care about seeking any other livelihood.*]

Next morning we started early with our Frenchman for a guide and traveled all day until near sunset, when we came to our place of destination, almost tired out and hungry, as it is not customary to halt at midday for a lunch, the days being short and cold. We

[16] At present-day Portage, Wisconsin. It was about a mile and one-half in length, and when the water was very high one could pass from the Fox to the Wisconsin River or vice versa.

[17] This may have been Augustin, Louis, or Charles Grignon, or still another member of the large Grignon family. (See John T. De La Ronde, "Personal Narrative," *Wisconsin Historical Collections*, VII [1873–1876], 349.)

traveled the whole day without eating, and then got amongst another class of people.

The Winnebagoes was here [*an ugly race of people. They had always been abusive to the white people, but there were but a few of them about, and they did not molest me*]. And such another gibberish I never heard in my life, and French mixed up with the Indian dialect, none of which I did understand the words. However, by signs and a few words of English that the Frenchman understood, I made out to make him understand my business up to the Portage, that was to examine the goods and see that all was safe and dry.

We got a good fire started in the storeroom and commenced opening the boxes and found the goods in good order and nailed them up again and gave a few raisins to the family that were trading there, and got ready to start back.

The Frenchman had some venison. I wanted a ham or thigh and I think we parleyed and made signs for about half an hour before I could make him understand what I wanted. I kept calling the venison cow meat, and the Frenchman gave it some name that I could not understand. So at last I took the man, showed him the venison, and by signs got him to understand what I wanted. So we got a thigh of venison and I packed it on to my French guide and we started early.

I kept along with them until about 3:00 o'clock, then I started ahead on the track that we had made going up; as there was about four inches of snow on it, it made good traveling and a plain track. The Frenchman worked hard to keep up with me and kept close to me for about half an hour, when he began to lag. He had the meat to carry, but was a much stronger man than I was. When he found he could not keep up with me he commenced jibbering about something and fell back with the other man, the discharged soldier, who was at this time far behind. I pushed on and got in about sundown and about an hour before the guide and soldier.

I had brought along some loaf sugar and some raisins for the old French trader. When we put up at the old gentleman's, Mr. Grignon had a warm supper got for us, but I noticed the Frenchman did not eat with us. And after we had got through with our meal I went into the next room and saw my guide and another Frenchman at supper. I saw there was only one dish on the table, so I had a curiosity to see what they were eating. So I sidled up towards the table and I suppose they noticed I was a little curious and offered me some of their repast. I politely declined, saying I had just finished my supper but merely wanted a taste to see what they were eating.

They said, "Corn, plenty corn, but little grease. Poor Frenchman, nothing but corn and little grease all winter, all winter." And afterwards I found that the traders hired their men in Canada for a term of four years, to be paid from fifty to one hundred dollars per annum, and clothe themselves, and to have one pint of corn and one ounce of grease per day, and the promise of something a little extra if the game in the country would justify the traders in issuing any different kind of food. And so the poor Canadians had to live four years on corn and grease mostly, and carry heavy burdens on their backs, and row boats and canoes, and do a large amount of other hard labor for a mere pittance of from fifty to one hundred dollars per annum, and feed on corn and grease!

Early in the morning I started with my discharged soldier for home again on Rush Lake. Today my soldier had to pack the venison, which worried him very much, and about 4:00 o'clock P.M., I started ahead and left my man to come on alone. I got in a little after sundown, but my man did not get in until sometime after dark, almost tired to death; and in fact, he was laid up a week from the fatigue of the journey.

After our arrival at home our old Master continued his economy on the provisions, and we had only about half an allowance—young and growing, healthy people. We had a few traps which we set, trying to get some kind of game that would give us food or sustenance for our bodies. But the wild animals were too much for us and kept out of our traps, so we lived on our half rations the best way we could until [a team] arrived from Prairie du Chien by the ice and land, Mr. [William] Belcher[18] in charge.

Belcher came to get a supply of goods for the troops. And I was ordered to proceed from Prairie du Chien to the Falls of St. Anthony with goods for the troops. Accordingly, preparations were made for the journey and I started with the train for Prairie du Chien with some seven or eight one-horse sledges, all managed by Canadians.

Although we had hard work in traveling in the cold, which was

18 William Belcher, a clerk for Devotion, had preceded Prescott to the west and had passed through the region in June, 1819. ("The Fur-Trade in Wisconsin, 1812–1825," ed. Reuben Gold Thwaites, *Wisconsin Historical Collections*, XX [1911], 131.)

very intense, we were glad to get where we could get something to eat. We made our journey from Rush Lake to P. du Chien in five days. As nothing particular happened on this piece of the road, I will commence from Prairie du Chien again.

SUPPLEMENT

Father Richard's Church (page 9)

When Henry R. Schoolcraft visited Detroit, he noted that in the summer of 1820 it contained "a Roman Catholic church, 116 feet in length, by 60 in breath [*sic*]—is 110 feet high with two steeples, has a chapel under ground 65 feet by 60, originally designed for a nunnery. Building of stone and not entirely finished." (*Narrative Journal*, p. 49 n.)

Silas Farmer in his *History of Detroit and Michigan* (New York: Farmer, 1884), page 847, states that Richard "issued his own money, paying out large quantities to the workmen.... The types with which the shinplasters were printed were stolen from the *Gazette* office by a printer named Cooper, who issued a quantity, with the counterfeit signature of Father Richard. The worthy father redeemed them as far as he was able, and his refusal to receive several hundred dollars of what was said to be counterfeit script is stated to have made a lasting breach between him and certain persons of his parish."

Fort Gratiot (page 11)

According to William L. Jenks in "Fort Gratiot and Its Builder General Charles Gratiot," *Michigan History*, Vol. IV, No. 1 (January 1920), pp. 141–155, "Fort Gratiot was built May or June, 1814, on the site of an old French trading post and fort. Captain Charles Gratiot, chief engineer of the Northwestern army under General Harrison, selected the spot as the most strategic for control of the water communications between Lake Huron and the lower lakes.... During its entire life of 65 years there was never fired a hostile shot from its walls."

The Menominee Indians (page 17)

The Menominee tribe was first visited by whites in 1634. From then until 1852 they lived near the mouth of the Menominee River of

Wisconsin and Michigan. They probably numbered from sixteen hundred to nineteen hundred and were, on the whole, a friendly tribe and had very little trouble with the whites.

Green Bay (page 17)

Although Prescott states that there were only five or six houses in Green Bay in 1819, he was probably counting only the homes of white persons. He must not have included the Indian homes, which stretched along the river for five or six miles. Captain Henry Whiting stated that there were about fifty houses and some two hundred to three hundred inhabitants, "depending on how you counted the Indians." (Benton H. Wilcox, librarian, State Historical Society of Wisconsin, letter of January 18, 1955.)

The Lawes and the Grignons were the leading families of Green Bay. According to Colonel Ebenezer Childs, who arrived at Green Bay in May, 1820, "There were quite a number of very respectable French families residing at the Bay when I arrived there: Judge Lawe, Judge Portier, and seven brothers and sisters named Grignon. . . . They are all engaged in the Indian trade under the American Fur Company, each cultivating a small quantity of land." ("Recollections of Wisconsin Since 1820," *Wisconsin Historical Collections*, IV [1857–1858], 159–161.)

Caching of Corn and Potatoes (page 20)

Corn was customarily stored in the ground. A large circular hole was dug, narrow at the top and bulging out below until it narrowed at the bottom. When this was nearly filled, it was sealed with dirt and covered over in order to disguise its location. Corn thus preserved kept fairly well. Potatoes and other produce were kept in the same manner.

The Winnebago Indians Inhabited Vast Territory (page 20)

"The Winnebago Indians inhabit the country . . . on both sides of the [Fox] river. They appear to go abroad for their game, and have no conveniences for dwelling, except a kind of lodges which they carry with them wherever they go. Their territory extends from the Mississippi to the vicinity of Green Bay, and the number of their warriors is seven hundred." (Edward Tanner, "Wisconsin in 1818," *Wisconsin Historical Collections*, VIII [1877–1879], 289.)

II

1820–1822

Trading at the Fort

After staying a few days at the Prairie* and witnessing the preparations by the Canadians for the holidays, which were quite comical in some respects, we got our train ready for another march up the Mississippi. [*After getting our complement of teams and Frenchmen to drive them, we started from the town that was older than Philadelphia, and there were only about 250 inhabitants in the place— that is, of the French, who were the first settlers. The government had what they called a factory to furnish goods to Indians at cost, for the traders sold their goods so high that the Indians suffered a great deal from want, and the government proposed this plan for their relief.* This made the traders angry, and they retaliated by underselling the government, and made them lose money and the government abandoned the traffic.*]

The weather was extremely cold but the ice was good, and we traveled all the way on the ice from Prairie du Chien to Fort Snelling with only one accident, that was a few miles below St. Croix. I arrived at a place called Mud Hen pond, between the head of Lake Pepin and St. Croix. We camped at an American Fur Company's trader's house by the name of Faribault[1] to rest our teams and get a little rest for ourselves, as we had been traveling for several days and sleeping out on the snow. [*As we had good comfortable rooms at Mr. Faribault's,*] all the teamsters agreed to have one day's rest at the trader's house, but the Indians broke up our plan of repose. [*The second day, in the afternoon, a large band of Sioux Indians arrived.*] A large number of them came in families and all made their camp

---

[1] Jean Baptiste Faribault, a noted trader of the Northwest.

near the trader's house. Fearing the Indians would steal our goods
[*from the sleighs*], we were obliged to hitch up our teams and start,
although it was nearly sundown and very cold.

The Indians looked curious and singular to me and I scrutinized all
their operations, both men and women. Before we started the trader
had been through the camp collecting his credits, and he got into
some trouble by taking goods from an Indian that had not been
able to pay up the amount due. Therefore the trader took from the
Indian his gun, traps, and a large kettle. The Indian remonstrated
and told the trader he was taking too much, but the trader said no,
and so a quarrel commenced. The trader came near being killed for
exacting too much of the Indians.

Amongst the Indians I noticed a family of a different appearance
from the other Indians [Mdewakanton Sioux]. They appeared to
associate with the trader's family on relative terms, and dressed
different and looked cleanly in comparison to the other Indians.
And amongst them was a young miss which attracted the attention
of the family of the trader, and when they assembled together they
appeared to be all one family. And there were some mixed-blood
girls that were as well built as white women that could be found,
only they had a little of the olive tint and were straight and had good
countenances.

The manner of raising the children amongst the Sioux is to lash
them to a board for about one year for four or six hours per day,
and in this way they must grow straight. But after they get to be
twelve years old they begin to carry heavy burdens and at the age of
thirty they begin to give way under heavy loads that is carried by
straps across the head. And they begin to get bow-legged and
crooked-backed and lose all their good form and features.

After we started one team broke through the ice. Not having ever
seen anything of this kind, it alarmed me. I had to take one team
and make for land, but I was afraid every step I took for fear I
should break through, but I got safe to land. The Frenchman got a
rope round the horse's neck and got his harness off, and they all got
hold of the rope and dragged the horse out. The animal was very
much chilled and must have suffered very much [judging] from the
groaning that he made. But as soon as the horse was pulled out,
which act appeared to be performed very easily—as the men pulled
on the rope, it choked the horse and he commenced kicking or

struggling and floated on his side and was quickly pulled out—a blanket was thrown over him and a man jumped on to him with a good whip and ran him for about ten minutes. Then he stopped and they took hay and rubbed him down, then gave him another canter. By this time we had got a fire started. We got the horse up to the fire and smoke and he soon dried up as well as ever, although the weather was very cold.

Now another trouble was on hand. Some of the load had sunk and the men cut some long poles and fastened some large nails to the ends of the poles. The ends of the nails were bent so that they got hold of some tobacco kegs and got them safely out, all but one keg, that night. The next morning the men raised the other keg, and we hitched up and started again and came as far as Olive Grove, now Hastings.

Here we found Lieut. Oliver [2] with a small party of soldiers watching a keelboat load of provisions that had got frozen in in the fall, [*while other parties were hauling them away*]. From here we had a good road and arrived without more trouble [*at the cantonment at the mouth of St. Peter's river*].

I found my brother well [*and full of work, as he was alone and had four companies to wait upon*]. And you never saw a more delighted company of people as the officers and soldiers were on our arrival. They had been out of groceries for a month or more and the scurvy had got amongst the troops, and there had already died about fifty [*or sixty*] men before I got there, and several [*ten*] died after I arrived. Their rations was nothing but rusty pork and bread. Some of them would go to bed apparently well at night and be found dead in the morning. Others would live a week, some 2 or 3 days.

Soon the commanding officer, Colonel [Henry] Leavenworth, sent a party of soldiers over to the St. Croix [River] and they found some spruce by Dr. E. Purcell's [3] direction. The doctor ordered a tea to be made of the spruce, and had it well sweetened, and made them use vinegar freely and some spirits. The scurvy soon left them, but about seventy men fell victim to the disease before its progress was

2 Lieutenant William G. Oliver, after whom the site of the city of Hastings was earlier called Oliver's Grove.

3 Edward Purcell (d. 1825), the post surgeon, was from Virginia. In 1818 he joined the 5th Infantry and accompanied that regiment to Minnesota in 1819. Among his duties was that of keeping a meteorological register.

baffled. Some of their bones were [found] not long since sticking out of a bank from whence gravel had been taken for the fort. The blankets that the soldiers had been buried in were but little decayed, also the hair, although they had been buried some twenty years. The coffins were all decayed, and nothing but bones, hair, and pieces of the blankets were found when they were disinterred.

The troops had arrived at the mouth of the St. Peter's River, Minnesota, in September before I arrived there, and commenced building winter quarters at the mouth of the Minnesota River near the south bank, as there was a large quantity of timber handy. They had got very comfortable quarters, both for officers and men, in the form of a fort with four gateways. It was quite formidable against Indians as the buildings were of logs a foot through. Some of the old chimneys still remain to mark the place of the first fort. The chimneys were of stone and long since have fallen and been over-grown with earth, and little mounds mark the spot and shape of the old fort.

I passed the winter in a little building outside the fort with my brother, trading with the soldiers. Nothing was done the first winter except to provide for themselves. In the spring the troops were all moved over to Camp Coldwater, where there were some beautiful springs, for their health, as the physician and commanding officer thought the former location very unhealthy, being surrounded by flats and swamps. So it took all summer [1820] to build new quarters and make some gardens for the officers and the troops.

When we would all assemble at our depot at Land's End, the clerks and men would have a jolly time for a few days running foot races, jumping, wrestling, and shooting at a mark in the sports. Whilst we were firing at a mark with my brother's pistols, I forgot the pistol was cocked and raised the muzzle carelessly straight up, and off went the pistol, and I suppose the ball did not miss my head more than two inches. It staggered me some and frightened me more, and I quit the pistols for that day.

Another day I got to wrestling with a man by the name of Noble, a clerk of the company. He was about my height and thick, stout built, and considerable heavier than I was. The first fall we broke hands; the second fall I threw him fairly. He got up and said he would throw me or break his legs, so we tried it again. He made a desperate lunge at me and threw his whole weight on to me; at the same time he gave my ankle a blow and wrench, and I fell with a broken ankle which kept me lame for nearly two months.

At night we used to get together and have duck soup, some half a dozen of us. There was one of our company we used to take pleasure in playing little tricks on him. We would get him in our suppers and after we would get through we would commence scuffling. We would manage so as to have all get on top of our man, and then we would roll and toss until he would holler murder and everything else; and after he had got a good fumbling we would let him up. The moment he could get a chance he would make tracks as fast as he could get away.

When I was trading at Land's End I went out to get some of my credits.[4] An Indian, also Mr. Campbell[5] and several others were along. We were going to a Wahpacoota [Wahpekute]* camp high up on Cannon River. The first night we camped, this Indian got at my pack and stole a paper of small brooches. There were about 500 in the paper and they cost about 30 dollars, as they were made of pure silver. There were so many in our company that I did not know whom to lay the theft upon, and said nothing. I came back home and in four or five days the Indian came into my house with his hair strung full of my new brooches. I went right to Col. Snelling and told him the circumstances and he sent some soldiers and had him taken up and put in the guardhouse.

He then sent word to the Indians to come in. The thief told them where they could find the brooches. At the end of three days the Indians came in and brought the brooches. They asked for food, saying they were very hungry. The colonel told them he did not feed them and told them he was a-going to keep the thief twenty days in the guardhouse. He took his gun, worth probably 2 dollars, and gave it to me for the brooches that were missing, and shut the

---

[4] The practice among the traders was to extend credit to the Indians in the form of goods such as traps, guns, ammunition, blankets, utensils, etc. The Indian was supposed to repay the credit as soon as the hunting and trapping season was over. Although no trader was supposed to extend credit as long as the Indian had not met his previous obligations to another trader, the unpaid amount might be carried over to the next season, when further credit could be granted. Under this system many Indians were forever in debt.

[5] There were several traders by the name of Campbell at this time—Duncan, Scott, and Colin. This was perhaps Duncan Campbell, or maybe Scott Campbell, the interpreter.

gentleman up. He stayed in about ten days and made out that he was very sick. Probably he was somewhat hungry. The colonel thought he had frightened him a little and let him out. When he got off a little distance he started on a run and made the snow fly behind him, and never was seen about the fort until the Sioux men were shot for firing into the Chippewa* camp. The man was one of the party and was shot with the rest.

During this summer Governor Cass arrived here from his northern tour.[6] A salute was fired, some counciling with Indians, and the Governor started on his journey down the river again. Nothing of importance was done during the summer except that some parties had been sent out to look for pine timber to build a fort on the point of land between the Mississippi and Minnesota rivers. A few sticks of timber had been hewed and hauled to the ground that Col. Leavenworth had selected for the fort on the rise about 300 or 400 yards west of the present Fort Snelling. The parties that had been in search of pine timber returned and reported large quantities on Rum River.

In the spring of [1820], Colonel Leavenworth was ordered to the Missouri and Col. Snelling was ordered to take command at St. Peter's on Minnesota River. Col. Snelling changed the location of the new fort and made it on the precipice at the junction of the two rivers. [*An examination of the Little Falls (Minnehaha) was made, and it was thought there was not water enough for a mill . . . and St. Anthony was selected.*] A party was ordered to go to the Falls of St. Anthony to commence a saw mill to make lumber for the fort.

The troops was obliged to return to their old quarters in the winter of 1820–21, at the mouth of the St. Peter's, while several parties were sent out to cut and hew timber for the fort and, besides this, the men had to cut and haul all the wood they burnt by hand on hand sleds. A large number (2,000) pine logs had been cut and hauled by hand by the soldiers to the bank of the Rum River, but the mill was not ready for running or sawing till the summer of 1822. At this time the water was so very low in the Mississippi River that the government teams used to cross over the main shore to the

[6] Governor Cass visited Fort Snelling on July 31 and August 1 and 2, 1820, with a party of about forty persons. He succeeded in getting the Chippewas and the Sioux to make a treaty of peace, but it lasted for only a short time.

Island for timber for the mill. For 2 years there was not much done worthy of note, the whole command being occupied in building.

There were about 300 men and officers to command them. The officers' names I will give so far as I can recollect them: Col. Leavenworth, Col. J. Snelling, Major Forsyth, Major Larabee, Capt. Gooding, Capt. McCabe, engineer of the first building, Lieut. W. G. Camp, Quartermaster, Lieut. McCartney, Lieut. Wilkinson, Lieut. Hobart, Lieut. Green, adjutant, Major Hamilton, Lieut. Oliver, Dr. E. Purcell, Louis Devotion, sutler, Lieut. Harris, Lieut. Clark, Capt. Clark, commissary, Capt. Pelham, Capt. Perry, and a bandmaster, Mr. Kerphew, from which company Mr. Jos. R. Brown sprang. [*Also, Maj. Vose, Capt. Gwinn, Lieut. McCabal, engineer and building, Lieut. Wilkins and Capt. or Maj. Foster.*] These are all the names I can recollect as the first officers that commenced the work on Fort Snelling.

All things went on peaceable until the fall of [1820][7] when an order was received from Washington to demand of the Sisseton* Indians a murderer. The Sissetons of Minnesota, it appears, had been over to the Missouri and murdered a white man there. Col. Snelling made the demand and 2 relations of the murderer were brought in as hostages. The Indians made a great show and parade on the delivery of the two hostages, firing guns, whooping, yelling, running to and fro with all sorts of gesticulations.

A formal delivery was made of the hostages outside the fort, the gates all closed, and the cannon all ready in case of an attack. The Indians said that their great father had demanded some of their bodies. "Here they are; kill and eat, if you wish; if not, we hope you will return them safe to us again."

Col. Snelling had them marched into the fort and took from them their British marks that the hostages carried. One had a large British medal and the other a British flag. The Colonel ordered a fire to be made in the middle of the parade ground and took the flag and burned it before all the Indians, and then went to the other hostage and cut the British medal from his neck. He ordered the two hostages confined in the guardhouse and ordered a few rations for the Indians that had come to deliver up the hostages. They went

[7] Prescott evidently intended to write 1820 instead of 1822. A letter dated November 13, 1820, from Colonel Snelling to Major Taliaferro, the Indian agent at Snelling, tells of the affair described here.

off very much humbled and were peaceable for about one year after.

The two hostages, after having been confined about a month, one morning at daybreak wanted to go out. A sentinel accompanied them outside the fort and they got out some distance, amongst the stumps and trees, from the sentinel and started off with a whoop. The sentinel, Francis Nason, or Lessard, fired at them and came near killing one of them; the ball passed so close to his head that he fell to the ground. The other, Mozahtunkah, or Big Iron, saw him fall and stopped and asked him if he was hurt. The other replied that he thought not. "Well," said Mozahtunkah, "we can get away, up and be off, for the sentinel is far behind!" So they started again and went clear. I happened to be out at this time and saw the Indians when they started and all the operation until they were out of sight. The alarm was given in the fort and all the officers and soldiers were out in pursuit, but Mr. Indian was too far off, and the chase was soon given up.

The Indians had run away but another demand was made upon them [the Sissetons] for the actual murderer, and after much delay and trouble the murderer was brought in and delivered up to Col. Snelling. Says the Colonel, "I will see that you don't get away," and put a large ball and chain on his foot and put him in the guardhouse.

The colonel sent him down to the States for trial, but no witness appeared against him and he was set at liberty, but never reached his native land. Some think he was murdered. Some think he died of fatigue and hunger.*

During the two years that I was at the old fort [Cantonment New Hope] I learnt to hunt and trap wolves. I got a couple of traps made and about every other day I would catch a wolf. Although they are a very cunning animal I often outwitted them. I sometimes would cut a hole in the ice the exact size of the trap. Then I would put a piece of clean white paper over the trap, then sprinkle snow over the paper. Then I would cut meat into small pieces and scatter all over the trap and around 8 or 10 feet wide. So while the wolf would be running around picking up the small crumbs of meat, it would step into the trap. Still, notwithstanding all this precaution, some of them would spring the traps and eat the bait and get off clear.

Another plan I had of hunting the wolves was to get into an old house or boat laying on the river bank and wait for them passing at night. About nine or ten o'clock at night they would begin to come around and I shot several in this way. Every chance I could get to slip out from the store I would be off hunting, and during the two years that I was at the fort I killed a large number of wild fowl, and wolves, which was my greatest delight for to trap.

About this time an order came that the sutlers for the troops should get only 25 per cent profit on their goods. Mr. Devotion kicked at this and quit the business, saying that 25 per cent would not pay the losses, otherwise wastage and brokerage, and wound up his business with about 80,000 dollars in paper money on the banks of Illinois and Missouri.*

The paymaster, Capt. Larned,[8] it is supposed, made a handsome [deal] out of this transaction. He had taken the government drafts and sold them to these banks, and took their paper and paid the troops with it. At this time there was no law compelling the paymaster to pay in specie, so the sutler had to take the paper money from the troops for his goods.

During the last summer that I was in the sutler's store the young woman that I had seen on my way up the Mississippi, a daughter of one of the chiefs, came into the store frequently to trade quill work of mockasins and many other little articles of their manufacture. Her appearance and conduct attracted my attention and, in fact, the young woman got acquainted with all the officers' ladies at the fort and she became very much respected by all for her good behavior and decent appearance, and cleanly, far exceeding the rest of the Indian girls. She used to get many little presents from the ladies and gentlemen of the fort, and I was not behind the rest in showing favors to the old chief's daughter.

Still, there was another young lass courting me and I was courting another. Finally, the one that was after me and wanted me to marry her sent a messenger to me one day and asked me to marry her, for she said she loved me very much. I made an excuse, saying I was too young to marry, and gave a small present. The messenger went off and they never troubled me again.

---

[8] The paymaster, Captain Benjamin Franklin Larned, joined the service in 1813 and remained in it at least until the 1850's, receiving promotions in 1847 and 1854, when he was a colonel and paymaster general. He died in 1862. (Francis B. Heitman, *Historical Register and Dictionary of the U.S. Army* [Washington: G.P.O., 1903], I, 616.)

But I fixed my mind upon the old chief's daughter. The chief's name was Kee-e-He-i, or The Man That Flies. The daughter's name is Nag-he-no-Wenah, or Spirit in the Moon. But as the owner of the store had made up his mind to leave the country, I did not make any advances to the young woman or give her any encouragement about marrying her, but continued to make them little presents from time to time until we left for St. Louis, which was in the fall of [1821].

We loaded our little keelboat. Mr. Devotion, Capt. Gooding, 2 or 3 discharged soldiers, and our servant was about all the company on board the little keelboat, and we started, leaving all old friends behind.[9] We had all become very much attached, both officers and citizens, and it appeared almost like my first setting out from home to leave old acquaintances, not knowing whether we should ever meet again.

And as we floated down the river we passed the tribe of the old chief on the island [10] below the fort. They were all out looking at us as we floated past; all we could say was a good-bye, and on we floated.

But we had hardly got a half-mile, and were still in sight of the fort, when floating along with our mast up we ran under a leaning tree hanging over the river. A limb of the tree caught the top of our mast, the boat swung around broadside to the current and careened over, and we came near sinking. But we got one of the men to climb the mast and cut the limb of the tree, and away we floated again; and after that we looked out for the old leaning trees on the banks and kept off from them.

We camped for the night below the mouth of the St. Croix. As usual Mr. Devotion gave us a stingy meal, as when we first came into the country. The next day we got into Lake Pepin and came to that noted place, the Lover's Leap.

The Indian tradition of which is that a young man had took a fancy to a young woman and induced his friends and relatives to make up a purse and purchase the young lady, according to the

[9] The Indian agent recorded for September 16, 1821: "Mr. Devotion late sutler and Mr. Wright [Prescott] & Philander Prescott Lieut. Joseph Hare late 5 Infy left this Post to enter into the civilized world, the good feelings of all at this Post attend them." (Lawrence Taliaferro's Journal, Vol. 6, MS, Minnesota State Historical Society.)

[10] Probably Pike Island, at the mouth of the Minnesota River. It was named for Lieutenant Zebulon Montgomery Pike, who in 1805 made a treaty with the Sioux on the west end of the island.

Indian custom, which purchase, if acceded to by the parents, is considered a marriage; although the girl may not have known the man, or may have had but a slight acquaintance with him, yet the parents' will or wish is to be obeyed. And aristocracy often brings or entails misery upon many of the Indian families by the parents' making marriages for their children where there is no love nor intimacy with the bridal parties.

The young man sent in his presents, or the amount that his friends had collected, to pay for the girl he wanted. The parents assented although the amount was small; yet the young man was a great hunter and the old folks looked to a man that would give them plenty of venison. But the daughter had been looking forward to a young man that she loved, and rebelled against her parents, or said that she wished to marry a man that she knew and loved, but the parents persisted in selling their daughter for a good hunter. The daughter remonstrated and said the man had already a wife and "I do not wish to live a life of polygamy, particularly as I am the second and will have to be a slave to his first wife." [11]

The parents said, "We are old and cannot hunt, and the man will feed us all." The daughter expostulated and said she did not wish to be made a slave to serve a married man as wife for the sake of a hunter. But the parents said, "You must obey."

This was in the evening, on what is called Point de Sauble, or Sand Point, opposite the fatal place. The daughter saw there was no chance of saving herself from slavery for life to a man and woman she knew not nor loved; therefore she resolved to free herself from misery by destroying herself. Accordingly she made preparation for the work, and long before the dawn of day she took the paddles of her parents and embarked into a canoe. She crossed Lake Pepin from Sand Point to the great perpendicular rock, opposite the place where the Indians were encamped.

In the morning early, the orator of the party or band that was traveling, arose and commenced his morning oration, as follows: "My friends, we are now going on a hunting excursion. It is time to be up and be off. The lake is calm. Up! Up! And make your

[11] James H. Lockwood wrote ("Early Times and Events in Wisconsin," *Wisconsin Historical Collections*, II [1855], 188–189): "A man may have as many wives as he can maintain . . . the more he has, the better he is off, as they can dress and prepare the more buffalo robes for market."

sacrifice to the god of the waters, that we may pass this lake in peace, or that the waves will be calm and not stop us on our journey."

The old orator proclaimed their duties to their gods in a loud voice and could be heard for three miles upon the water—and I believe I have often heard them three miles when they were speaking before raising their camp. It is a general custom for some of the camp to rise early in the morning and give directions for the day, where to go and where to camp and where to hunt that day, and when to assemble at night.

The old orator said, "In my midnight dream of last night a mountain appeared before me, and on the top of the mountain I saw a damsel attired in her best clothes, and she looked forlorn and alone and appeared to be in trouble, and I awoke. Arise, and prepare for the day's journey."

All was up at the loud voice of the orator, and cooking and preparations went on for the journey of the day. After the repast and other little preparation of packing and loading the canoes, the old woman of whom we are speaking missed her paddles and looked round for them and began to mistrust something was wrong and ran down to the water's edge and found her canoe was gone. She then commenced inquiring for her daughter whom she supposed had slept with some of her friends for the night, owing to her sorrow or troubled state of mind.

But no daughter was to be found and a general search was made, but nothing was to [be] found of the supposed bride, and orders were given to march. The mother with much reluctance raised her camp and started with the rest. The usual sacrifice or offering was cast upon the waters by the old warriors. Pipes of peace were filled and smoked to the deity and the god of the waters, and the old orator commenced a song to the spirits of the water and to his dream of the last night, saying, "I fear my dreams will bring sorrow to our hearts this day."

They paddled slowly along on the lovely bosom of Lake Pepin, and as they approached the opposite shore of the lake the warriors raised a song of glee and joy. All at once an echo was heard from the high promontory opposite where the little fleet of canoes were passing down the lake. The old heralder raised his voice and said, "On that summit I saw a damsel in my dream. I now hear her voice. Hark! Listen!"

A breathless spell came over the whole flotilla of the company, about a hundred canoes in the company. A song was heard from the mountain top: "My parents, I remember your kind care and sing to the gods that have kept us, and the morning star that guides us in our early rising and employment, to guide you for the future. And I now free myself from misery and contention."

"What?" says the old orator, "Is my dream coming to pass? Where, from whence come those sounds? Hark again! Look on that mount! See! See!" he says, "From whence comes that voice and song?"

Here a great consternation took place. The canoes all landed and a race [began] with the men to gain the summit to see who was the person that was responding to their songs below; and the mother looked up, and behold, her daughter was there, clothed in all the riches of Indian attire, standing upon the precipice of about one hundred feet.

The young men warriors strove for gallantry to ascend the mountain. The young man, although a husband, reached the place first and said to the girl, "What has brought you here?"

"You are the person that brought me. A married man I never will live with!" She rolled herself in her blankets and made the awful leap and landed a mass of broken bones and mutilated flesh. Oh, what anguish both to parents and lover (if there were any love), and a warning to forced marriages! The body was taken up and disposed in the common way on a scaffold, there to remain one year, and after that to be interred in the ground.

We went on down the lake and passed a point where some white men had been killed by the Chippewas, not far from the foot of the lake. The Chippewas came over to war against the Sioux, and finding none, they turned in and killed three whites that were on their way to Fort Snelling—Mr. [John] Findley, [*Joseph Barrette*], and Mr. [Francis] Depouse[12] and some others that I do not recollect their names. Troops had been ordered out to arrest the Chippewas, but

[12] John L. Findley was a clerk and had charge of the business of Colonel Alexander McNair, who had the sutling of the fort at Prairie du Chien. He was the first clerk of court at Prairie du Chien about 1819, and in 1821 in the company with a Frenchman by the name of Depouse went up the Mississippi River and was murdered. (Lockwood, "Early Times," pp. 116, 122, 127, 149.)

by the time the troops arrived there, the Indians were nowhere [to be seen]. And a short time after, a boat full of soldiers was robbed of their provisions by a party of Chippewas near the same place where the white men were killed—a good specimen of bravery by our troops!

We passed on down without any trouble and came to Prairie du Chien, my first landing place on the Mississippi. I found no change in the old French settlement, which is older than Philadelphia, and only about fifty houses in 4 miles square. This place derives its name from the oak timber,* being the exclusive growth of timber on the prairie,—black jack and scrub white oak.

From here we worked down to the mouth of Fever River and rowed up to the traders' establishment, about 7 or 8 miles from the mouth of the river.[13] Here we found 2 or 3 Indian traders, Mr. Bautelier, Vanmeter, Mr. Shull, and some others in log cabins, 3 I think in all.[14] Mr. Devotion traded off some cloth for lead and loaded his little keelboat and went out for St. Louis.

We floated along down to Rock Island. At the head of the rapids we passed a Sauk and Fox village. They were swimming horses. Though the wind was blowing strong and a heavy swell was on the river, the horses and canoemen appeared to enjoy the pleasure, and crossed the great Mississippi, a Menominee word for "great river." The Chippewa name is Kitchecepee. The Sioux word is Hah-hah-watte-pah, "river of the falls" instead of "laughing water," a burlesque upon the Indian language.

When we arrived at Rock Island we were soon surrounded with the natives of the country, Sauks and Foxes.* At the place was a government fort.[15] Here we met some old acquaintances, officers and soldiers, and passed a pleasant evening with the military.

We floated off the next morning for St. Louis, and we met with no inhabitants until we got near Hannibal. A man by the name of White was the first, and we encamped and got some new milk and some fresh butter, an article we had not seen for 2 years. I had

[13] The Fever, or Fevre, River began to attain great importance following the discovery of lead deposits in the area in 1822. The traders' establishment was at, or close to, the site where Galena was then growing up.

[14] Although Prescott gives their names as Bautelier, Vanmeter, and Shull, it is quite probable that the three were Francis Bouthilier (also spelled Bouthelier and Boutielle), A. P. Van Metre (also spelled Vanmetre and Van Meter), and Jesse W. Shull.

[15] Fort Armstrong, construction on which had begun in the summer of 1819.

Philander Prescott's America

been troubled with dysentary all the way down, and I got a pint of new milk and boiled it and put pepper in it, and it cured me in one night.

We sailed on down and passed Clarksville, with one brick house and 3 or 4 log cabins. We continued our journey on down to St. Louis without accident and landed in St. Louis in the fall of [1821].[16]

[*St. Louis was but a small town, and I do not recollect seeing more than one church, and that was Roman Catholic. There was a small market, two or three mills, one bakery, and about half a dozen steam boats, which supplied the place with all the goods that were wanted for the trade.*] Here we spent the winter, and the most of our time was spent in trying to get something for the bank notes that Mr. Devotion had received in payment from the troops for the goods he had furnished them. [*Mr. Devotion found the banks all broken and closed. He could do nothing to help himself.*] All was a failure and Mr. Devotion lost all his earnings in the soldier trade for 5 or 6 years, and Mr. B. F. Larned, the paymaster, reaped all the benefits, and the banks of course had a hand in the matter.

Upon this failure, Mr. Devotion commenced drinking, and his whole business went to destruction by the lawyers, who eat up everything he had. We passed the winter [1821–1822] and commenced in the spring to make a garden at the place where we were living as it was rented for a year. My brother had hired out and gone back to Fort Snelling to tend the sutler's store again.

I was still living with Mr. Devotion and he one morning ordered me to go to work in the garden, so I went to work and helped plow the garden and prepared the ground as well as I could. Then a lot of manure was hauled on the ground and I was ordered to go and beat it up and spread it out over the ground; and here commenced a trouble.

I told Mr. Devotion that I was not hired to him to be a carter or a manure master. I would not attend to it. This made the old gentleman somewhat displeased that I would not be a dung carrier for him, and [he] would not speak to me for several days. Finally he came out and said he had intended to do something for me, but he did not know whether he should send me home or not. I told him to act his

[16] St. Louis was not incorporated as a city until 1822, when its population was a scant 5,000, including a large number of Frenchmen engaged in the fur trade. St. Louis was the natural center of the fur trade of the Missouri and Mississippi valleys.

pleasure but to remember the services I had rendered him. He went away and left me and went to his hired man and told him to go on with the garden.

During this time my brother arrived in St. Louis again, the sutler business having passed into the hands of other persons. We passed the most part of the summer in hunting and looking over the country and we did not know hardly what to do. My brother [Zachariah Wright] engaged to a clerkship with Messrs. Powells. My old master, Mr. Devotion, came to me one day (in the spring) and said, "I have had it in my mind to do something for you and, if you will take a lot of goods and go to Fort Snelling and trade with the Indians I will get an assortment for you."

This proposition met my views and I agreed at once to go to work and go into the trade, remembering the girl I left behind me. So Mr. Devotion went to Messrs. Bostwicks & Co.[17] and purchased two thousand dollars worth of Indian goods on credit, and turned them over to me. I baled them up and got our little keelboat ready again and hired four men and a steersman, who took charge of the boat and the boatmen. In one week we were all ready and left in June [1822] for Fort Snelling again [to trade with the Sioux Indians]. My brother remained in St. Louis with Messrs. Powells, and Mr. Devotion kept batch with his servant.

Before going any further with my trip up the Mississippi I must relate some little incidents that took place whilst I was in St. Louis. Mr. Devotion's man [Tom] was an Irish Roman Catholic. He had prevailed on me to go to the Catholic church, and I finally became more and more attached to their service and became a regular attendant. And had any of them proposed the thing to me, I would have joined their church. But no one said anything to me on the subject of religion and I slipped from what I do not know.

About this time Lent came on, and our man was keeping Lent; I inquired of him something about it and so I thought I would keep Lent, too. I commenced on bread and water and stuck it out for forty days on nothing but bread and water, and got along just as well as those that lived on meat. One day during Lent Mr. Devotion

17 Bostwicks and Company failed within the following year. (Sydney A. Patchin, "The Development of Banking in Minnesota," *Minnesota History Bulletin*, Vol. II, No. 3 [August 1917], 139.)

wanted me at table. I told him that I did not wish to be at table when he had company, as I was keeping Lent. He commenced swearing and said I was a nuisance to the house for keeping up such foolish acts, but I stuck it out; and when Lent was ended I commenced eating meat and other rich food, but it made me very sick for 2 or 3 days, the sudden change of diet.

Our servant, although a strict Romanist, would indulge a little most every day, and after dinner would take a very sound nap. And one day whilst our man was fast asleep, I got some pieces of rope and tied his legs together, and then took the rope up to a large nail in the joist overhead. Then I tied his hands and made them fast and commenced pulling the rope on his legs, and worked very easily until I got his legs pretty well drawn up. Then I went off quietly and left him there snoring away.

I went over to Mr. Devotion's room and, after a while, I went out to see if Mr. Tom had woke up yet, but he was not stirring yet. So I stood a while on the piazza in front of the room where I had left friend Tom. In a few minutes I heard rattling in the room where he was. After a little, open flies the door. The moment Tom saw me he made for me, swearing vengeance. I run for Mr. Devotion's room. He followed me to the door but dared not come in, for he was afraid of the old master, Mr. Devotion.

He stopped and went back to his room again, but he kept me out for three days under penalty of a good thrashing if I ever put my foot in his room again.

Mr. Devotion discovered there was something wrong and asked me what it was. I told him what I had done. He had quite a hearty laugh over the scrap and told Tom he must make peace with me. After a while Tom saw me out[side] and came along laughing and said he would let me off if I would promise not to play any more pranks with him. So we agreed to drop the matter, forget all, and make friends again.

This summer [1822] the water was very high and, working along with our little keelboat, we found it very difficult to work with poles, as we could find no bottom and had to pull along by the brush a good deal of the time. We were three days getting above the mouth of the Missouri.

We had stopped for dinner and there appeared to be a great storm arising. We laid to, and the storm did come with a vengeance. We were near being sunk by the storm. The [wind] blew down a large cottonwood tree which fell within ten feet of our boat, which, if it had struck us, would have sunk us all in one minute's time. The water was over the banks of the river in many places, and the water was up to the windows in the houses along the river banks. The storm shook the trees so violently along the margin of the river that acres and acres of land and timber fell into the river during and after the storm above and below us, but we escaped unhurt.

After the storm we moved on slowly. Sometimes we were 2 and 3 miles from the river in order to find bottom, so we could work with our poles. One day we [had] a good fair wind from the south and we sailed about fifty miles that day and reached Clarksville. One brick house and two or three wood buildings was all there was of the town. There was a post office here. I got the mail for the Upper Country and set out the next morning.

We worked slowly along until we reached the head of the Lower Rapids, or Rapide Des Moines. We stopped for dinner and we saw an old Indian village a little distance off, and saw some flags flying in the air. So we thought, while the men were resting a little, we would go and see the Indian town. So we all went but one man to watch the boat. But we found before we could get to the village we had a small stream to cross. The men plunged in and over they went and I followed, but I found the water was very deep and I could not swim. And if the pilot of the boat had not caught me by the collar of the neck, I should have drowned. But he got me out safe and we had quite a joke over the scrape of their getting me in over my head, and getting a good ducking, etc., etc.

We went on up to the village, on an eminence on a beautiful, large prairie. We run into the houses, from one to the other, as the Indians were all off hunting. All at once we commenced scratching worse and worse. By and by they began to look at their legs and they found that they were covered with fleas. They commenced swearing in French, and jumping and running off for the water, and as soon as they gained the river in they plunged and rolled and washed until they drowned all the fleas.

I stayed a little while and examined a new grave. The body was that of a man in a sitting posture, a warrior partly decayed. A large number of trinkets were left in the grave, which was open so we could see all. This Indian, we learned afterwards, had been to war against the Sioux and got wounded with an arrow, and had got home and died. A great deal of nicety had been displayed for Indians in the burial of this warrior. I think there [were] 3 or 4 very pretty flags flying over the grave and there to be worn out by the winds. The trinkets, we could not get to see what they were made of. Some looked like silver, some brass, and wampum and beads of various kinds. I would think, at the prices the Indians had to pay for those articles, it had cost them $150 for what they had left on the body and in the grave.

We went back to the boat and picked up some round stones that appeared to be light. We broke some of them and found inside particles of stone in every variety of shape, and almost as transparent as thick pieces; and, in fact, the inside looked very much like glass, but the outside was a dark color and rough.[18]

The river here all comes together and is about 3/4 of a mile wide, and in low water it is shallow and large sharp rocks in the bottom. Boats have to be very careful in descending in low water, for the current is very strong and boats frequently get stove on these rapids.

We got under way and went all the remainder of the day in our wet clothes. The next day I was taken down with fever and ague. I had no medicine and I dragged along in misery until we got to Rock Island, where there were some troops. I got some medicine but it did not help me much. By this time the water had fallen some, so we could pole and cordell our little boat* to considerably better advantage. We crossed the Rock Island rapids in about a day and a half, which was considered a good run for poles and cordell. After we got over, the hands were very tired and stopped for dinner, and after dinner some of them went to sleep.

One of the Frenchmen said he would like to play a trick on one of the boys that was asleep, a boy that was a little dumpish, otherwise simple. He told some of those that were awake if they would keep the fellow from hurting him when he should find it out, he would play the most laughable trick on him that they ever saw. So all promises imaginable were made that they would assist each other.

"Very well, you will see some fun," says the Frenchman. The man they were to play the trick upon lay broad on his back with arms and

---

[18] These stones evidently were geodes, many of which have been found along the Mississippi River in that area.

hands both spread out. The mischief maker unbuttoned his pants and went and eased himself in the sleeping man's right hand, and hastily buttoned up. "Now," says he, "all pretend to be asleep as soon as I am done." So he pulled a hair from his head and laid it across the sleeping man's nose, and crawled off.

All were apparently asleep, but were like foxes with their eyes open. It wasn't long before the hair began to make the sleeping man's nose itch and, thinking it was a fly or some insect, he brought his right hand over on his nose, and I guess there was a hubbub.

In a moment all were routed and a race began, first after one, then another. Some that had been asleep did not know what to make of it, as they did not know what had been done. They thought the fellow was crazy. When he found he could [not] catch them, he commenced with his tongue, and as soon as they all understood the joke they all joined in the sport. Nobody knew nothing about it; nobody saw anything. He would look at his hand and then chase one again, then another. Finally he found he could make nothing of them and went and washed, swearing vengeance on the perpetrator if ever he found him out. The time came for starting and all were ordered on board, but there was not much fun the remaining part of the day. In fact, the fellow did not get over it for a week, but took good care to get on the boat when he went to sleep in the day time.

I have written this to show the character of the French, who are always replete with tricks and levity, and as it came into my mind. In my first voyage up the Mississippi on the ice with a French train, I will tell another of their tricks.

An old Frenchman was driving a team behind. He called to one that was driving a team a little distance before him and told him he wanted a chew of tobacco. The one ahead said, "Yes; in a few minutes I will let it fall in the snow and you can pick it up." "Very well," said the old man, and on we went. After while we came to some horse manure. The one ahead picked up some and halloed to the old man behind and told him there was some tobacco for him, and let a piece fall in the snow. The old man watched very carefully and came to the place and picked up what he thought was his tobacco.

It was all covered with snow, so that he did not discover what it was at first and came near getting it into his mouth but, stopping to brush the snow off a little, discovered that it was not tobacco, for it all fell to pieces when he commenced brushing the snow off. The old fellow commenced scolding and swearing at the other for cheating him in such a dirty way. This set the whole crowd to laughing and shouting, as they knew nothing of the affair until the old man began to rage. This made him worse, and the old fellow pulled his blankets off the sleigh and was for turning back. They all gathered around him and told him he would perish if he attempted to go back alone. Some threatened him if he attempted to go back [and said] they would tie him on the sleigh, but the old man was pretty resolute and held off for some time. Finally, one of the party gave the old man a good plug of tobacco. This pacified him a little and he agreed to go on and took his team again.

We worked and toiled in the hot sun from morning till night. So warm that the men's arms would have new sun blisters on them every few days; and I had the ague, which was no comfort to me during the hot weather. Finally we got to Prairie du Chien.

Here I got some more medicine and I took two passengers on board; one, by the name of B. F. Baker,[19] going up to teach school at Fort Snelling, was sick and had the ague. The other was a Mr. Joel Whitney, from Green Bay, with a few goods and groceries to sell at Fort Snelling.

We moved off slowly, two of us shaking with the ague every other day. It appears to me that we used half a bushel of bark, but it did not appear to help us in the least. Mr. Whitney had some good brandy on board but he would not tap it. He said he was afraid the men would get at it, but this was a mere excuse, for the men had a plenty of whisky and were not in want. The real thing that he was afraid of was that we would not give him enough for it, and we learnt afterwards he was the greatest skinflint that ever went up the Mississippi.

Finally, after toiling 55 days in the hot sun, and sick with ague, we arrived at Fort Snelling some time in August [1822].

SUPPLEMENT

Prairie du Chien (page 27)

Henry Schoolcraft, who visited Prairie du Chien in 1820, left this description of it: "The village of Prairie du Chien is pleasantly situated on the east bank of the river, on the verge of one of those

19 Benjamin F. Baker soon became a noted fur trader in Minnesota.

beautiful and extensive natural meadows, which characterize the valley of the Mississippi. It consists of about eighty buildings, including the garrison, the principal part of which are logs, arranged in two streets parallel with the river, and is estimated to have an aggregate population of five hundred. This is exclusive of the garrison, now consisting of a company of infantry, ninety-six strong, under the command of Capt. Fowle. . . . The present settlement was first begun in 1783. . . . There had formerly been an old settlement about a mile below the site of the present village." (*Narrative Journal of Travels*, ed. Mentor L. Williams [East Lansing: Michigan State College Press, 1953], pp. 220–221.)

James Lockwood reports ("Early Times and Events in Wisconsin," p. 130): "Prairie du Chien was, at this time, an important post for Indian trade, and was considered by the Indians as neutral ground, where different tribes, although at war might visit in safety; but if hostile, they had to beware of being caught in the neighborhood, going or returning. Yet I hever heard of any hostile movement on the Prairie after they had safely arrived."

Government Factory System (page 27)

The system operated at Prairie du Chien, with John Johnson in charge, from 1815 to 1822. The factory was given a liberal allowance of merchandise which was worth about forty thousand dollars. This large stock was purchased for the factory so that the Sauk Indians near Saint Peter River and the Fox Indians near the lead mines might be supplied with merchandise, both tribes having expressed a desire to be furnished with goods. Thomas L. McKenney sincerely hoped that the state of affairs would improve around the new factory. He said that conditions had been such that the citizens' "scalps were bought and sold in the village of Prairie du Chien, strung on poles, and carried in triumph to Mackinac." Only a short time passed before he complained that "the Multitude of Traders, British and all other sorts made a sort of wall about the factory. Few Indians could get to it." (Ora Brooks Peake, *A History of the United States Indian Factory System, 1795–1822* [Denver: Sage Books, 1954], pp. 23–24.)

The Wahpekute Sioux (page 31)

The Wahpekute Sioux were one of the smallest of the seven branches of the Dakota, or Sioux people. According to Major Long, they had roving habits and hunted near the headwaters of the Cannon and Blue Earth Rivers in southeastern Minnesota. Long, in 1823, estimated they numbered 800 people, living in 100 lodges, and having 200 warriors. He stated: "This tribe has a very bad name, being considered to be a lawless set of men." (William H. Keating, *Narrative of an Expedition to the Source of St. Peter's River* [Philadelphia: H. C. Carey and I. Lea, 1824], I, 386.) Their name means "shooters in the leaves." (Frederick W. Hodge [ed.], *Handbook of American Indians North of Mexico* [New York: Pageant Books, 1959], II, 890.)

The Chippewas or Ojibways (page 32)

The Chippewas, or Ojibways, belonged to the Algonquian group of Indians. They were traditional enemies of the Sioux, or Dakotas, who belonged to the Siouan group. The Chippewas at this time occupied the northern parts of present-day Wisconsin, Minnesota, and North Dakota, while the Sioux were their neighbors to the south, especially in Minnesota and North Dakota. The number of Chippewas at that time has been estimated at from fifteen thousand to thirty thousand.

The Sisseton Sioux (page 33)

The Sisseton Sioux were one of seven tribes of the Sioux, or Dakota Indians. They may have numbered 2,500 persons, with 800 warriors. They were closely allied with the Wahpeton Sioux; and when they ceded their lands in 1851, their territory stretched from the Big Sioux in eastern South Dakota to the Mississippi. The northern boundary was from the Red River, just north of Moorehead, to St. Cloud, and thence down the Mississippi.

Punishment for a Murderer (page 34)

On November 13, 1820, Colonel Snelling wrote to Major Taliaferro, the Indian Agent, as follows:

> The unfortunate wretches were delivered up with a great deal of ceremony and affecting solemnity. The armed guards watched a procession in the road led by a Sisseton bearing a British flag, followed by the murderer and the chief. These two had their arms pinioned and large splinters of wood were thrust through them

above the elbows, intending to show their disregard of pain and death itself. The murderer wore a large British medal around his neck, and the two men bore offerings of skins in their hands. Finally in the procession came the Sisseton chiefs while the two prisoners sang their death song with the others joining in the chorus until the guardhouse was reached. There the British flag was burned in a fire and the medal worn by the murderer was given up. [Hansen, *Old Fort Snelling*, p. 113.]

Major Taliaferro, in a communication to his superiors dated November 10, 1820, wrote:

The old chief I have detained as a hostage; the murderer I have sent to St. Louis for trial, presuming that it is a course you will approve. I am much indebted to Mr. Colin Campbell, the interpreter, for his great exertions in bringing this affair to a happy issue. The delivery of the murderer is to be attributed solely to his influence over the Sussitongs. ["Early Days at Fort Snelling," *Minnesota Historical Collections*, I (1850–1856), 424–425.]

Taliaferro may perhaps have been mistaken about the exact date.

Paper Money Issued by Local Banks (page 35)

From 1811 to 1816 the number of local banks increased from 88 to 246. The state legislatures which chartered these banks placed few restrictions upon them. The United States was operating on a paper currency issued by the state banks which was overissued and depreciated. It was difficult for Devotion to know at Fort Snelling the value of the money on banks far down the Mississippi.

The Naming of Prairie du Chien (page 40)

"It has never been determined whether Prairie du Chien was named after 'dog' or 'oak.' Both are so much alike in French that no one knows which it took its origin from." (Philander Prescott, "Autobiography and Reminiscences of Philander Prescott," *Minnesota Historical Collections*, Vol. VI, Pt. 1 [1894], 477.)

Scanlan, the historian of the town, quoting Major Long, states: "Prairie du Chien, or the 'Prairie of the Dog' derived its name from a family of Indians, headed by a chief called 'the dog.'" (Peter Lawrence Scanlan, *Prairie du Chien: French, British, American* [privately pub., 1937], p. 218.)

The Sauk and Fox Tribes (page 40)

The Sauk and Fox tribes belonged to the Algonquian family and at this time were enemies of the Sioux, or Dakota, tribes. They lived on both sides of the Mississippi River until the Black Hawk War of 1832 brought their removal from Illinois.

Maneuvering a Keelboat (page 45)

"When the wind was up-stream a keelboat might make headway with a sail. But in a river so crooked as the Mississippi and with winds so fitful as those that blow in the western country, this seems to have been more an aggravation than a cure of trouble. Most of the time a keelboat was poled against the stiff current, or men would go ashore and haul on a line. Thus, favored by fortune and the weather, they might make from eight to twelve miles a day, if the day were not too short. Yet keelboats were used as late as 1832 and a great commerce was carried upon them. . . . Keelboats traversed not only the main streams, the Mississippi and later the Missouri, but many tributary rivers as well." (Charles Edward Russell, *A-Rafting on the Mississip'* [New York: Century Co., *ca.* 1928], p. 22.)

Every keelboat had a tall mast from the top of which was tied a long rope that men pulled upon along the shore. This was called cordelling.

III

1822–1824
Initiation into the Fur Trade

As soon as I arrived at St. Peter's, or Fort Snelling, I commenced building my winter quarters and trading house. I kept my boat hands one week for that purpose and we got the body of a house up and part of the roof on. Then I had to let my boat's crew go back. So I purchased a wood canoe of the Indians, gave them provisions for the voyage down to St. Louis.

I hunted about and hired another Frenchman and went to work and finished my house the best we could. Timber was very scarce and we had a poor place for to shed rain. The Indians came in and commenced trade in small things, as the furs were not good or seasonable.

One day an Indian came to me and said he wanted to get something. I took him down to the boat where I still lived and asked him what he wanted. He said he wanted powder. I asked him where the pay was. He said he wanted a credit. I told him I could not give credits. He hung around for some time and asked for something else. I refused. After a while he pulled out his knife and commenced rolling it about on his lap and asked for powder again. I refused and got up and took my gun down and laid it across my lap. "Now," says I to myself, "I will be ready for you if you do try to injure me."

So the fellow hung about for some time and kept asking for powder, but I kept refusing. Finally, he found he could not frighten me into miscues. He then commenced coaxing me and showed me his gun and said he had not one load of powder. I looked at his gun and found that it was not loaded. It was probably well for me that it was not, for the Indian is a great rascal and might have taken some advantage of me, as I was entirely alone. However, I stuck to my gun, and finally the fellow went off mad enough, and I was glad to see his back, for he had kept me a full two hours in the little cabin of my boat, working and trying to make me give him something.

I lived here with my Frenchman until October [1822], when my brother [Zachariah Wright] arrived from St. Louis. By this time some of the furs began to get good and some trade commenced, and most every day we had a visit from the fort from the officers, [*who had all got into quarters*]. Most of them were young men and fond of sport. My brother had a fine pair of large dueling pistols. We used to spend a good deal of our time in shooting at a mark.

And my brother and myself we got so perfect with the pistol that we used to hold a candle for each other to shoot at in the house in the night. This used to alarm the Indians very much to see us holding a piece of candle about six inches long for each other to shoot at. We used to snuff the candle every shot.

One time we were shooting and a little cat jumped up onto my brother's shoulder just as I fired. The ball made the tallow fly about some, and some of it struck the cat in the face and sent her a-wheeling and squalling. This pleased the Indians greatly to see the little cat cut up such antics from the effect of the tallow striking her in the face. No doubt it made the kitten's face smart some, as its face was only about six inches from where the ball struck.

Riding about was about all we done that winter, except to tend to the Indian trade, which did not take a quarter of my time. Now and then I would take an excursion or a trip around amongst the Indians, and once in a while the girl I left behind me (Nag-he-no-Wenah, Spirit in the Moon) called in to see me and trade a little, get a little present and be off again in a short time. One time I offered her a scarlet blanket for a kiss, but it was no go, and off she went home.

When the spring [1823] came my brother got our furs together and made packs of them and pressed them as well as we could,[1] and my brother then started for St. Louis with them. Before my brother left for St. Louis we received a letter stating that Mr. Louis Devotion, our old Master, was dead. It appears after I left he took to drinking very hard on account of his losses, which was considerable, about 40 or 50 thousand dollars. As I have related, the troops had been paid

[1] Furs were put in a press to reduce their bulk, then packed in bundles weighing about one hundred pounds. Each bundle was wrapped in a skin of little value to protect the furs in transit.

off in Illinois and Missouri money and the banks failed, and when Mr. Devotion found he was going to lose all, it broke him down. He gave up to hard drink and died the fall after I left him.

[*After my winter trade was over*] my brother went down and paid for the goods that I took for the trade. When my brother went down he had some discharged soldiers to row his boat for him, and they found he had some money with him. They formed a plan to rob him. He happened to overhear them and [it] happened so that they were not far from a town; he landed and discharged them and got another crew, and so got down without any trouble.

Mr. Devotion was dead, and the house that had furnished us with goods had failed and we could get no Indian goods. [*The companies had all joined together, and made a monopoly of the whole trade and would not furnish any goods to any person to trade with on his individual account.*] My brother could not make up his mind what to do. About this time one Kenneth McKenzie[2] from Red River of the North came to St. Louis and started up a trading company. My brother joined them and came up with them. I had got tired of waiting at Fort Snelling and went down to Prairie du Chien to see if I could get any news of my brother or what he was doing. I stopped with Judge Lockwood,[3] an old acquaintance of mine.

After waiting some two weeks my brother arrived with Mr. McKenzie with a large keelboat loaded with goods and provisions for the trade and some 30 men and clerks to carry on the trade. Also they had sent a strong force up the Missouri to carry on the trade. A company was formed, called the Columbia Fur Company,* and a strong opposition was got up against the American Fur Company by Mr. McKenzie's efforts.

2 Kenneth McKenzie, born in Scotland in 1801, immigrated to the Northwest, where he engaged in the fur trade with the Northwest Company until that firm was absorbed by the Hudson's Bay Company in 1821. He became a leading figure in the formation of the Columbia Fur Company in 1822; and when that company was taken over by the American Fur Company in 1827, he became a leader in the new concern on the upper Missouri River. (Hiram M. Chittenden, *The American Fur Trade of the Far West*, New York: Harper, 1902, I, 384.)

3 James H. Lockwood (1793–1857) was born and educated in New York. In 1815 he went to Mackinac as a school teacher. He visited Green Bay in 1816 and went on to Prairie du Chien, where, as a trader, he took up permanent residence in 1819. (James H. Lockwood, "Early Times and Events in Wisconsin," *Wisconsin Historical Collections*, II [1855], 119, 157–158, 172–173; III, 55–56.)

I embarked with the company and we left Prairie du Chien. The hands worked hard early and late, as the season was getting late, to get the goods in the Indian country. At night when the boat would stop the clerks would go to the skiff and go out fishing, so that most every day we would have fresh fish with our salt pork.

After toiling hard for eight or ten days we reached Buffalo Slough, a small stream coming in from the east bank of the Mississippi, so named from their having a range there for buffalo in times of the oldest Indians' remembrance. This place is about 6 miles below what is called the Grand Encampment* on the west bank of the Mississippi. This place derived its name from the traders' and Indians' camping there to hunt a day or so when going up or down the river, as there were then great quantities of game there.

When we started from Buffalo Slough we got a fair wind and hoisted sail. The boat had a very large sail and we sailed all that day and passed the St. Croix River, a distance of about 60 miles.

We had a pet bear on board the boat and we used to have a great deal of sport playing with it. This day we were sailing along very finely. We had on board Dr. Purcell, physician for Fort Snelling. He was out and playing with the bear. The bear jumped at him and the doctor ran back. In doing so his heel caught on a cleat on the running board of the boat and he fell backward into the river.

"The doctor's overboard," I holloed. The cook was on deck—an old black man. He jumped down on the running board and in he went and swam down to the doctor, and told him to lay his hand on his shoulder and hold on until the boat came. He done as directed, but the boat, having great headway, had left them some ways behind. Before the sail could be taken down and her headway stopped finally, the skiff was got loose and sent after them. The old black man kept swimming all the time with the doctor resting one arm on his shoulder until the skiff came to them, took them in, and got them all safe on the boat.

The doctor went overboard on his back. He had on a large soldier coat, and as he fell backward, it spread out on the water and held the doctor square on his back until the black man swam to him and saved his life.

The next day we had a fair wind again and sailed up as far as Carver's Cave* without any more accidents. Here we got a canoe and four or five of us got in and paddled up to Fort Snelling with the mail.* We got in late, after ten o'clock. They were most of them in bed, but the old friends were glad to see us and get the mail.

I went up to my old place that I left in charge of a Frenchman. I ordered him to cut me some timber for another house whilst I was gone. And when I came back [I] found a house partly up at a place called Land's End, about half a mile above my first wintering ground.

The boat came up the next day and I bought of the company $500 worth of goods on credit. They, the Columbia Fur Company, went on up the Minnesota in small boats and carts for the winter trade with the Indians.

I went on and finished my house, fixed it pretty comfortable for the winter [1823–1824], and commenced giving some credit to the Indians, but the few goods that I had did not last long.

In a few days one Alexis Bailly,[4] a certain half-breed, a trader from Prairie du Chien, came along with some goods and I entered into co-partnership with him for the winter trade, and got some more goods.

By this time the girl I left behind me had come up to see me, but she only stopped a few minutes and was off again. I began to think about getting married after the Indian manner [by purchase], so I took ten blankets, one gun, and 5 gallons of whiskey and a horse and went to the old chief's lodge. I laid them down and told the old people my errand and went off home. The third day I received word that my gift had been accepted, but that the girl was bashful and did not like the idea of marrying, and I must wait until they could get the girl reconciled to their wishes for her to marry me.

In a few days they moved their tent up and camped near my house, and it was ten [days] after they moved to my place before I could get my wife, as she was then timid. At last, through much entreaty of the parents, she came for to be my wife or companion as long as I chose to live with her. Little did I think at that time I should live with her until old age. We passed the winter very comfortably together. The old chief lived in his tent near us all winter. I fed and clothed them all winter.[5]

4 Alexis Bailly (1798–1861) arrived in the Fort Snelling area about 1824. He had a fur trading post at Mendota which he sold in 1835 to Henry H. Sibley.

5 By caring for his parents-in-law, Prescott was only fulfilling the duties of an Indian son-in-law. Indian parents were often eager to have their daughters enter marriage relations with white traders, for they knew they would be better cared for than would otherwise be the case.

In the spring [1824] my partner [Bailly] came down from the winter trade, and my brother and myself had much trouble in settling up our affairs. Finally, under fair promises, we let him take all the furs, and that was the last of all the trade with our partner. He went off and made up accounts that far overcame mine, in a parcel of trash that he had left me to sell and would not take back— brought them as a charge and an offset against my account, and brought us in debt about $130.

The Columbia Fur Company came along and we gave them orders on Mr. Bailly. He showed his accounts and they soon saw that we were taken in, and they could not get anything of Mr. Bailly. My brother went to St. Louis with the company's boat. They had a pretty good trade on the Minnesota. They made 400 packs of furs and robes. This made the American Fur Company look with big eyes when they learned of this large lot of furs taken from their pockets.

The company went to St. Louis and got a new supply of goods and coming back, as they were about to leave Prairie du Chien, a warrant was sent by Mr. Bailly, our former partner, to take my brother for debt. Here they like to have had a fight. The whole boat's crew joined in to help keep the sheriff off from serving his warrant on my brother. Finally, friends interfered and my brother gave his note for the amount, and they left for Fort Snelling.

I passed the summer doing nothing. Finally the company's boat arrived and we had to make some new arrangements. I had no goods and could not get any, and what was to be done? It was proposed to me to join the company on a certain condition, that was, I was to go to the Chippewa country with an outfit for to trade. I had no other alternative and had to accept. The arrangement was made and I got my outfit ready.

Another outfit had also been started for Red Lake, in charge of Mr. B. F. Baker, the gentleman that came up with me in the keelboat, when we both had the ague. But the worst of all—what was I to do with my wife? Of course, she did not like the project, but said she could live with her parents. This relieved my mind some, to think she would be in a place where she would be at home. So I made arrangements for her by leaving her plenty of clothing and other things to purchase fresh meat or game from the Indians as she might want.

We parted, and off we went in our bark canoes. Mr. Peter

Quinn[6] was my interpreter. The first day we went to the falls [*of St. Anthony*]. Here we had to take our canoes out and carry them around the falls by hand. Two men took up a large bark canoe and carried it half way, then laid down and rested, then picked it up and carried it to the upper landing, a distance of half a mile.

The way the canoe is carried, it [is] rised up to the shoulders and the men have a little cord that they hold in the left hand, attached to the canoe. By this cord the canoe is held firm to the shoulder. The bales of goods weigh about one hundred pounds. These packages are carried with a headstrap tied round the bales and the strap over the head. These they carry from one end of the portage to the other, one-half mile. This work generally takes one day, so at night we were all over and ready for to start in the morning.

The water was very low and we made slow progress. We broke our canoe on the rocks frequently, then would have to stop and repair [it] by patching and pitching with gum. Finally we got froze up at a place called Prairie [Percée], or a Hole-in-the-Prairie, formed from a place having been worn out by the water in the bank on the east side of the river.

Here we built a log house out of small pines, of which there were plenty, where Fort Ripley is now built, about one hundred miles from Fort Snelling. This is the first pine they found in a body near the river.

We found that we were only on the east and southern borders of the Chippewa hunting ground, but we had not been there long before some Indians came in and [were] very glad to see us. They said their old traders were so very hard on them they could hardly live. They could not get ammunition enough to kill game to live on. I went to work and give them a pretty liberal supply, and they started out hunting, all well pleased, and by night we had bear and two or three deer. And you may be assured we all had a great feast that night, for we had been living very poorly for several days, working in the cold water and ice, getting our worn-out canoes along.

The Indians began to come in and some trade was done. I hired an

---

[6] Also known as Patrick Quin or Queen. Born in Dublin, Ireland, in 1787, he went to Fort Snelling in 1823, where he engaged in U.S. government service in Minnesota, and was, at various times, an Indian trader, an interpreter, and an Indian farmer.He was killed by the Sioux at Redwood Ferry, August 18, 1862. ("Minnesota Biographies," *Minnesota Historical Collections*, XIV [1912], 621.)

old chief to take some goods and go and trade with Indians far above, up the Crow Wing River.[7] He went off and returned in about two weeks with a good lot of furs. I outfitted him again. By this time my goods began to get low. However, I took some wampum, a few goods, and some silver work, and a little outfit for the Sioux country.

I started with one man and a Chippewa Indian that had been amongst the Sioux a long time and could speak considerable of the Sioux language. The Sioux and Chippewas being at war, I took this man as a guide, and knowing the Indians knew him, a great many of them, I thought it would be safe to take him with me. We made up our pack and left the interpreter and one man in charge. We started for the Sioux camp—where, we did not know.

We traveled two days, through a dense forest of thick pine one whole day, crossed quite a stream with our mockasins on, and snow about 4 inches deep. We traveled the balance of the day with wet feet, but did not suffer from cold, as we had large pieces of blanket inside our mockasins. At sundown we camped, made a good fire, eat our lunch, dried our mockasins, and laid down and went to sleep very soon, as we were very tired, had carried our packs, and were wet.

At daybreak we started again and just at night we got out of the timber. This day it rained some and thundered, about the middle of December [1824]. We camped and slept sound from fatigue. The next morning we started down Sauk River. The Indian went out hunting for elk and told us to go on down to a point, that he would meet us there. So we went on, as we supposed, to the place he pointed out, and waited and waited for our guide, but could hear nor see anything of him.

We had struck the Sauk River too high up. We were two days' march from the Mississippi. We waited until we got out of all patience, and started on down the river. We did not know what to do. We were in a country that we knew nothing [about], and where to go we knew not. Here we were in a quandry, but we kept on our journey down the Sauk River.

About two o'clock our guide came to us, much to our joy, as we were relieved from any further anxiety about the route that we were to travel. The Indian said we had missed the point, otherwise had not reached it. We had not gone far enough. He said he had been to the

[7] Prescott's winter camp of 1824–1825 was approximately six miles south of the mouth of the Crow Wing River.

place that he pointed out some distance below us, and not finding us there supposed we had gone on down the river. He started on after us and traveled on until he had got tired and, not finding us, knew that we could not get far ahead of him, and started back in search of us. The rain the day before had taken the snow nearly all off in the prairie and our tracks did not show. [This] was one cause why we did not find each other sooner.

We went on until night and camped on Sauk River, a stream about 30 yards wide, but shallow in the summer. Our food had very nearly given out, so we had a but little for our supper and breakfast and no signs of any Sioux.

The next morning we followed on down the river. About ten o'clock we heard guns off south of us. This we knew to be the Sioux and turned our course in that direction. Shortly after we started in the [direction of the] firing that we heard, a buck sprang up. The [guide] had his gun down in [a] moment, although it had a cover on it, and fired as the deer ran from him. As he fired, the deer tumbled heels over head but was not quite [dead]. The Indian put a small load in his gun and finished him. The Indian turned the deer over and said he had killed the deer without making a hole in the skin.

"How can that be?" said I. "Why, can't you account for it?" he asked. "No," I said. "Well," said the Indian, "the ball went straight into the backside, through the entrails, and lodged in his shoulder." The Indian hastily took off the skin and a considerable quantity of the meat with it, and shouldered it. We went on, expecting to meet with some Indians, but we travelled and travelled and travelled until we got tired and sat down to rest. We started again and travelled until dark and found no Indians that night. So we had a good roast of our venison and went to sleep, not dreaming of the trouble that we were to meet the next day.

We started early in the morning and traveled till about nine o'clock. All at once we heard a gun not far from us. We gave a whoop and in a few minutes an Indian came running up to us and commenced holloing and firing his gun. Directly another came and commenced firing his gun, and so on; and in about half an hour we had about one hundred wild Sisseton and Wahpeton* Indians [about us]. The wildest kind of confusion prevailed for about half an hour.

Some were for killing us. They said we were come as spies from the Chippewas to get them killed, etc., etc. I denied all their assertions and told them I came to trade with them, but they would not listen at all and kept on with their threats. They stole my cap from me, took the Indian's meat from him and his gun, and took my man's gun and cap from him, and now threatened to take my goods.

Some of the old men interfered, saying this [is] one of our traders of the same company that we have at Lac qui Parle[8] with us. I told them if they did not stop their mischief I should report their conduct to the officer at the fort. They still were saucy, and two or three times some of them cocked their guns to commence the work of murder. We stood [it] and never let on we noticed their murderous intent. The old men interfered and stopped the young from killing us, but I assure you it was a close run.

They held council and decided to take us into camp to the chief, Limping Devil.[9] This name he derived from having tricked the traders, and very badly. The Fox and Sauk Indians [at an earlier period] had come to war and found a camp of Indians encamped on the Redwood River. They fell on a small camp that was at some distance from the main body of them, and killed nearly all of them, and made off without getting injured. The main camp started in pursuit the next morning. They travelled all day and all night, and the next morning about ten o'clock they came in sight of the hindmost ones.

The Sioux had to hold back for some time to wait for the footmen to come up, as the horsemen were some distance in advance. Finally, a part of them got up and the Sioux made the attack. The Fox and Sauks halted, and the Sioux rushed right on to them and attacked them with lance and war clubs. And by the time the hindmost of the

8 A trading post of the Columbia Fur Company called Fort Adams is known to have existed at Lac qui Parle in 1826. Prescott's remark indicates that it may have been there earlier.

9 Limping Devil,* also known as Thunder Face, or in the Siouan language, Itewakinyanna or Estaykeenyan, was chief of the Tizaptani band of the Sisseton Sioux, from three hundred to four hundred persons, or about fifty lodges. (Newton H. Winchell, *The Aborigines of Minnesota* [St. Paul: Minnesota Historical Society, 1911], pp. 549, 553, 555; Stephen Return Riggs, *Mary and I: Forty Years with the Sioux*, introd. by Rev. S. C. Bartlett [Boston: Congregational Sunday-School and Publishing Society, 1888], p. 87.)

Sioux got up, the Sioux had killed 13 of the Fox and Sauks, and the foremost ones had fled by this time. The Sioux said they were completely tired out and did not follow them any farther. There were no Sioux killed but several were wounded. Amongst them was this Limping Devil, [who] was wounded in the knee. This gave him the name of Limping Devil.

He was a brave but awful wicked man, and as we moved off for the Indian camp, this man came out on horseback to meet us, as he was still lame. He took me by the hand and then my guide and my man, and bade us proceed on to his camp.[10]

The Indians were all waiting, expecting the chief would give orders to have us killed, but no such order came and we went safe into camp. No doubt, it must have been the interposition of God that subdued this wicked chief's heart for the time, that our lives might be spared.

When we got into camp the chief told his brother to take me to his lodge, and the man went to another lodge, and the Indian guide to another place and so we were all separated. A council was called and we were all called in and I was told if I would tell the truth that we could go home again, but if I lied we could not go. They wanted to know what I had come for. I told them I had come to trade, but I had got out of the route that I had intended to go and had fallen in with them instead of the Indians I wanted to see. I told them the Indians that I was in search of were the [Mdewakantons] that had left St. Peter's after I did, when I expected to meet my wife.

"Are you married?" they said. "Yes," I said. "To whom?" "To Kee-e-He-i's daughter." At this time an Indian, Black Tomahawk, of the lower bands came in and confirmed my statement, and said, "These Indians are afraid you have come to find where they are, so the Chippewas can come and kill them."

They kept me there until about midnight, talking and questioning me as to my residence, and made me promise to come back and bring them some powder and balls. The council finally broke up and they let me trade the few goods I had, which was done in about an hour's time.

The chief's brother, whilst I was trading, stole one of the otters that I had traded and sold it to me for wampum.* I could not say

[10] The custom of shaking hands was not native to the Indians, but was acquired early from white traders and explorers.

anything, for the least thing would have started a fuss and we would have been killed. So I said nothing, but gave him the wampum and gathered up my furs as quickly as possible and tied them up and sat down on them.

They kept me a prisoner for three days, and we had to move with them in camp every day. Finally, the 4th day in the morning, the chief gave us an escort of 20 braves, mostly old men, to accompany us one-half day's journey. So they conducted us on our road until about noon and halted. We sat down and had a smoke together and shook hands and we separated. And I will assure [you] we travelled hard the remainder of the day and got on to the Mississippi and camped, almost tired to death. We had traveled so hard to get out of the reach of those hateful creatures.

In the morning we were off by light without any food. We traveled all day, and at night camped by Pike's Rapids, a place where General Pike wintered when exploring the Mississippi River.* In the night it commenced snowing and snowed all day. We shouldered our packs at daylight and we trudged through the snow storm. This was the third day we had been without food. I asked my man and Indian what they would choose, providing they could have their wish, for breakfast. The Frenchman said, "A good drink of brandy." The Indian said, "A good loaf of bread and a good cup of tea or coffee." I told the Indian he was [a] good deal of my opinion, still I would [like] a good piece of fat bear meat. "Oh yes," said the Indian, "that would make the belly and hair both slick."

We traveled on, almost wearied out, through the snow storm, and about three o'clock P.M. arrived home once more, a place I once thought I should never see again, when I was first taken prisoner by the Sioux.

The Chippewas came in in large numbers to hear the news, and they said it was one of the greatest wonders in the world that we were not all killed. The mother of the Indian was along with them. She came to see her son and told me plainly that if her son had been killed, she would have killed me on my return without him. So it was a providential escape all around.

I staid at home and recruited strength a little, and fixed up for another trip for Fort Snelling, as I was entirely out of goods. There were three chiefs that wished to go, and 4 other Indians, myself, and one man made up the party, nine in all.

We all got good snowshoes made, and while we were getting ready one Mr. Wm. Aitkin, a trader from Sandy Lake,[11] came down and stopped in an old partly broken-down trading house about half a mile above me on an island. He invited me to call over and see him, so I went with my interpreter and made him a visit, and gave him an invitation to visit me. So he called' in and we talked over the trade and some other matters a short time. Mr. Aitkin left but invited me to visit him at Sandy Lake. I told him I probably would after I came back from Fort Snelling.

By this time I had about twenty packs of furs and peltry. I showed them to Mr. Aitkin. He looked with astonishment and said, "Those are mine by rights, for all these Indians have credit of me." I said I had paid for them, I believed they were mine now. "Yes," he said, "and I will watch you after this!" And so he did keep three or 4 men amongst the Indians all the time, watching them; and as fast as they would kill skins they would take them from the Indians. But the Indians would always find some chances to hide a bear skin or some other furs and bring them to me.

Finally, we got ready and started for St. Peter's, or Fort Snelling, on snowshoes. The first day I got along very well for a new beginner. We expected to camp with some Indians the first night, from Mille Lacs on Rum River,* but we got disappointed, and it was bad business for us, as we had taken no provisions with us, expecting to get a supply from the Indians. But they were gone, and what to do we hardly knew.

So two good walkers said they would go in search of them. The sun was about two hours high when they started, and I with the balance of the company remained in the old camp without any supper. We built up a good fire and lay down and took a sleep. We slept until about nine o'clock. We got up and made a fire and warmed up, but no Indians came back. We waited and waited; at last they came about midnight.

We inquired what had kept them so long. They said they had followed the trail of the Indians, which had taken them a long way around and to Mille Lacs, which they said was not far off to go

11 William Alexander Aitkin* (1785–1851) was born in Scotland and immigrated to America as a boy. About 1802 he arrived in the Northwest in the service of trader John Drew. ("The French Regime in Wisconsin—II," ed. Reuben Gold Thwaites, *Wisconsin Historical Collections*, XVII [1906], 14.)

straight, and that there was a trail [there] that they [had] come in [on], that we could go there in two hours, but that they could get no provisions.

What to do again was a subject to be considered about getting provisions for the journey. The old chiefs [said] we could go by [Mille Lacs] and Snake River [12] and by so doing find Indian camps all along, and sleep with them nights, and if they [had] any food they will feed us for the night.

We were all anxious to go to Fort Snelling, [but] all the journey by this route was long and somewhat doubtful about getting provisions. I consented to go and we started off in the night, about half past nine. I found the snowshoes had strained the cords of my instep very much, and it was with much difficulty that I could keep up. However, I hobbled along and finally we got to [Mille Lacs] about midnight.

An old Frenchman by the name of LeRoy was trading there for Mr. Wm. Aitkin. The old man got us some rice made, or gathered, by the Indians, and had it cooked. So we had some warm rice and a little sugar with it, which made us a very good supper. We were very hungry, having traveled all day and part of the night without eating. The old man said they had to live poor, as the trade would not afford any great expense, and they had mostly to live on fish and rice. He said they only got flour about once a week; as for pork, they never thought of such a thing. This old man's daughter was married to Mr. Aitkin as his second wife.

Mr. A. was expected there that night but he did not come. I wish he had, for I could of got some provisions of him. But the old man was afraid of his Master and dare not furnish us any [food], as we were opposition traders. And the custom in this country [was to] starve out, ruin out, and drive out every opposition, either by fair or foul means, that they possibly can.

In the morning the old Frenchman gave us another dish of rice. This wild rice is very similar to our white rice as to nutriment, but it is quite dark [in] color. Its nutriment is quite feeble and does not give much strength to the body. The people of this country have to eat it. They simply boil it in water, and when they can get some

[12] The route via Snake River was about twice as long as that by way of Rum River.

grease to put in it, it helps to give nutriment. Also sugar is used with it, which makes it palatable. A person can eat a quart after it is cooked and in two hours after will be as hungry as ever. The Indians had been round to the camps and gathered a little rice* that had been parched, which is very good to eat when traveling. It prevents thirst and relieves the appetite for a little while.

We started early in the morning for Snake River. We had a track most of the day. We travelled the whole day and only stopped once; that was about two o'clock to eat a mouthful of wild rice. And on we went and traveled until dusk, when we came to a trading post. The trader's name was Johnson.[13] This was the hardest day's travel that we had all the journey. The distance I do not know, but I think it must have been all of 40 or 50 miles.

Mr. Johnson welcomed us into his house and gave us such as he had. That was wild rice simply boiled in water. We made our repast, but we had been eating rice so long without seasoning that we did not relish it very well, but still we had to eat some. Mr. Johnson said there was no game about where [he] lived, and they seldom ever had meat. Once in a while they got a little grease from the Indians, but had to pay a great price for it.

Mr. Johnson said he came into the country from Lake Superior by the way of the lakes and small rivers in bark canoes. I think he said they had nearly one hundred portages to make before he reached his trading post. He said the whole trade was worth only about two thousand dollars a year and it hardly paid for the trouble and expense, but as he was in the trade he did not know what to do for a living except to follow up the trade.

We had a good large chimney fire and a very warm room, so we laid down to rest, but I was so tired that I did not rest for a long time. The Indians went to sleep in a few minutes and did not wake until morning. When we awoke, Mr. Johnson had a large kettleful of rice, boiled in water as usual. We eat as much as we could. Mr. Johnson made many apologies for the poor food he had to offer, and when we started he give us a little to carry with us.

In the morning we started early and traveled through pine forests all the day, as we had done the day before. They were some of the

[13] This may have been William Johnston, a trader for the American Fur Company.

handsomest pines that [I] had seen in the country. We traveled all day without eating again, and part of the time on snowshoes.

Just as the sun was setting we came to an Indian camp and stopped for the night. We went into their tents and sat down. The Indians told us they were starving and could not give us anything to eat. The tents, which were principally made of bark from the birch tree, or rushes from the ponds and lakes, were open and cold. All that I saw about the camp was one little pike fish in the eatable way. The woman cooked it in a small kettle and eat it.

We laid down but did not rest much, being very cold and hungry. In the morning we started on our snowshoes, without supper or breakfast, and traveled until about noon, when the Indians halted and took out their little bag of rice. We all eat a little and started on through swamps and hummocks, a most awful country to travel on snowshoes. Sometimes I would get a trip and my snowshoes would throw me ten feet ahead; into the snow I would plunge. By the time I would get up the Indians would be some distance ahead of me. Then I would have to work and run and worry myself most to death to catch up again, for I hated to give out and tell them to wait for me.

So we worked on until night, but I was awfully tired. The Indians made a good fire and we sat down and dried our snowshoes and mockasins. They pulled out the balance of the rice and we eat it, which was but a few mouthfuls apiece. However, we had a better camp than we had when we camped with the Indians the night before, for we could make a good large fire and warm up well. It is a great thing in traveling to get warm and dry at night; then you can sleep and you will feel much better for traveling in the morning.

We started early on our snowshoes. About noon we came to oak openings, and our snowshoes did not trip us up so often, as there was not so much underbrush. At night we camped in the oak openings. Whilst the Indians were hunting about for wood for the night, one of them found a dead deer and cried out, "Good luck!"

"What is it?" we all sang out. "A deer!" he said. The Indians all give a whoop of joy and went to see the deer. It had been dead for a long time, but was whole and frozen and covered with snow. The Indians dug it up and got it up to the fire and thawed it a little, and got the hide off and chopped it up. The meat was fairly black. They had a small kettle along. They melted snow and filled their kettle and boiled the meat, but oh! what an awful smell came out when the meat got hot. But the Indians stuck to it and cooked it and eat hearty of it. I tried to eat some but, as hungry as I was, I could not eat the meat, it was so old and smelled so bad.

From this point, by hard walking on our snowshoes, we got into Fort Snelling. The colonel commanding was about the first that I met as I went into the fort. He was quite surprised to see me and made some inquiries where I was from, etc., etc. Finally, I told him I was very hungry. "Why, have you been starving?" I told him we had been nine days living on a little wild rice. He told me to come in to his quarters where he told his wife, Mrs. Snelling, one of the most accomplished and charitable ladies of the fort at that time. In a few moments she brought me a large bowl of soup, but none but a hungry person could tell how good it tasted.

With many thanks I left them and went on to our trading post 2 miles above the Fort, where Mr. Lamont[14] was in charge. All were glad to see us. They soon had some food cooked for us and we retired to rest. The next morning we all felt very tired, stiff, and sore, but in a day or two we all felt well again.

I had been here but two days when my wife arrived. She had been out with the Indians on a hunt, and it was this camp that I was in search of when we got lost and fell in with the Sissetons, and missed finding my wife as I expected. After they had put up their tents I went to see them in their lodges or tents. My wife presented me with a fine boy [William Alexander], born while they were on the hunt in December, 1824.[15] I staid with them about a week.

SUPPLEMENT

The Columbia Fur Company (page 54)

The Columbia Fur Company was created in 1822; it consists of but few individuals, who being all practically acquainted with the Indian trade, in which they had previously been engaged in the service of the Hudson's Bay or North-West Company, resolved

[14] Daniel Lamont was one of the original founders of the Columbia Fur Company. (Chittenden, *The American Fur Trade*, I, 388.)

[15] The first of three sons and six daughters born to Prescott and his wife, according to Mrs. Ralph O. Stratton, curator, Ontario County Historical Society, Canandaigua, New York, in a letter of January 13, 1955. However, the 1850 census, which must have been in error, indicates that there were three sons then living; one son is known to have died before 1850. See Appendix C.

after the consolidation of these two companies into one, to
establish themselves on the United States' territory, and seek to
trade with the Indians south of the boundary line, under licenses
granted by the Indian agent at the mouth of the St. Peter. Their
capital is not very large, but being all active, intelligent, and
experienced, they will, we doubt not, succeed. Their principal
establishment is at Lake Traverse; its situation is judiciously
selected, as it is at the head of the navigation of the St. Peters and
Red Rivers, in the midst of a country which abounds in buffalo,
so that they can lay in ample provisions for their wintering
parties. By extending their excursions to the headwaters of the
Mississippi, and as far on the Missouri as the Indians will permit,
they will be able to obtain large supplies of beaver and other
valuable skins, and as their object appears to be merely to trade
with the Indians, and not to hunt upon their lands, they will, it is
hoped, continue on amicable terms with them.

(William H. Keating, *Narrative of an Expedition to the Source of St.
Peter's River* [Philadelphia: H. C. Carey and I. Lea, 1824], I,
426–427.)

The Grand Encampment (page 55)

The Grand Encampment was on Cypress Prairie, where the town of
Tepeeota flourished briefly from 1856 to 1859. Long wrote in 1817:
"The elevation of the prairie above the river is about twenty-five
feet. Upon the upper end of the prairie is the Grand Encampment, or
place of general resort for the Indian traders, during the winter, for
the purpose of trafficking with the Indians." ("Relations with
Western Canada," *Minnesota History Bulletin*, Vol. II. No. 1
[February 1917], 22; "Review of Books," *Minnesota History
Bulletin*, Vol. II, No. 2 [May 1917], 87.)

Carver's Cave (page 55)

Carver's Cave was named for Captain Jonathan Carver, who on
May 1, 1767, received a deed there written by himself and signed by
two Sioux chiefs, granting to him and his heirs a large tract of land
in the present states of Wisconsin and Minnesota. The Sioux called
the cave Wakon-teebe, or the Tepee of the Great Spirit. ("Minnesota
Geographic Names," *Minnesota Historical Collections*, XVII [1920],
80, 443–444.)

Mail Delivery at Fort Snelling (page 56)

Mail at Fort Snelling was first carried as an accommodation by any trustworthy traveler. The regular mail arrived semiannually, then quarterly, and for many years no more frequently than bimonthly. (Charlotte Ouisconsin Van Cleve, *"Three Score Years and Ten"* [Minneapolis: Harrison and Smith, 1888], 32–33.)

Wahpeton and Sisseton Sioux (page 60)

The Wahpeton and Sisseton Sioux were always closely associated. The Wahpetons, whose tribal name means "dwellers among the leaves," lived along the Minnesota River, though they claimed the land as far north as the Crow Wing River and the mouth of the Chippewa River. Each tribe numbered from nine hundred to fifteen hundred persons. Major Long, who visited them in the summer of 1823, described them as good-looking and straight. The men, who were hunting at the time, wore nothing but breechcloths, and a few dispensed with that. "The dress of the women consisted of a long wrapper, with short sleeves, of dark calico; this covered them from the shoulders to the waist; a piece of blue broadcloth wound two or three times round the waist, and its end tucked in, extended to the knee. They also wore leggings of blue or scarlet cloth." (Keating, *Narrative of an Expedition*, I, 368–369.)

Limping Devil (page 61 n.)

Samuel W. Pond gives the following description of Limping Devil:

Itewakinyanna (Thunder Face), chief of the Five Lodges or the Woods band, was a noted character in his day, a bad leader of a bad band. If his character was not better than his reputation, it was bad enough; but though his people could not well have chosen a worse thief, probably they would not have tolerated a better one. They were as restless and roving, and supposed to be as lawless, as prairie wolves. They were good buffalo hunters, but bad horse thieves, and a terror alike to friends and foe. Though Thunder Face was at their head, it may be that they would have gone farther and done worse without him; for Indian chiefs sometimes seemed to be leading their people when they were only guiding them, as a man when he can no longer hold a runaway horse, still tried to steer him the safest way.

("Two Missionaries in the Sioux Country," ed. Theodore C. Blegen, *Minnesota History*, Vol. XXI, No. 2 [June 1940], 330.)

Limping Devil and his brother, Respected One, also known as Kenehanpe, were dangerous characters. Stephen R. Riggs wrote of them: "There seemed to be no love lost between these two brothers. Each was jealous of the other. They often sought, by poisoning, or in some other way, to destroy each other. That they might accomplish this object they have been known to offer a horse for 'bad medicine,' as poison is properly called." ("Dakota Portraits," ed. Willoughby M. Babcock, Jr., *Minnesota History Bulletin*, Vol. II, No. 8 [November 1918].)

Wampum (page 62)

Wampum was strings of shell beads used as a medium of exchange among Indians. "Wampum proper seems to have been of late introduction, originating on the Atlantic coast. It was common amongst the Iroquois and the eastern Algonquin, but there is no record of its use by the Dakota of Minnesota. . . . Yet Philander Prescott mentions it as one of the articles deposited as stakes at the Santee game of Lacrosse. It was probably common among the Sauk at that time." (Winchell, *The Aborigines of Minnesota*, p. 493, 493 n.)

Pike's Winter Camp (page 63)

Zebulon Montgomery Pike in the winter of 1805–1806 had his camp on the west bank of the Mississippi in present Swan River township, Morrison County, about a quarter-mile south of the mouth of Swan River. Pike's Rapids were opposite the camping place. Prescott's trading post was about seventeen miles north of the rapids.

William Alexander Aitkin (page 64 n.)

"Aitkin married into an influential Indian family; was soon a trader on his own account; and rapidly advanced until in 1831 he took charge of the Fond du Lac department of the American Fur Company with headquarters at Sandy Lake [about two miles east of the Mississippi River]. . . . He died September 16, 1851, and is buried on the east bank of the Mississippi, opposite to the mouth of the Swan River, in Morrison county, where he had a trading post during his last nine years, after 1842." ("The French Regime in Wisconsin—II," p. 14.)

Mille Lacs and Rum River (page 64)

"The French voyageurs and traders . . . called the country having 'all sorts of lakes,' the Mille Lacs (Thousand Lake) region; whence this name came to be applied more particularly to this largest lake of the region. . . . Rum River was so called by English-speaking fur traders as early as 1766. The Sioux called Mille Lacs, Mde Wakan, meaning Spirit Lake, and the name was applied to the river as well, Spirit River. From Spirit came Spirits or Rum, in due course." ("The French Regime in Wisconsin—II," pp. 343, 348.)

How Wild Rice Was Gathered (page 66)

"Wild rice grows about four feet above the water, and has ears from three to five inches long. The kernel is about three-fourths of an inch long, of a dark slate color, and used by the Indians as a substitute for bread. They gather it by rowing their canoes by the side of it; and, after bending the ears into the canoe, beat the rice off. After a canoe is full, it is rowed to the shore; the rice is spread on blankets, and, when dry, is beaten till separated from the chaff. It is then winnowed and becomes fit for use." (Edward Tanner, "Wisconsin in 1818," *Wisconsin Historical Collections*, VIII [1877–1879], 291.)

IV

1825–1827

In the Fur Trade

About this time [1825] an old Sisseton chief arrived from the Upper Country at Mr. Lamont's. Mr. L. had married his daughter and the old chief had come down to see them. He also went to the fort to see the commanding officer and I went along to interpret. We were taken into the colonel's office, and in a few minutes the colonel came in and spoke to the old chief. He got up and shook hands with the colonel and they entered into some conversation about business of the time, etc. Finally, Col. Snelling asked the chief if he knew anything about some cattle that had been killed by the Sioux Indians the summer before.

The chief said that some white people were driving a drove of cattle through the Indian country, going north to the British settlement on Red River.* The Indians had demanded pay of the white men to let them pass [but the men insisted on passing] without pay[ing]. The Indians held a council amongst the braves and they agreed to go and take pay themselves by killing 2 or three cattle. So off the band started, some on horseback and some on foot, whooping and halloing.

As soon as the drovers saw the Indians the cattle started upon a run with the Indians after them, some on horses, some on foot, and they commenced firing at the cattle. They killed several and wounded several more, and a part they could not overtake and run wild into the prairie. The drovers turned about and went home and lost their whole drove.

The colonel asked the chief why he did not stop them. The old man said, "When hungry Indians see buffalo or beef before them, they are like a parcel of hungry wolves and cannot be made to listen." "Well," said Col. Snelling, "I am going to have some kind of satisfaction for this kind of conduct. You are not a-going to destroy

73

whole droves of cattle that are passing peaceably through your country."

The old chief began to smell the rat and made all sorts of excuses, but Col. Snelling told him that excuses came too late and that he should put him in prison, and sent for a guard of soldiers. They came and the colonel told the old chief he must go with the soldiers. He rose and went. The colonel told him if he attempted to run away from the soldiers they would shoot him. The old chief said nothing but went quietly along to the guardhouse.

The sun was not then an hour high. About half an hour after, Lieut. Camp[1] came in and said that the Indian was shot. We all ran out to see and found that the old man had made an excuse to go out, and got a little in advance of the sentinel and started on a run. The sentinel fired and brought the old man down. The old man had heard of others escaping and thought he could do the same, but he got caught this time. The sentinel broke the old man's arm and fractured the whole bone from the elbow to within about 2 inches of the shoulder. And the ball went through and struck his side and hit a rib, and ran around the rib to the pit of the stomach, skin deep, and there lodged between the skin and the bone.

The arm had to be amputated, but the surgeon, Dr. Purcell, was dead; so the sergeant of the hospital undertook the job. He tied the old man to a table and went to work, and in about two minutes the arm was off. During the operation the old man did not let on that it hurt him in the least. When they got through he asked if they were done. I told him he had but one arm now. "Well, then give me a smoke," he said. He did not appear to mind what was going on any more than if they were cutting away at a piece of leather.

The old man was kept in the hospital about a month until his arm was about well. Then the colonel let him go. Lieut. Camp, above mentioned, gave the sentinel an extra gill of whisky for a month for the good shot he made, breaking the chief's arm and stopping him from getting off, for they [the Indians] had imbibed the idea that they could run away from the soldiers with the greatest ease.

After this fuss was over I started back to my wintering place again. I got a few goods and made little packages for each of my Indians,

[1] This may have been Lieutenant William G. Camp, who was honorably discharged from the army in June, 1821, but may have remained at Fort Snelling.

and we started. This time we took a new route and went by way of the Mississippi. The first day we went to the falls and camped with Sergeant Spaulding, in charge of the saw mill. They had a good warm room and gave us a good warm supper, which we all enjoyed.

In the morning we started early and went to Elk River. From there we went home in three days, so that we made the journey in five days home again. We found all well and [a] number of Indians awaiting for us to trade. I done up what little trading there was to be done. Then Mr. Wm. Aitkin came down again and insisted on my going up to Sandy Lake with him.

So I fixed up and [took] one man with me. We started for another tramp of three days. Mr. Aitkin had a dog train. We put all our bedding on it and once in a while Mr. Aitkin would take turns and ride. The first day we went about 45 miles to a place called Rabbit House by the Chippewas. In passing a place called Patterson's Rapids,[2] Mr. Aitkin told me the rapids were named after a man that had been killed there by the Sioux Indians. A party of men had been sent out to the Indian camps and, having collected a considerable quantity of furs and meat, several Indians came back with the men to help them in with their loads, as all was carried by straps over the head. It would take quite a company to carry what two horses would draw.

This company of whites and Indians camped at this place for the night. They had built a large fire out of old dry pine, eat their supper and dried their snowshoes and mockasins. One of the Chippewas went down to the river to get a drink. When he came back to the fire he told his comrades that there were some persons walking on the ice, for the water worked up and down all the time just like when people walk on the ice.

Some others went and looked at the water. Sometimes it would shake, sometimes it would be still; then again, all at once, the water would begin to shake again. Some believed and some did not. The first one that made the discovery said he believed there was a war party on the river, and he was a-going to prepare for the worst. So he put on his mockasins and fixed up his pack. Some of the party done the same, but some would not believe the signs and laid down and went to sleep.

[2] Aitkin may have been mistaken, or Prescott may have misunderstood him, when they located Patterson's Rapids on the upper Mississippi. It is on the Minnesota River just below Lac qui Parle.

About midnight there came a volley of balls and arrows into the camp. There were four or five Indians killed [at] the first fire, and one Frenchman, Patterson.[3] All that were left took to their heels and ran for their lives. The Sioux charged upon the camp and dispatched those that were yet alive and scalped them; then they gathered up the booty, which was considerable, of furs and meat, and hunted around to see if they could find any wounded.

Two Frenchmen that had put off their mockasins threw themselves under a large tree that laid a little up from the ground. Here they laid trembling all the time the Indians were hunting. The Frenchmen said the Indians stepped over the log two or three times, and they thought the Indians must have seen them but did not want to kill them. Some of the Indians and Frenchmen ran off barefooted and froze their feet very bad, and some of them died. The two lay under the log until the Sioux went off, when they came forth, put on their mockasins, and started for home, empty and light, as the Sioux had carried off everything that was of any use to them.

We left Rabbit House early the next morning and went to Cedar Lake where there were two traders, viz., Mr. Oakes and Ashman.[4] Here [we] passed the remainder of the day in company with these gentlemen, where we were treated very kindly for the night and had some fine white fish for breakfast. We started early for Sandy Lake, where we arrived some time after dark. This day we traveled about 55 miles. Our men did not get in until about midnight. The next morning we were all very stiff and tired.

I remained with Mr. Aitkin three days. Mr. Aitkin had made very good improvements for an Indian country. At this place, Sandy Lake, the North West Fur Company once had a trading post* and it was broken up after Lieut Z. M. Pike ascended the Mississippi. The American Fur Company came in and tore down the old North West Company's fort on Sandy Lake and moved over onto the Mississippi, where Mr. Aitkin was now living and building. He had a fine garden and a large quantity of good vegetables.

I spent three days very pleasantly with Mr. Aitkin, and on the 4th

[3] Although Prescott calls Patterson a Frenchman, his name seems to indicate that he was of Scottish origin. However, a number of Scots intermarried with the French of Quebec Province, and in many cases they and their children adopted French customs. This may have been the case with Patterson.

[4] Possibly Charles W. Oakes and Samuel Ashman, both fur traders.

day in the morning I started with my man for home again. We went home in three days. By this time it was beginning to get warm and the snow was beginning to melt. After we passed Crow Island, or the mouth of the Crow Wing River, the Mississippi is very much like the Minnesota—woody bottoms and very crooked—only the Mississippi has the most water.

I got home and found the Indians waiting for me to get some ammunition to go into the sugar bush, for these people make large quantities of sugar.* The last one to start was The-Hole-in-the-Day, the chief of Sandy Lake Chippewas.[5] He started on the 2nd of March, 1825. He had not gone far before some wild geese passed over him. He fired and killed two of them, and returned back and brought them both to me.

We now commenced making our packs of furs, and on the last of March the ice moved out of the Mississippi. The first of April I went down in a canoe to get some more goods. We found the ice had blocked up the river at a place called the Little Falls. We took our canoe out and made a portage around the ice and went on down, and in two days we went to Fort Snelling.

I found all well. My wife and boy were all in good health. I staid only three days and started back in my canoe with two men and a few goods. I went as far as the falls and made a portage around the falls. I heard that Mr. Bailly had arrived at Fort Snelling and I went back to see him to see if I could do anything with him about our old co-partnership business. But he only laughed at me and said that I was very impudent to talk to him about an old debt that had been settled by cheating a year ago.

So I went back and took my canoe again for my wintering ground. We had strong headwinds; it took us six or seven days to get up. One day we run under a leaning tree; our canoe got a turn on the men and came broadside against the tree and came near capsizing us. And it was with much difficulty that we could get hold of an ax to cut the branches so we could get from the tree. Our situation was so precarious that we could hardly stir for fear of upsetting the canoe. The

---

[5] Hole-in-the-Day the Elder was born about 1800. Although not a hereditary chief, he became an acknowledged leader of the Chippewas in war and council and was an inveterate enemy of the Sioux. (Stephen R. Riggs, "Dakota Portraits," ed. Willoughby N. Babcock, Jr., *Minnesota History Bulletin*, Vol. II, No. 8 [November 1918], 511.)

water was very deep and the current very rapid, and for a few moments we were in great danger of losing all, and probably our lives also.

We got [back] after some hard work against the wind and current, and found all well but anxious to see us, as they were out of provisions. We waited a few days, gathered what furs we could, and started for home, or Fort Snelling, again. We went down in one day and a half, 120 miles by the river.

About this time [1823] some immigrants came through from Red River of the North. On their way the Sioux had attacked them and killed some of them, and took one white child prisoner. Lieut. [Platt R.] Green was ordered to Lake Traverse, where the Indians had the child, and to take the child and bring it down to Fort Snelling. So he went and the Indians gave up the child without any ceremony, as they feared Col. Snelling the whole extent of the Sioux country.*

The Sioux had committed the outrage because Col. Snelling had taken one of their chiefs and cut his arm off for killing cattle. The white people who were left when the Sioux fired upon them fled back to the British settlement, and the British made no demand for the murderer, therefore nothing was done about it. And, in fact, it is supposed that the British did not care anything about the affair, for they did not like to have their people leave their colony, as there [were some who] had already left them and moved into Iowa and Wisconsin, otherwise Michigan at that time.*

After I got down with my furs I stopped about a month with my wife and boy. This summer [1825] the Indians had all been to Prairie du Chien to make a treaty of peace. The Nations for 300 or 400 miles around came into council. A very large concourse of Indians assembled. Governor [Lewis] Cass and General [William] Clark and some others were commissioners. The object of the treaty was for the Indians to make peace amongst themselves and the white people. Whilst the Indians were making peace at Prairie du Chien, the Indians were warring at home, so if peace was made, hostilities were as soon commenced again, and the peace amounted to nothing, although it cost the government many thousand dollars.*

The Sissetons had treated the traders very badly after they heard that the old chief had been imprisoned and had his arm cut off. They thought, of course, he would either die or be killed. They dared not kill any of the traders. They found the fort was too close and too strong for them, and that Col. Snelling was determined to punish them for bad conduct.

After remaining about a month I packed up a few goods and some powder and lead and started up the Mississippi again. This time I was destined for Leaf Lake, with two large bark canoes, four men, and Mr. Peter Quinn for interpreter. There were quite a number of Chippewas in [our] company. They had been down on a visit. The mosquitoes were terrible; the men had to wear mittens and had to keep smokes in our canoes all day, and at night we were compelled to surround our camp with smoke in order to get some rest.

After ten days' toil we reached our place of destination, Leaf Lake,[6] about 9 miles east of Otter Tail Lake.* We commenced building on the east side of the lake. The lake has narrows in the middle; the whole lake is about three miles in length. We built four houses in the form of a square and left places for gates at each corner. The logs and puncheons were all up and [we] were going on to make the floors out of puncheons, when one morning a Chippewa came in and said the Sioux had been to Otter Tail Lake and killed a Chippewa and his wife, and the Chippewa had killed one Sioux in the struggle for life.

The Chippewas all started off to see what was done. They found the Chippewa and his wife scalped, and the Sioux was set up near by the Chippewas, and a great deal of Indian trinkets thrown over him. The Chippewas, as soon as they got near the Sioux, fired a volley into his body, and charged upon the dead carcass, and scalped it and cut it to pieces and done many disgraceful acts to the dead body.

The killing of these Chippewas frightened them so that they all moved off and said they would not winter there. So I had to pull up stakes and move down the river and commence anew again at the mouth of Leaf River. Leaf Lake is the place where Col. Dickson and

---

[6] The Columbia Fur Company's post at Leaf Lake, managed by Prescott, was given the name of Fort Bolivar by Taliaferro in 1826. Prescott, however, does not mention this fact. (Grace Lee Nute, "Posts in the Minnesota Fur-Trading Area, 1660–1885," *Minnesota History Bulletin,* Vol. XI, No. 4 [December 1930], 373.)

D. Graham[7] once wintered for the North West Fur Company, but they were also disturbed both [by] parties of Sioux and Chippewas, so they quit the country.

After moving down to the mouth of Leaf River[8] I went down to Fort Snelling to get my winter's supplies. I had to wait nearly a month before the boat arrived with the winter's supplies from St. Louis. I got my goods as soon as possible and fixed up some things for my wife and boy, and left in company with Mr. B. F. Baker of the American Fur Company.

The season was far advanced and we did not arrive at our wintering ground until freezing weather, and I had to build. Mr. Baker had built at Crow Island[9] during the summer [1825], so he had a house all ready to go into, and I had to go to work and build. I built a storehouse and a house for myself and interpreter. My men wintered in a lodge made of poles and split wood set upright, pitching together at the top and wide at the bottom.

Here the Indians brought me a young girl and the parents wanted me to take her and live with her for the winter. I put them off; they came again. Finally, I consented and she lived with me about 2 months, and went off to make sugar, as she said. After a while she came back again and stayed a few days, and went away again.

I had a great struggle with the opposition this winter.* They watched me in every hole and corner. They even made their men get up into the forks of the trees in the coldest weather and watch us when we would be going out to the Indians after furs. And if they

[7] Colonel Robert Dickson (d. 1823) was one of the most prominent men in the Northwest. A native of Scotland, he migrated to America and by 1788 was engaged in the fur trade, with headquarters at Lake Traverse after 1800. He remained loyal to the British during the War of 1812 and after that war became associated with the Earl of Selkirk in the Red River colonization.

Duncan Graham (1772–1847), also a Scotsman, was associated with Dickson in the fur trade for many years. Although he fought with the British in the War of 1812, he later became an American citizen.

[8] Prescott spent the winter of 1825–1826 there. On April 26, 1826, Taliaferro wrote, "Philander Prescott arrived from Leaf Lake this day—after spending the winter in trade among the Sioux and Chippeways." (Lawrence Taliaferro's Journal, Vol. 7, MS, Minnesota State Historical Society.)

[9] Crow Island was at the mouth of the Crow Wing River. Taliaferro called this post Fort Biddle in 1826.

could possibly discover where we were gone or going to, they would follow us and try to get the furs from the Indians. They kept this up all winter, but it done them no good, for I sold my goods and made my packs notwithstanding the great efforts made to break us up or run us out of the country.

We had a very deep snow in the winter of 1825–26. The winter was very severe. A number of Indians perished amongst the Sioux on the prairie. In the Sheyenne River [region] the buffalo had left the country, and the Indians could not follow them; the snow was too deep. They tried to make their way back again to their summer quarters or cornfields. They eat up all their horses and dogs; still they had not enough to bring them in.

And as they were traveling along in the snow they would fall down and stay there of their suffering. They were too weak to get up again, and those that could keep up did not think enough of those that had fallen to perish, to help them up. Self-preservation was all the go, and go ahead was their determination.

But finally they had to go to eating each other. They got so far gone they had to come to this. When one would fall down dead almost they would freeze in a few minutes. Then some one coming along behind would cut off a limb and at night would cook and eat it. Some forty perished; about 200 got into their summer residence where they had corn.

One woman (Tash-u-no-ta) got down as far as Fort Snelling, crazy. There she was always hankering after human flesh. And when the children would be playing about she often would say, "What fine fat children!" So as soon as the children were told who [she was] and what she said, they were all afraid of her and would run and hide themselves when they saw the crazy woman coming. Finally one day she attempted to swim the Minnesota River and drowned in the attempt.

During the winter I made one journey down to Mr. Baker's at the mouth of the Crow Wing River. There I saw a deserter that had run away from Fort Snelling. He had frozen his feet and could not walk, and in talking about matters of the world, I found that he was a Universalist. We had a long talk on the subject of religion, which I suppose did neither of us any good, for I told him in the end I should not like to trust him to raise a child of mine. He retorted in the same way, so I dropped the subject and went to bed. And early in the morning I was off for home. It is a hard day's walk from Crow Wing to the mouth of Leaf River.[10]

We worried out the winter by going with a party of Chippewas to visit a Sioux camp a long day's journey. The Sioux came over first to see the Chippewas; the Chippewas returned with the Sioux to their camp, and some of the traders went in the train to help them make peace.

We found the Sioux camped near the waters of the Chippewa River, in number about 100 lodges or about 500 souls. We stayed with the Sioux one day and two nights, counseling and feasting, and made peace—to be broke the first good opportunity that should offer. We left the Sioux camp for home, came to the Chippewa camp and stopped over night. The next morning we got home again.

We waited to make our packs and start down the river again. In the meantime I sent Mr. Quinn, my interpreter, over to Lake Traverse, where Mr. McKenzie lived, about five days' journey.[11] He took two dogs and a train and one Chippewa Indian and started. He was gone 12 days and brought back some powder that I had sent him for.

About the middle of April [1826] the ice began to move. The Indians had all left for Leech Lake to make sugar. We were all alone and quite lonesome, and the moment the ice would permit we were off, with about 30 packs.

In a few days we all arrived safe at home near Fort Snelling. As I passed the fort some of the officers haled me and asked me if I had seen any Sioux Indians. I said no. They said they had thought of sending a man up the Mississippi to inform us of some trouble they had with the Sioux Indians. There had been a party of Chippewas—Hole-in-the-Day [was their] chief—to see the commanding officer and to trade sugar.[12]

[10] The distance in a straight line between Baker's post and Prescott's was about twenty-seven miles.

[11] The distance to Lake Traverse was about 110 miles in a direct line. There Kenneth McKenzie ran the main headquarters of the Columbia Fur Company.

[12] Although Prescott and some others record these events as occurring in 1826, it is clear from Major Taliaferro's journal entries that the correct date is late May, 1827. (William W. Folwell, *A History of Minnesota* [St. Paul: Minnesota Historical Society, 1921–1930], I, 149.)

Seth Eastman

Courtesy of the Edward E. Ayer Collection,
Newberry Library, Chicago

Mackinac

Seth Eastman

Courtesy James Jerome Hill Reference Library

Wenona's Leap, Lake Pepin

Dog Dance of the Dahcotas

Indian Sugar Camp

The Rice Gatherers

Medicine Man Administering to a Patient

Unloading a North Canoe at the Trading Post

Interior of Fur Trading Post

Frank J. Millet

The Treaty of Traverse des Sioux

Courtesy Minnesota Historical Society

Philander Prescott

of corn Deer and some other Vegetables when as at our watering ground there was nothing but musty corn and no grease to eat with it and the men complained of it, having or leaving a burning sensation in the stomach as it was only coursely ground and not sifted I turned back next morning and came back to the gate and camped the next day we were early at home Mr Brown started back to Fort Snelling again with a poor prospect a head for a successful trade in that quarter the french man that came out with us to hunt left also as there but few Beaver and they all turned their attention to hunting Rats about the middle of winter a band of Superior Sioux arrived all most starved and I had to turn in upon them in two considerations one was if I did not give them some corn they would kill my horses and eat them and then I could not get away from there in the spring for want of teams in case they should kill and eat my horses and another consideration was this it was the party that took me prisoner and save my life when I was in the Chippewa country the old chief Limping Devil told me do you recollect says he the time when the Indians found you in the woods and took you and wanted to kill you and I saved your life now I want you to help me he said I told him I was willing to go as far as I could but he must recollect that I had a good many people to feed and that he must not think of my feeding all my provisions out to them the old fellow looked surly and did not say much

A Page from Prescott's Original Manuscript of Recollections

They were camped below the fort in the bottom, some fifty in all —men, women, and children. The Sioux had visited them day after day, and the Chippewas had feasted them on sugar until they were filled, and gave them some to carry home with them.

One evening a parcel of young men had been to the Chippewa camp, feasting and dancing. Then they rose to depart and when they got outside the lodge, one of the Sioux blew a whistle and they all wheeled about and fired into the Chippewa lodges and ran off. It was dark, so no person followed them. At one fire they wounded nine of the Chippewas but, fortunate, none were killed. But some, [it] was thought, would not survive the night.

They were all taken up to the council house and laid on the floor. The blood stood in large puddles all about the floor. The surgeon of the fort dressed all their wounds and Col. Snelling made them as comfortable as he could for the night. In the morning they were all taken into the fort, where they were out of danger from the Sioux.

In the morning Col. Snelling ordered all the Sioux to come into council. A few of them came in, but the principal men did not come in. They knew pretty well that some of them would be taken as hostages until the others that fired on the Chippewas was brought in. They would not come in but rather prepared for resistance.

The Col. ordered two companies of soldiers out with officers and our interpreter. The Indians ran and hid themselves in the grass. At last they came upon a party of them up at Land's End. They were ordered to surrender but they refused, saying the Col. would kill them.

Bad Hail,[13] the old orator and principal soldier of the Nation, told the interpreter if he would put his hands on him he would shoot him. The interpreter had two companies to back him up, and pushed forward and laid hold of Bad Hail, the most prominent Indian of all the bands. The soldiers stepped right up with the officers and Mr. Bad Hail was confined.

When the Indians saw this, they did not know what to do and kept retreating. Finally, the officers managed so as to surround about a dozen of them, mostly chiefs and braves, and closed in on them and made them prisoners. When the Indians saw this, they gave up and came in, and all marched down to the council house. Still they could not get them into council; they were fearful of a trap.

The agent, Major L. Taliaferro, told them as long as his flag was

13 Bad Hail, a Mdewakanton, was often the Sioux spokesman at councils.

floating over their heads they should not be hurt. So after much parleying, they consented to go into council; they all got in—a large building full. "Ah," says the Colonel, "I have got you now," in a low-toned voice.

The Indians commenced by justifying themselves. They complained that the Chippewas were always the aggressors; after making a peace the Chippewas were the first to break it. The Chippewas said the same of the Sioux. So it went back and forth, and it was found that the Indians could not settle their difficulties themselves. Neither did the agent and colonel agree as to what was the best policy to pursue in the settlement of this difficulty amongst them.

Finally, Col. Snelling took the whole thing into his own hands and went at it in earnest. He told the Indians he was going to keep some of them as hostages for three days, and at the end of three days, if the party was not brought in that had done the mischief, he would hang the hostages. This made them hang their heads.

They appealed to their agent, Major L. Taliaferro. The agent told the colonel he had promised them protection as long as they were under his flag. "Well," says the colonel, "I can easily obviate that," and went out and had the flag pulled down. And when the Indians saw that, they made loud complaints of injustice. The colonel told them he was not a-going to allow them to come right here under the guns of the fort and commit murder with impunity, then run off and cut up as they pleased, then laugh at the white people and call them cowards, etc., etc.

"Now," says the colonel, "I am going to stop as much of this kind of work as possible." The Indians said it was a band of foolish boys that done the mischief, and offered 30 horses to settle the matter. "No," said the colonel, "you see that blood all over the floor? If your people had been shot that way, would you have sold your blood for a parcel of poor old horses? No!" said the colonel, "You would never of stopped crying for blood in return for life. You would have asked [for punishment] and I shall do the same."

Col. Snelling picked out some 6 or 8 chiefs and braves and told them to go to the guardhouse, and sent the other Indians off to hunt up the murderers. The Indians raised a party of braves and went in search of the depredators. At the end of three days they brought in two of them and said the rest had run off and they could not find them.

The colonel was not satisfied and said he must have some more, so the Indians started again. In two days they returned and said the rogues had fled the country and they could not get them. The colonel said he must have another, so one of the braves turned over his brother who had been charged with having been seen with the party that fired on the Chippewas. But it was found out afterwards that this Indian was not with the party when they fired on the Chippewas. A-nag-a-nah-jie is the name of the man that gave up his brother. They were of Little Six's* band of Sioux.

Col. Snelling ordered a sergeant and a guard to take the three Sioux and march them out from the fort about a quarter of a mile, and also ordered the Chippewas out to shoot them, which act they performed very willingly. The Sioux were placed some fifteen paces off from the Chippewas. At the first fire, 2 of the Sioux fell. One was mortally wounded but started to run, but another shot from the Chippewas brought him down.

So the Chippewas took the bodies of the three Sioux and threw them into the Mississippi, and all went home as quiet as if nothing had happened. This act of Col. Snelling struck terror into the Sioux Nation, and it humbled the Sioux down, so that there was no more trouble with them for many years from the Mississippi to the Missouri.

Col. Snelling was blamed by many of the friends of the Sioux;* firstly, because no Chippewas had died of their wounds; and 2ndly because they said that Col. Snelling had no authority to take the life of any one; and they stigmatized him as a murderer. Then others said again that Col. Snelling had done right, and that by that [act] he no doubt would save the lives of many Indians and some whites also. When Indians formerly had committed murder they would be taken before the courts. The result would be acquittal for want of witnesses.

I am willing to join with those upholding Col. Snelling, as I have lived to see the effects of his rule while he was commanding officer at Fort Snelling. And [I] must say, by the colonel's ordering the three Sioux to be shot, the act has saved many a life from brutal murder. Sioux remember it to this day and still talk about the matter with a very subdued tone, when they speak of it amongst themselves.*

In the spring of [1826] we had the highest water that was ever known in this country. In the commencement of the winter [1825], a large body of ice broke off from the Fall of St. Anthony and clogged up the channel. Water rose about 20 feet and kept breaking the ice and forcing it along before the rise and rush of water. By the time it reached [the fort] it was frightful to look at; but as soon as the flow had passed the fort, it got vent by a channel that flowed into the Minnesota River.

But in passing the fort it carried off a long washhouse belonging to the fort. A man was in it at the time. The man and his wife had both got out, but the man thought of his watch and [went] after it, but the rise of water was so sudden that it raised the house that was made of solid hewed logs bodily up and floated some distance before it came to pieces. The man that was carried off in it was never heard of or found. The flow passed on.

Down about a mile, on a little prairie on the east bank, lived a trader by the name of [Jean Baptiste] Faribault.[14] They had been notified from the fort of the breaking up of the ice and they made their escape to the opposite side of the river. But down there the water did not rise high enough to injure their houses. But the following spring the water rose to 4 feet deep. Mr. Faribault's house was entirely swept away, but he had used precaution and moved all his effects to the west side of the river.

At Red River of the North the water was so high that the river overflowed its banks for 30 miles on each side of the river, and many of the people had to live on rafts for several days before boats could carry them to dry land. It was reported that they could not find a good landing until they reached Turtle Mountains. The inhabitants lost their all, and had to commence anew again. The Hudson's Bay Fur Company sent to the states and purchased cattle, horses, and sheep and sold them to the colonists to commence anew again. But quite a number of them left there and came over to the United States and settled for life. The driving [of] these cattle across to Red River was the cause of the Sioux chief's losing one of his arms at Fort Snelling.[15]

During the spring a duel was fought between Lieut. Hunter and Col. Snelling's son, Joseph.* The colonel heard that the parties had gone out to fight and sent a guard out and stopped them. The parties moved off and the guard went home, and the combatants met in

[14] Faribault was occupying the land opposite Pike's Island.

[15] There is some confusion in dates. As related earlier, the incident of the chief's losing an arm occurred in 1823, rather than in 1826 as indicated here.

another place and exchanged shots. The colonel's son had the end of one of his forefingers shot off. This ended the strife and they went home.

Sometime after this another duel was fought between Lieut. Baxley and Capt. Leonard.[16] They fired some 6 or 8 shots apiece. Lieut. Baxley got one shot the most. Capt. Leonard's second forgot to cock his pistol, but Lieut. Baxley missed. Seconds interfered and [tried] to reconcile matters, but nothing would or could be done satisfactorily, and at it they went again. I believe [at] the eighth shot Lieut. Baxley's ball struck Capt. Leonard in the corner of the eye near the temple, but did not kill him, although it came very near killing him. Lieut. Baxley had 32 ball holes through his clothes but did not draw blood once.

Capt. Leonard was sutler for the fort. He was boarding with Lieut. Baxley. He was a very vain, wicked man, and it was for some bad language used before Mrs. Baxley that brought on their trouble. I believe there were one or two other challenges and I believe one of them exchanged shots and then made up; and in one party the seconds made the parties settle or drop the matter, as they said the charges were too trifling to quarrel about.

Lieut. Baxley had got into a scrape the year before coming up from St. Louis with his Lady on board the Columbia Fur Company keelboat. Lieut. Baxley went into his wife's room to go to bed and found this clerk's shoes in there. Lieut. Baxley went out and talked to the man about it. The clerk was about to take a glass of liquor at the time, but instead of drinking the liquor he threw it in Lieut. Baxley's face. Lieut. Baxley drew a pistol and shot the clerk dead, I believe; still it runs through my mind that he stabbed him with a knife.

Lieut. B. never lived a happy life with his wife, and finally they separated and each took their own course for a livelihood. Shortly after this, Lieut. Baxley was dropped at the reduction of the army after the war and that was the last I heard of him.

After spending about a month [at home] I made preparations for the Chippewa country again. By this time I began to get tired of the

16 Lieutenant Joseph M. Baxley (d. 1839) was from Maryland. He joined the army in 1814 and resigned as a captain in 1836. Captain Luther Leonard (d. 1865) was from Vermont. A graduate of the U.S. Military Academy in 1806, he had a long army career, retiring in 1861.

country, both on account of the poor living and the hard labor required to keep up the trade. And as I could not take my wife with me, I was determined it should be the last time I would winter with the Chippewas. So I got ready and started in company with Mr. Baker again.

This time I had to go to a new place and build again. This was at Leech Lake, the head of the Southern Fork of the Mississippi. We went into the country by the way of Gull Lake and made portages from one lake to another until we reached our place of destination. I went to work and built on the point of land making in from the south; I believe it is an island, and I should think there were ten thousand acres of land in it.[17] The northernmost point of this island reaches near to the middle of the lake, which is about thirty miles long.

On the way up the Mississippi I got sick with some kind of fever. I had but little medicine, and I did not get well for a month. As soon as my house was up I started down for my goods for the winter's trade. We had to wait a long time for the keelboat with our goods, and it was late in the fall before we got into the country with our goods.

The Indians most of them, had taken their winter credits and gone off to hunt.* Had it not been that I met some of them on the Mississippi as I was going up and made some credits, I should not [have] got any Indians to hunt for me this winter at all.

As soon as I arrived we had to go to fishing, as the traders and Indians all have to live on fish and potatoes through the winter. We caught about 2000 tulepe, a species of white fish, only much smaller, weighing from a half to one pound apiece. We ran a knife through the tails of the fish and put them on a stick and hung them up head-downwards to dry. In this way they kept fresh and good all winter. This is our bread and meat for about eight months of the year. The distance is so great and our canoes so small that we could not carry any more provisions. Sometimes we can get a little wild rice from the Indians, which is quite a relief for a change of diet once in a while. 2 sacks or one barrel of flour was all that any of us could take for our winter's supply.

Here we dragged out a long, tedious winter [1826–1827], most of

[17] Prescott's winter camp in 1826–1827 was evidently on Big Point or on the peninsula, the latter almost an island in the southwest part of the lake.

the time fishing for a living. We used to cut holes through the ice about three feet thick, and set our nets by means of a long pole. We would cut holes with axes until we came to water, then we used an ice chisel. This is about 2 feet long, made of iron, beveled on one side, with a little crook in the other end, and lashed to a handle or pole about 6 feet long, With this instrument the bottom of the hole (was) made larger. The holes are made nearly as far apart as the pole is long. The net is tied to one end of the long pole and pushed along under the ice from one hole to another until they get to the length of the net, which generally is about 180 feet; but when the net is floated and the sinkers attached, it does measure not more than half that distance. When set, [the net] has to be pulled about one-half of its length, so as to give the fish a chance to play, and this keeps them from breaking the meshes very much.

The pike or pickerel were very hard on the nets. Their numerous long, sharp teeth caused a great many holes in the net. But the fishing in the winter is a cold and poor business. Sometimes in the morning we do not get more than one fish, sometimes none at all, sometimes five or six. When there were no fish, the poor dogs have to suffer, of which every trader in the north has a train.

In Leech Lake there are a few white fish that will weigh from 10 to 15 pounds, but they are scarce. The dory or pike are very abundant in March. The traders and Indians set their nets in the air holes in the lake and large quantities of them are taken. At this season of the year this species of fish are hunting for places to spawn, generally in shallow water and grassy bottoms it suits them. Also they find small fish about these air holes, and they spawn and find their food all at the same place. One net frequently loads a dog sled with this species of fish every morning.

About the first of May the Indians, most of them, came in from their spring hunts.* They kill from 4 to 800 muskrats, sometimes one or two otter, a beaver or two, a few mink, a few coon, sometimes a bearskin. These skins makes a good hunter's spring hunt worth from one to two hundred dollars.

Mr. Rousan,[18] an old Canadian who was trading there for the American Fur Company, told me he was there when Lieut. Z. M. Pike came up to Leech Lake in the winter of [1805–1806] and found

[18] Possibly Roussain, a trader subordinate to William Aitkin of the American Fur Company.

a British flag flying and ordered his soldiers to shoot it down. He said the soldiers fired several shots but could not bring it down. Mr. Rousan said he ordered the Indians to try their skill at shooting, and they fired only a few shots before the flag fell to the ground.*

Whilst I was waiting here for the ice to break up in the lake, 2 of my men deserted me and went off to Red River. This made me short of hands to take my canoes out, the distance being about 5 or 6 days' travel by the river. At last, about the 20th of May, 1827, the ice gave way to the force of the wind and the heat of the sun, and in a few days we were afloat, under way for Fort Snelling again. The first day we crossed the lake and passed by the old wintering ground near the outlet of the lake. This point had been used for a long time by the North West company for a trading post, and this is the noted place where their flag was shot down by Lieut. Z. M. Pike.

It must have required a great deal of energy and perseverance on the part of that officer to have reached that post in the winter without snowshoes or mockasins, the distance being about 250 miles through a thick forest of pines and underbrush, with thick, heavy shoes which became very slippery in walking on the snow, and they froze hard on the feet. The feet are always cold and frequently the men get frosted.

[From Leech Lake] we moved on down into the river and encamped for the night. The next day we worked all day in the serpentine course of the river; the grass being higher than our heads we could not see out any distance from the canoes.

In the evening we came to the Po-kega-ma, in the Chippewa tongue, a fall in the Mississippi.* Here the river is not more than 20 yards wide, and it rushes through between two rocks, one from each side of the river. The pitch or rapid is about 4 or 5 feet, and in the middle and at the bottom of the chute is a large boulder. The whole river dashes onto this rock and divides the stream, which reunites below the rock again.

The traders all have to land here and make a portage and carry their goods about fifty yards round to the still water below the rapids. Some traders one day coming down all had landed except one small bark canoe with only one man in it. He was noticing something on the shore, and before he noticed it, he was drawn into the suck of the rapids, and in an instant more he was against the big rock below. His canoe went down sidewise and struck about half way or middle of the canoe and broke square in two. One half went each

The Fort Snelling Area

side of the rock, and the man floated to shore in one half of the canoe and his load in the other half, all wet. The rest of the company had a great laugh at the man for his ducking and the great fright he got in going over the fall without thinking of what he was doing or where he was going.

We soon got our loads carried around, and floated on down to Sandy Lake the next day. We stopped only a few moments. The clerks of the American Fur Company had become dissatisfied with their employers and wished to leave them and join the Columbia Fur Company, and gave me a letter to that effect which I promised to lay before the company. I done so on my arrival at our depot, Land's End, near Fort Snelling.

We passed Sandy Lake the next day, passed the houses of Mr. Oaks and others near Cedar Lake. They had all left for Mackinaw with their furs and to get a new supply of goods for the winter.

From here we went to Pine River and camped, for the Pine River is a route that light canoes travel to go to Leech Lake. Also Willow River is traveled for that purpose, but loaded canoes cannot travel these routes, as the water is too shallow and rapid.

The second day we came to Crow Wing, where we heard of Gen. Jackson's election.[19] We found that Mr. Baker had been gone several days, so we floated on down in a day and a half to Fort Snelling. We found all well and the packs pretty much all made ready to ship to St. Louis. A steamboat came to our depot and took the furs, the first steamer that ever came that far up the Minnesota, in 1827, although there had been 3 or 4 to Fort Snelling.

The first was in the spring of 1823[20]—a stern wheeler, the name I do not recollect, from Cincinnati with supplies for the fort. [*The Indians say they had dreamed of seeing some monster of the deep the night before, which frightened them very much. It appears they did not discover the boat until it had got into the mouth of the St. Peter's, below Mr. Sibley's. They stood and gazed with astonishment at what they saw approaching, taking the boat to be some angry god of the water, coughing and spouting water upwards, sideways and forward. They had not courage enough to stand until the boat came near them. The women*

19 Prescott is in error in referring to Jackson's election on this trip in 1827; Jackson was not elected until 1828.

20 The first steamboat to arrive in the area was the *Virginia* on May 10, 1823, and she ascended only as far as Mendota and Fort Snelling.

*and children took to the woods, with their hair floating behind them in
the breeze, from the speed they were going, in running from supposed
danger. Some of the men had little more courage, and only moved off
to a short distance from the shore and the boat passed along and landed.
Everything being quiet for a moment, the Indians came up to the boat
again, and stood looking at the monster of the deep. All at once the
boat began to blow off steam, and the bravest warriors could not stand
this awful roaring, but took to the woods, men, women, and children,
with their blankets flying in the wind; some tumbling in the brush which
entangled their feet as they ran away—some hallooing, some crying, to
the great amusement of the people on board the steamboat.]*[21] At this
time all the provisions were brought from there for all the troops on
the Mississippi, and we used to get the best of flour for $5 per
barrel, and 8$ for prime pork.

After all the packs were off, the partners of the [Columbia Fur]
company got together and had a little council of what was to be done
the following year. I told them for one that I was a-going to quit the
Chippewa country, as I had been there three years, starving half
the time. Someone else must take my place for a while. No one made
any reply.

Some other business was transacted. Also a proposition to sell
out came up, and it was agreed that if the agent, Mr. [Kenneth]
McKenzie, could sell for enough to clear us from debt for [him] to
do so. By this time we had incurred a very heavy debt. Our outfits on
the Missouri had been very expensive, and our whole debt was now
about $100,000.

So Mr. McKenzie sold out. The American Fur Company agreed
to take all the goods we had left at cost, and give us the Missouri
trade. They [were] to furnish the goods and we were to get one-third
of the profit. The two parties went to work and took an inventory of
stock, and found that we did not pay our debts to Messrs. Powell by
several thousand dollars. This dissatisfied most of the partners to
think that Mr. McKenzie had sold out to such a disadvantage. Also
Messrs. Powell had almost stopped business on account of this heavy
debt that we owed them.

But Mr. McKenzie had made the bargain and said he was going to
stick to it. So the rest of us all backed out, except Mr. William

[21] Philander Prescott, in the St. Paul *Chronicle and Register*, April 6, 1850.

Laidlaw.[22] So the two Scotchmen took the American Fur Company's offer and the rest of us were left to grub for our lives. Five in number, we had labored and half starved for four years and had run the American Fur Company so hard that they were glad to come to some kind of an arrangement. But we may say our four years of hardship and labor went to the benefit of Mr. McKenzie and Mr. Laidlaw, and off they started for the Missouri country.

My brother remained with Powells, clerking again.* Mr. [Daniel] Lamont went into business with his brother in St. Louis and died about two years after; he left a daughter uncared for. Mr. Laidlaw came around this way to go to the Missouri to see about some private matters of his. And Mr. McKenzie, when he arrived, we fired him a salute from a swivel that we had that belonged to our keelboat. Six full loads we fired, and a squib for the agent of the Columbia Fur Company for the honor of selling us out in the manner he did.

Myself and Mr. [Joseph] Jeffries, Mr. [Joseph] Renville, and Mr. Tilton[23] were all out of employment. Mr. Tilton got into business with one Mr. Parker in the lead business at Galena. Mr. Renville got an assortment of goods from the American Fur Company, and Mr. Jeffries went with him as clerk in the Indian trade at Lac qui Parle.*

So they had all got into business but myself. I was left on the bank of the river—myself and wife and one child. However, in the summer I had been up to Leech Lake and brought away what few goods were left there, and turned them over to the company. The Indians all

22 William Laidlaw was described as one of the ablest of the traders who came to the Missouri with the Columbia Fur Company. (Hiram M. Chittenden, *The American Fur Trade of the Far West* [New York: Harper, 1902], I, 383–386.)

23 Jeffries, who had acted as interpreter for the Long party on its way north in 1823, was for a time in charge of the Columbia Fur post two miles from the head of Lake Traverse.

Joseph Renville (*ca.* 1779–1846), had interpreted for Pike in the upper Mississippi Valley in 1805–1806 and for the Long expedition up the Minnesota and down the Red River in 1823. He established a trading post at Lac qui Parle after 1827. ("Minnesota Biographies," *Minnesota Historical Collections*, XIV [1912], 634.)

A Mr. Tilton, doubtless of the firm of Tilton and Company, had visited the Mandans, along with James Kipp, in 1823, and then built a post on the south side of the Missouri. Forced to abandon the place before winter, they built a house in the Mandan village, where they conducted trade until 1827. (Chittenden, *The American Fur Trade*, I, 326–327; II, 932.)

over the country looked very sad over the events that had taken place, and said they would starve and freeze.

Mr. McKenzie never offered me a place as clerk or interpreter, or any other position or place, in the new business he was about to enter into—although I worked and starved to my heart's content for three years for the company. So when the company was taking an account of stock, I asked Mr. McKenzie for some powder and lead to leave with my wife and child, as I had to go somewhere and find some kind of employment. With some hesitation Mr. McKenzie let me have a few pounds of powder and lead.

So they two went into the Missouri trade and in a few years they made some fifty thousand dollars apiece. Mr. Laidlaw quit the trade and settled at Fort Leavenworth, and in a few years, Mr. Jeffries did also. Mr. Renville and my brother died some years since, also Mr. Lamont. Mr. Tilton, I believe, is also dead, so there is only Mr. McKenzie and myself still living of the old Columbia Fur Company.

SUPPLEMENT

The British Settlement on the Red River (page 73)

The Scottish Earl of Selkirk in 1811 acquired from the Hudson's Bay Company a tract of 116,000 square miles in the Red River Valley and north to Lake Winnipeg and Winnipeg River. In 1812 he brought to America a group of Scottish and Irish immigrants, and in the next two years about two hundred Scots highlanders reached the new settlement. In 1815 approximately half of the settlers moved to upper Canada, but more immigrants arrived from the British Isles and Switzerland both before and after Selkirk's death in 1820. (John Perry Pritchett, "Some Red River Fur-Trade Activities," *Minnesota History Bulletin*, Vol. V, No. 6 [May 1924], 409.)

The first cattle drive to the Selkirk colony took place in 1815, when Lord Selkirk arranged for the delivery of five hundred head of cattle. In 1821 a drove of cattle, or possibly sheep, was driven north fifteen hundred miles from Missouri, and an interesting map (in Cardinal Leonidas Goodwin, *The Trans-Mississippi West* [New York: Appleton, 1922], p. 248) of Iowa Territory showing "Dixon and McKnight's Route to Pembina Settlement in 1822" indicates that another drive was held the following year. Subsequent drives are recorded for 1833 and 1844. The usual route for the drovers was through Iowa, up the Des Moines Valley to the Minnesota Valley, and north down the Red River. The drives that Prescott mentions seem to have taken place about 1825 or earlier. (Donald D. Parker, *Lac qui Parle, Its Missionaries, Traders and Indians* [privately published, 1964], pp. 249–255.)

The Northwest Company on Sandy Lake (page 76)
Before Aitkin took charge at Sandy Lake in 1831, the old post had been abandoned for a new site at the mouth of the outlet of Sandy Lake, on the narrow point between the outlet and the Mississippi River. ("Minnesota Geographic Names," *Minnesota Historical Collections*, XVII [1920], 18.)

The Northwest Company's post on (the west shore of) Sandy Lake was one of the most important fur-trading station in the Northwest from 1794, when it was built, until after the War of 1812. (Nute, "Posts in the Minnesota Fur-Trading Area," p. 371.)

How the Indians Made Sugar (page 77)
The Indians each spring, about April, spent a month making sugar. Entire Indian villages were moved to the sugar groves where temporary tipis, etc., were erected. While some made sugar, the men often hunted. "When the season is good and the family has the apparatus in sufficient quantity and readiness, one family can make from 500 to 600 pounds each season. When the season is bad they can make no more than enough to supply themselves. The sap is boiled in cans and kettles within the large wigwams, which stand from year to year, in which they all sleep." (Newton H. Winchell, *The Aborigines of Minnesota* [St. Paul: Minnesota Historical Society, 1911], pp. 497, 595–596.)

White Children Rescued From Indians (page 78)
In 1823, news was brought by the traders that two white (Tully) children were with a party of Sioux, on the St. Peter's. It appeared from what they could learn, that a family from Red River—Selkirk's settlement—had been on their way to the fort, when a war party of Sioux met them, murdered the parents and an infant, and made the boys prisoners. Colonel Snelling sent an officer with a party of

soldiers to rescue the children. After some delay in the ransom, they were finally brought. ("Early Days at Fort Snelling," *Minnesota Historical Collections*, I [1850–1856], 432.)

One boy died soon after the incident, which may account for Prescott's statement that only one child was rescued.

Red River Settlers Make Their Way to Fort Snelling (page 78)

> Travellers from the south brought news of a better locality, and towards this place there soon began a movement which, while not great in any one year, was long continued. In 1821 five families made the journey to Fort Snelling, and their success inspired others. In 1823 thirteen families made the perilous journey of four hundred miles. . . . The many hardships endured by these travellers, and their pitiful condition, appealed to the sympathy of the Americans, and they were welcomed and aided by the officers at Fort Snelling. During their stay one party was granted the use of the old barracks at Camp Cold Water. Employment was given the men upon the reservation, and those who preferred to remain were allowed to settle upon the military grounds. Comparatively few, however, made their homes here, the greater number proceeding to Galena, Illinois, and Vevay, Indiana.

Marcus L. Hanson, *Old Fort Snelling, 1819–1858* (Iowa City: Iowa State Historical Society, 1918), p. 189–190.

Taliaferro mentions the Red River settlers of the Selkirk colony in several entries in his journal. On July 28, 1835, he wrote: "The Canadians who reached here last night report . . . that 20 families are now on their way & will be here in a day or two perhaps . . . from the Red River Colony. 114 Souls in all, some have their cattle, pushing on into this country & to Green Bay &c. 375, & 114 makes 489. Since 1821 that have passed this Post for Vevay & other points in the Several States."

On July 31, 1835, the Agent recorded: "Emigrants from Red River arrived this morning having their Carts & oxen with loads of various articles 50 or 60 head of Cattle & some 20 or 25 horses. At this rate the loss of one & two hundred Souls at a time with their property will reduce the numerical strength of Gov Simpsons Colony to an alarming extent, he will have only the half bloods & the Trading Community left."

On August 3, 1835, Taliaferro reported:

Mr Robert Campbell of Red River called at the Agency to inquire of John and Andrew Tully, nephews of his, taken prisoners 12 years ago by the Sioux.

Two men Michael Killcole an Irishman & Joseph Ierpah called & reported the loss of three yoke of oxen at the Little Rapid by the Sioux Indians, being Emigrants from Red River & no law bearing upon their case, I wrote a collection paper for the officers & citizens to give a mite. . . .

If the Indians had not been drunk not a hoof of all the cattle from Red River would have been lost. The Am F Cpy have permitted the Indians to get more whiskey, and to a greater extent this year than for Some two or 3 years past. I hear of it from Wabasha village below Lake Pepin to Lac Traverse.

(Taliaferro's Journal, Vol. 12, pp. 148–149, 151.)

Aftermath of the Treaty Signing (page 78)

Taliaferro wrote on September 30, 1825, that he was giving Zachariah Wright Prescott a draft of $80.62½ "for the transportation of Sick and convalescent Indians" from the Indian agency at St. Peters to Lake Traverse. The Indians were probably returning from the treaty signing, where a number of them became quite ill. (Taliaferro's Journal, Vol. 4, p. 44.)

The Indians' illness may have resulted from drinking adulterated whiskey. On September 19, Taliaferro had written in his journal:

A letter has been received from Mr. Laidlaw who was employed to take the Sick Indians, of the Yanctons, Wahpetons, Sissetongs & Wahpacootas to Lac Traverse stating that the Indians generally were still very ill, and that the Little Crow War Chief of the Sissitong Band of the Sioux had died and it was expected that Wahnatarh Chief of the Yanctons and one other of his party would die in a few days. The Indians stated to Mr. Laidlaw, that they had been poisoned at Prairie du Chien by drinking mixed whiskey and Sugar, and what confirms them in this belief is that all who drank it have been taken sick and many have died. They attach great blame to Laidlaw and Renville for inducing them to attend the Council at Prairie du Chien, and it is expected that the consequences resulting . . . will be cerious [*sic*] in relation to these two persons.

(Taliaferro's Journal, Vol. 7.)

Otter Tail Lake (page 79)

Otter Tail Lake was so named from a long, narrow sand bar with an outline suggesting the tail of an otter, formed long ago and now covered with large trees. ("Minnesota Geographic Names," *Minnesota Historical Collections*, XVII [1920], 390.)

Indian Traders in Minnesota in 1826 (page 80)

There were a good number of traders in Minnesota at this time. In 1826, probably early in the year, Major Taliaferro compiled a list of licensed Indian traders among the Dakotas, or Sioux. It included the following: P. Prescott, Leaf River; D. Lamont, mouth of the Minnesota; J. Renville, Lac qui Parle; Wm. Dickson, Lake Traverse; B. F. Baker, Crow Island, Upper Mississippi; Duncan Campbell, Falls of St. Croix; John Campbell, mouth of the Chippeway; Francis Grandin, Traverse des Sioux; Hagan Moores (Hazen P. Mooers), Lake Traverse; and Louis Provençalle, Traverse des Sioux. (Edward Duffield Neill, *The History of Minnesota from the Earliest French Explorations to the Present Time* [Minneapolis: Minn. Hist. Co., 1882], p. 382.) While some of these were listed as trading among the Dakotas, actually they were trading among the Chippewas, or Ojibways, notably, Prescott and Baker. Taliaferro on June 27, 1827, wrote that "for some years past two respectable young men, P. Prescott of New York, and B. F. Baker of Virginia, have been trading with the Chippeways of the Mississippi. . . ." (Taliaferro's Journal, Vol. 4, p. 85.)

The American Fur Company's posts in Taliaferro's agency early in 1826 were: Fort Columbia, Upper Sand Hills, Sheyenne; Fort Biddle, Crow Island; Fort Rush, mouth of Chippeway River; Fort Calhoun, Leech Lake; Fort Pike, Red Lake; Fort Rice, Devil's Lake; Fort Greene, below Big Stone Lake; Fort Southard, Forks of Red Cedar River; Fort Lewis, Little Rapids of the Minnesota River; Fort Benton, Sandy Lake. Fort Factory, near Fort Snelling, is also listed though not assigned to a particular company. (E. D. Neill, "Occurrences in and Around Fort Snelling, from 1819 to 1840," *Minnesota Historical Collections*, II [1860–1867], 113–114.)

The Columbia Fur Company posts at this time were as follows: Fort Adams, Lac qui Parle; Fort Washington, Lake Traverse; Fort Union, Traverse des Sioux; Fort Barbour, Falls of St. Croix;

Fort Bolivar, Leaf Lake; and Fort Confederation, second forks of the Des Moines River. (*Ibid.*)

Little Six (page 85)

Little Six was also known as Shakopee, meaning six. It was a hereditary name of successive chiefs in lineal descent from father to son.

Colonel Snelling Blamed by Friends of the Sioux (page 85)

Henry H. Sibley, who arrived in Minnesota in 1834 and knew the foregoing story only by hearsay, wrote in 1856 of Colonel Snelling's conduct as follows:

> The excitement produced by so unusual a proceeding, was prodigious, not only among the Dakotas, but among their white friends in the country. The commandant was charged with unjustifiable haste in the summary execution of innocent men, and for a short time there was a fair prospect of an Indian war. Col. Snelling justified the steps he had taken, on the ground that the American flag had been insulted, by the violence offered to Indians under its immediate protection, and it was his duty to punish the offenders.
>
> As a mere question of policy, there is no doubt that Col. Snelling commited a grave error, in sacrificing four Dakota lives as an atonement for the wounding of the two Chippewas, both of whom recovered. True, the severity of the measure tended to prevent future outbreaks of a like kind, in the immediate vicinity of the Fort, but it also excited a far deeper exasperation in the minds of the Dakotas against their hereditary enemies the Chippewas, and a spirit of revenge against the soldiers, both of which found vent in blood.

("Reminiscences; Historical and Personal," *Minnesota Historical Collections*, I [1850–1856], 475–476.)

Joseph Snelling's Account of the Execution (page 85)

The fullest account of this whole affair was written by Colonel Snelling's son, Joseph, who concludes his account, in agreement with Prescott, with these words: "For a short time after the execution . . . the Indian country remained quiet. The Dakotas avoided all intercourse with the whites. They were angry at the death of their fellows, indeed, and spoke of vengeance among themselves; but they either were convinced of the justice of what had been done, or knew the superior force of the whites too well to think of taking any active measures." ("Running the Gauntlet: A Thrilling Incident of Early Days at Fort Snelling," *Minnesota Historical Collections*, I [1850–1856], 456.)

Joseph Snelling (page 86)

Joseph was the son of Colonel Snelling by his first wife. He was born in Boston in 1804. His mother died soon afterward, and he was left in the care of relatives. At the age of fourteen he went to West Point but left when he was sixteen, while his father was at Fort Snelling. In the summer of 1823 he accompanied the Long exploring party up the Minnesota Valley and down the Red River Valley. He was well acquainted with the stirring Indian troubles of 1826 and 1827 and later wrote accounts of them. In 1827 he left Fort Snelling for the East, where he gained some prominence in the literary field. He died in Boston in 1848.

Winter Hunts (page 88)

The deer hunt began in September or October. Having returned from that, if they had been successful, the Indians "spent the time mostly resting and visiting until the first of March. During this time they handed over their furs and such deer skins as they could spare to the traders, and, if they had corn or rice, dug it up to eat with their tallow. . . . It was with them all, perhaps, the easiest time of the year, though if the hunt had proved unproductive it was on the other hand the hardest.

"The season of rest and recreation . . . lasted till March, when it was necessary to prepare for the muskrat-hunt and sugar-making. . . . the men were the fur-hunters, the women were the sugar-makers." (Samuel W. Pond, "The Dakotas or Sioux in Minnesota as They Were in 1834," *Minnesota Historical Collections*, XII [1908], 360, 373–375.)

Spring Hunts (page 89)

"The spring hunt was the most important, for the furs were then the most valuable. There were a few muskrats in all parts of the country, but they were not everywhere plentiful, and the Indians residing in the vicinity of Fort Snelling often went more than a hundred miles in quest of them, hunting south and west of Fort Ridgely. They were under the necessity of starting from home early in March, as it took some time to make the journey and the hunt commenced before the ice was out of the lakes. They usually carried a small supply of provisions, if they had any, also their guns, spears, and traps. Some had horses, but most carried their loads on their backs. They took some large traps for otter, and the muskrat traps were much heavier than those in use at the present day. These, with other necessary articles, made heavy burdens for men to carry a hundred miles." (Samuel W. Pond, "The Dakotas or Sioux in Minnesota as They Were in 1834," pp. 370–372.)

Pike Shoots Down British Flag (page 90)

Zebulon M. Pike's journal entry for February 10, 1806, reads: "Hoisted the American flag in the fort. The English yacht still flying at the top of the flagstaff, I directed the Indians and my riflemen to shoot at it, who soon broke the iron pin to which it was fastened, and brought it to the ground." ("Pike's Explorations in Minnesota, 1805–6," *Minnesota Historical Collections*, I [1850–1856], 400.)

Po-kega-ma (page 90)

Pike rated these falls next to the Falls of St. Anthony as an impediment to navigation. As early as 1804 the Northwest Company had a post located near the falls, and later the American Fur Company had a post there.

Zachariah Wright Prescott Leaves Minnesota (page 93)

Philander Prescott's brother probably left the upper Mississippi area in 1826. Taliaferro's journal on January 31, 1826, states that "W. Prescott from 2d Fork Desmoines arrived this day." On two earlier occasions Taliaferro had mentioned him—September 9, 1823, "Mr. Wright P. & Phi Prescott both arrived." Both were given licenses on July 4, 1823, and a special note was "attached to W. Prescott's License" on September 13, 1823. (Taliaferro's Journal, Vol. 7.)

Lac qui Parle (page 93)

Lac qui Parle was about ten miles long, with a maximum width of one mile and a maximum depth of twelve feet. It was an expansion of the Minnesota River lying about thirty miles southeast of the lower end of Big Stone Lake. The French name means "the Lake

That Talks," perhaps derived from "a very remarkable creaking, groaning, and whistling of the ice on the lake in winter and spring, due to the fluctuations of the water level allowing the ice to rise and fall, grating upon the abundant boulders of the shores." ("Minnesota Geographic Names," p. 288.)

V

1827–1829

On the Mississippi

After all had left and all the goods had been removed from Land's End to the American Fur Company's store, I had to start. It so happened that the steamboat *Josephine*[1] came up to Fort Snelling with supplies for the fort, so I shipped for St. Louis, where my brother was living with Messrs. Powell [1827].

It made me feel sad, sad to think and review the past five years that I had been there. I had formed the acquaintance of most all of the officers in the fort and all the traders of the country, and have to go amongst strangers [with] nothing before me and only the clothes I had on. Everything looked gloomy; and then again, to leave my Indian wife and boy was another thing that troubled me much, as I could not leave them well provided for. The company being in debt, I could not get anything from that source. I had taken nothing for three years but barely enough to keep me from suffering in the winter, and what I did get was of the most common kind and [my clothes] were not fit to go into decent company.

The boat was getting ready to be off. I went and bid the old woman a good-by and left her with her parents. I went and embarked. The clerk of the sutler's store called me [to] one side and asked me if I had any money. I told him no, so he took ten dollars and gave [it to] me, saying, "You are travelling amongst strangers and you may want a little."

This was an act of kindness at the hands of Mr. H. K. Ortley, the

---

[1] The *Josephine* is one of fifteen steamboats listed as having arrived at Fort Snelling up to May 26, 1826. (Russell Blakely, "History of the Discovery of the Mississippi River and the Advent of Commerce in Minnesota," *Minnesota Historical Collections*, VIII [1895–1898], 376, 378.)

clerk of the sutler's store at Fort Snelling, which I felt deeply to appreciate and asked another favor of him, that was if he heard of my wife and child's being in want of provisions at any time to let them have some. He promised to do so, as he had at one time thought of getting my wife when she was a girl. But he would not promise to marry her for life. This the old folks did not like and they would not let their daughter marry under those circumstances—to be kept a few years and then be cast off with three or four children. So Mr. Ortley did not get her.

The boat was ready. I shook hands with my old friends and Mr. Ortley, and long shall I remember the time when he slipped the ten-dollar bill on the State Bank of Missouri into my hand. I thought of the old proverb "A friend in time of need is a friend indeed." He lived at Fort Snelling four or five years, left two or three children, went to St. Louis, set up a large grocery store, but died in two or three years.

Off we sailed. I took a last look at the land I loved and [which] appeared more like my native land and home, by a long residence in it, than the one I had left to the east, in the state of New York, Phelpstown, Ontario County.

The bell rang and the boat passed slowly over the bar at Mendota, which gave us time to view the old place where we had often assembled to see Indian dances and to trade Indian curiosities.

After we got under way I found that Col. Snelling was on board the boat with his family, going east and to Washington. The colonel was to settle his accounts. Whilst there he took sick and died.[2]

Nothing transpired on our route from Fort Snelling to St. Louis, only that I hired out to the captain of the steamboat as clerk at twenty dollars per month. But I had to stand watch half the night, and the captain the other half of the night.

We arrived all safe and sound at St. Louis again. [I] found my brother well; he was the principal bookkeeper in the Messrs. Powell's dry goods store. As I had got employment on the steamboat in the day time, I had to be at the boat always in the day time, either receiving or unloading freight, and it was only in the evening that I

---

[2] "The Snelling family located at St. Louis while Colonel Snelling proceeded to Washington to settle some accounts. While here he was suddenly taken sick and died on August 20, 1828." ("Early Days at Fort Snelling," *Minnesota Historical Collections*, I [1850–1856], 436–437.)

could get a chance to stroll about the city a little while in the evening with my brother.

The [boat] made regular trips from St. Louis to Galena. The water was very low at the Rock Island and Des Moines rapids, and we had hard work to get over. We frequently had to lighten the steamboat with a keelboat, by taking the freight from the steamer to the shore and leaving a part there, then moving ahead with a part of the freight until we found deep water, when we would put the freight into the steamer again. Whenever freight was left on the shore I had to stay and watch it. So betwixt three duties that I had to perform—clerking, standing watch on the boat half the night, and watching the freight on shore—I worried out in about two months.

Frequently I would take hold and help load lead in order that we might keep up our regular trips. This was very hard work; to handle pigs of lead for one or two hours at a time was very straining on the hands and arms. I was careful with the freight and never had to pay for any but once, and that was for some furs that were stolen by the barkeeper, about fifty dollars worth the boat had to pay for.

We worked hard all the fall, running from St. Louis to Galena, and the boat made about two thousand dollars. Capt. [J.] Clark owned and commanded the boat. Finally the ice commenced running and we quit the trade to Galena, laid up a few days in St. Louis, painted the boat, repaired her machinery some, and took in freight for New Orleans, mostly bulk meat or pork in pieces, and some lard and hominy.

So we got a full freight, but there were so many boats in that trade that we had to carry freight very cheap, and our boat, being small, did not pay very well to work cheap on small freight. On our way down we got aground twice and had to unload twice. This was hard work and we had to work night and day, for the ice was not far behind us, and we were fearful if the ice overtook us it would cut our boat to pieces. In a short time, however, we got clear.

We ran into the bank one morning in a fog and got in amongst a parcel of snags and logs afloat. Here we expected to be lost every minute, but the snags were old and rotten and gave way when the boat floated onto them. The wheels of the steamboat had got full of roots, and even whole trees, roots and all, had got fastened to us. It took us half an hour to get clear from them. By this time the fog had cleared off a little and we could see that the river was full of old dead trees, floating down with the current at a very rapid rate.

The water was very high and the [river] was out of its banks most all the way from the mouth of the Ohio to New Orleans. By this time I was pretty well tired out, not only standing watch half the night, but I had to get up every time the boat landed to wood or take in freight or passengers. As I was clerk, the captain would not have anything to do with the accounts. My rest being broken so much made me sick, but I stuck to my place. And before we got down we got into another pile of logs in a large eddy in a fog in the night. I think we were two hours getting out of this scrape.

At last we arrived safely at New Orleans[3] and we were informed that the water had never been so high. It was only about two feet below the levee. I felt very unwell but went to work and got out part of the freight. The barkeeper had been ashore and returned, saying there was a ball that evening close by. So they all, captain along, agreed to go to the ball.

I felt unwell and did not care about going, so I agreed to stay and keep watch. But it appears that the barkeeper had looked for an opportunity to get all hands off the boat so he could steal some of the freight, and his plan worked very well, for after all hands of the boat had got to dancing, they thought nothing of the boat until near morning. I was left alone nearly all night and got so sleepy that I got sound asleep in my chair.

No doubt the barkeeper was watching me all the time to see if I got to sleep so he could pillage some of the freight, and his plan worked out well, for the next morning there was a barrel of lard missing. The captain, when he found it out, commenced swearing and cursing me, and said I had not attended to my duty in watching the boat. I told him I could not watch above and below at the same time. "Well," he said, "if you had not gone to sleep you could have heard them in taking a barrel of lard from the boat."

I asked him why he allowed all the boat hands to leave the boat and be gone all night. He said he did not know all the hands were going to leave the boat and said I ought to have told him that they were all going to the party. But this was all an excuse to throw the

---

[3] New Orleans was a fast growing city, still more French in language and nationality than English. In 1820 its population was 27,176, while in 1830 it was 46,310.

blame on me, for he knew all the hands were absent from the boat, as they were all at the ball where there was dancing all night.

I told the owner of the freight how it was, and he was satisfied that the captain was altogether to blame in the matter, and said he would make the captain pay for the lard. He did so by deducting the amount out of the freight, which made quite a hole in the freight bill. The captain was mad at me and did not speak to me for three days. But the barkeeper got off clear with the lard, which cost the captain about $30.

This was the second pull for the barkeeper, making $80 in one trip he got out of the captain by stealing. This same man came near ruining the captain once before. He got mad at one of the engineers one day and set the engine a-going when we were taking in wood. He gave it a full head of steam, and the way that old machinery flew for a few moments was wonderful! The flywheel, which weighed about two tons, went so fast we could not see it, and it is a wonder it did not fly all to pieces and kill some persons on the boat. The engineer heard it and ran from the table at breakfast and shut off the steam. [It was] a fortunate circumstance that nothing was broke and no one hurt. The captain tackled the barkeeper and gave him a terrible cussing, and that was the last of it.

The captain had got into a scrape coming down which like to have [got] all in the cabin into trouble. A woman had taken passage for New Orleans, where her parents lived. Her parents were a respectable family and belonged to one of our religious societies in good standing. But the daughter had become wild and profligate—too often the case in cities—and ran way from home and went to St. Louis. Some of her friends found her out and persuaded her to return to her parents. She consented and went on our boat. The captain had found out who she was, and was known to leave his berth and go to this woman's, and was accused of it by some of the passengers. This made him mad and he accused me and others in the cabin of watching him and circulating lies about him. I told [him] he was mistaken so far as I was concerned. He went all round the boat but could get no satisfaction on the subject, and the thing [was] dropped where it was commenced.

Three days after, the captain told us he was going up river. As they had no boats that season, there was some freight for the upper part of the Red River. He handed me a check on one of the banks and told me to go get the money for the freight of our trip down. I went to the bank and got it all in silver and put it into a shot bag. I was walking along by one of the chain gangs working on the levee. One says to me, "If I could meet you alone somewhere with that bag you would not keep it long." I thanked him for the compliment and told him I was glad to see he was safe enough, and that I did not fear him in the way he was fixed there. He laughed and went on about his work.

We got in our freight and left the city for Natchitoches[4] on the Red River of the South. We went on very well until we got into the Red River. One day our skiff broke loose. We came near being blowed up by one of the engineers whilst we were working to get the skiff. The engineer held on all steam and it was escaping at a fearful rate from the safety valve. I was fearful of danger and raised the valve a little to let off some of the steam that was forcing the boilers terribly. We could see the steam flying from almost every joint or splice. The captain scolded me for raising the safety valve and [said] I would scald somebody.

We had also a large flat[boat], or broadhorn as they are termed on the lower Mississippi, in tow. We kept onto work, helping to get the skiff to its place; and the flatboat needed some new lashings. The engineer held onto all the steam, and I discovered there was something the matter with him. I went and told the captain that the engineer would blow us all up very soon if he did not go and see to him. The captain started, but before he got to the engine, a piece burst out of the steam pipe as large as a man's finger. It made all hands scatter. The steam flew with so much force that no one could approach near enough to do anything to stop the leak. The captain was now glad to get the opportunity to let off steam through the safety valve, and by so doing let off enough. So we got a piece of copper plate and three or four doubles of canvas and a strong cord, and lashed the copper and linen on over the hole, and stopped the leak.

If we had of got blown up and the [boat] sunk, and if we had not been killed by the steam, we should have been drowned. The Mississippi was so high that it backed the water up in the Red River 90 miles, and the mouth of the river was about 30 miles wide, so there was no possibility of escaping a watery grave, and all must have

---

[4] Natchitoches, about two hundred miles up the Red River on its west bank, was more French and Spanish than English at this time.

perished for the fault of one man. The engineer had been indulging very strongly in New Orleans and had got the delirium tremens. He was perfectly out of his head at the time, and so came near to blowing us all into Eternity. However, providence overruled the disaster and we got safely under way again.

We went on up a piece farther and took in a widow woman and some slaves in the night. They said they had been a week on a raft. The whole country was flooded with water. We went on and found a steamboat, *Robert Burns*, aground. By this time we had got above the flood of the Mississippi and found the banks of the Red River about fifteen feet above water.

The weather was very mild and pleasant. The fact of seeing nice high and dry banks once more was gratifying to the eyes and body, for we had been about 15 days sailing about in this high water, and could not scarcely find dry ground enough to land the steamboat on.

The *Robert Burns* lay in the channel and we could not pass until she got off, so we laid there the balance of the day and a part of the next, when the *Burns* got off. She passed us and missed us, and that was all, and went off.

We had a passenger on board, a kind of trader; he had come all the way from St. Louis with us. He is one that the captain had accused of watching his movements about the lady cabin passenger before referred to. He had purchased, with the captain, some 30 barrels of whisky from a little boat trading up and down the Mississippi River. This ladened our steamboat so that we had much trouble to get along. The river was narrow and crooked and full of snags.

We got up to Alexandria and got off some of our load, and went on a little better for one day. Then the water got very [full of] shoal[s] again and at one place was barely wide enough to let the boat through.

We had now been about a week out and had got out of provisions, and we had much trouble in getting such supplies from the inhabitants as the boat wanted, for the inhabitants lived mostly on hominy, and the Negroes the same.

Our fair weather turned into raining. The captain and Mr. Gray hired a couple of horses and went up to Natchitoches, a distance of about 30 miles by land, and told me to work along up as well as I could after we got off, for we were now aground. With much hard pulling we got off, but there were so many snags that we made slow progress. It rained all night and all day; the next day it slackened up a little, and the captain and Mr. Gray came back again. It set into raining about dark and it actually came down in streams. In the morning it slackened up a little and the water had commenced rising, so we got under way and got up to Natchitoches, and a hard trip we had of it.

The Red River of the South resembles the Minnesota River very much in width, depth, and serpentine course and height of banks, but the timber is different. The great cypress trees [are] laden with moss hanging from the top to the ground, and the dry land is not more than half a mile wide, and from that to a mile, when it terminates in those cypress swamps. The farms for sugar and cotton are from a half to one mile wide along the banks of the rivers.

Natchitoches was nothing but some log huts with only 3 or 4 common houses when we were there in the winter of 1827 and 1828. The first night we arrived the pilot went ashore and got up a Spanish fandango ball. This was something I wanted to see. Having heard a great deal about the Spaniards. I wanted to see them perform, so the captain ordered some one to keep watch and we all went. The boat's crew, most of them, joined in the dance. [The others were] an old Spanish woman, and one or two quadroon women, and about a dozen men for the ball, a very good sample of the inhabitants of the place.

The women had tortillas, a mixture of flour and cornmeal made into small rolls, then rolled up in cane leaves and boiled. The Spanish were buying them. I supposed it was something good and purchased half a dozen and thought I would try them, and of all the insipid things that I ever tasted were those tortillas! The Spanish appeared to be very fond of them. They had a little lap dog running about the floor where they were a-dancing; it was barking and I commenced feeding him the tortillas. After while the pilot came to me and told me the Spanish were mad at me for feeding the tortillas to the dog. They took it as an insult to their mode of cooking and told me to stop. I threw [away] the balance that I had in·my hands and took up my hat and walked away, down to the boat, and left them to dance and eat the tortillas to themselves. I never saw a more vulgar looking little company than had got together to have what they called a ball. The boat's crew danced nearly all night.

The next morning we went to work to unload the boat. We went on very well and got nearly half out before breakfast was called. I turned to go to breakfast and saw one of the men rolling a hogshead of sugar on a plank alone. I spoke to him and told him not to attempt to roll the hogshead of sugar out alone, but he persisted in doing it. I remonstrated and told him he would let it [roll] into the water. "Oh no," he said, and went on.

He was almost out when the hogshead of sugar took a cant and over it went into the river, one end on dry land and the other wet. It was rolled out as soon as possible, but it was spoiled. It was full of water, and in a few minutes it was all molasses and commenced running out.

The captain commenced swearing at me and wanted to know why I let that man roll the sugar into the river. I told him I had forbid him and told him to wait for help, but [he] persisted and went ahead after being told twice. "Why in hell did you not call some hands to help?" I said they had all gone to breakfast. He kept on swearing, saying, "You always have some kind of foolish get off for negligence of duty," and went off to breakfast, and I followed.

After breakfast the captain went ashore and got an auctioneer and had the molasses sold for about nine dollars. I told him to make the man pay the balance by working on the boat. He let fly an oath and said, "He has not got a cent, and how can I make him pay for the sugar?" I said nothing more. The captain was mad all the way down to New Orleans and hardly spoke to anyone on the boat for two or three days.

We hurried on, got unloaded, and made off down stream. By this time the water had risen about ten feet and rushed on down with a frightful current. The bayous that run out of the river run out at a frightful rate, and if a small boat should get drawn sidewise into one, I believe it would break the boat in two.

We came back to Alexandria and found our old friend, the flat-boat [man], there. He said he had not sold enough to pay his freight and was about to leave for New Orleans. He was a funny old fellow, active, and had been entrusted with a large amount of property, otherwise groceries, from the Ohio River. Several farmers had clubbed together and made a large flatboat, and put in all their spare produce and sent this man down to sell it for them along with his own.

We went on down to New Orleans and took in some more freight and went back to Alexandria again. Here the captain came near getting into a bowie knife scrap on account of some freight that had been landed. The owners had taken it away and then would not pay the freight. The captain went and got a knife and went and demanded pay or the goods, so he could get his pay out of them. He flourished his bowie a while and the other party [did] the same, but bystanders interfered and got the matter settled, and the captain got a check on the bank and got his money.

By this time we had begun to get sick of the country and the people in it, as a large number of [them] were cutthroats and black-legs. Alexandria was a pretty little town with pine trees growing amongst the houses, which gave it a pretty appearance from the river.

We got off as soon as we could for New Orleans. When we got there we found our old friend with the flatboat had sold out and spent most of the money and left for parts unknown, so his friends at home had to suffer. He had had a fine lot of farmers' products, horses, cows, pigs, fowls, apple cider, cheese, butter, peach brandy, cider brandy, whisky, corn, flour, and, in fact, he had the finest lot of good provisions that I had ever seen—nice and clean—all lost to the owners, several thousand dollars worth. And I was told that was a frequent occurrence by the Ohioans and Indianans. When they get to New Orleans they get to gambling and lose all.

This was Saturday. In the afternoon a gentleman came on board the boat and appeared to be an old friend of the captain's, and set and talked very friendly with the captain. About half an hour later he went away again. In about an hour after, another gentleman came to the wharf and called the captain and told him he wanted to speak to him. The captain went out and they walked off together. In about half an hour the captain came back and said, "Did you see that man on shore that called me out?" I said yes.

"Well," said the captain, "that was the sheriff. The man that came here first has sued me for debt." The captain said he [the man] claimed $400 on the steamboat, on the engine; and the captain said he would not pay it, for it was an old one and was not worth anything like he charged for it.

So the captain went to a lawyer and gave him $25 and told him the facts in the case. The lawyer told him the laws were very strict in that city about such things, and said the plaintiff had all the advantage of him. "And now," said he, "you have one way of escape left. That is to get up steam quietly in the morning, Sunday, and start off." So we done [that] and got off clear, but had no freight.

So we worked our way back to St. Louis, without any freight to pay our expenses. So the captain lost about $500 in his New Orleans trade, and got back to St. Louis about the 10th of February [1828]. We remained in port a few days.

One day the captain came to me and said the boat could not pay a clerk now, as there was not much business doing in freight, but if the 2d pilot and I would take the bar, we might have all we could make out of it. So we agreed to do it and got our supplies and had them charged to the boat. My brother was still living with the Messrs. Powell. The captain got about half a load of freight and a few passengers and started for Galena.

The day before we arrived at Galena it commenced snowing, and there was ice running from the Mississippi. We took a large keelboat in tow, so we just moved, but we got to the mouth of Fever River after dark. It began to turn cold and I commenced working up the Fever River. When we got to Galena on the morning of the 23rd of February, 1828, the ice, newly formed, was strong enough for the boys to skate on all around the steamboat. The boat laid there for two weeks, frozen in.

The inhabitants had been celebrating Washington's birthday before we arrived, and in the evening they pretended that a steamboat was coming. By carrying lead and firing cannon [they] hoaxed a good many of the citizens that came out to see if a boat had arrived. And little did they think that a boat was so near at hand. We should have got up on the 22nd in time for the celebration if we had not taken the keelboat in tow.

An old Frenchman who lived on the opposite side of the river got up in the morning and came out and said, "God damn the steamboat! What for he come here in the winter?" The old man felt hurt, for he was a trader and had about all the flour there was in town and was asking $13 per barrel for it. But the boat had a lot on board, so the old Frenchman had to come down a peg on his flour, which made the old man swear a little.

The captain of the boat got to gambling whilst he was frozen up in Galena and lost all his loose cash. And being tied up there so long made him very cross. One day he got to scolding me because I was always away from the boat and did not sell anything. I got my dander up a little, too, and went ashore to a merchant by the name of Hempstead that had borrowed my brother's pistols, the ones we had used so much at Fort Snelling. I did not tell him what I wanted of them. He let me have them and I went down to the boat with a full determination to give the captain a challenge.

The 2d pilot, my partner in the bar business, saw me with the box. He mistrusted from the size and shape of the box what I had, and would not let me alone until I told him what I was going to do with the pistols. Finally I told him I was agoing to challenge that old brute of a captain. He set his head against it at once, and got hold of the pistols and took them back again. I told him that I was not going to stop on the boat to be abused by that old fool of a captain. "You may go where you like," he said, "but as for your getting into a quarrel on this boat, you can't do it as long as I am on it."

So I quit the boat and went to a friend of mine and boarded with him about one week. From there I went to a public house to live, and there I found a man by the name of Holliday; he had been sick for a month or more, but was now convalescent and was making preparations to go to mining. He was to get an outfit from my friend, Mr. Tilton, one of the late partners of the old Columbia Fur Company. I proposed to join in and go halves in all we could find in mining, so we agreed to go over and see Mr. Tilton on the subject.

He fell in with the plan at once, and we got a lot of tools and bedding and hired a team to move us out to the mining country. About the 20th of March, 1828, we moved, and the 2d day we went and camped on a branch of the Little Platte. We built a temporary shanty and commenced digging for lead ore. We dug about a month and could find no mineral, so we moved our camp farther north one day's travel on to one of the branches of the Pecatonica River.

Here we built a small house out of little poplars, and split some long oak shingles and covered our house, so we were quite comfortable and commenced digging. The first hole I dug I found some very pretty mineral and it looked fair for a good lead, but on further working we found it was a few scattered lumps and no lead. And so we kept on digging all summer. I dug about 200 holes from three to ten feet deep, and did not find mineral enough to purchase a plug of tobacco. Notwithstanding, there were some good leads in the neighborhood. A young man by the name of Thos. McKnight[5] came and went to digging near us but found nothing of value, also a man by the name of Jones had been mining 4 years and had found comparatively nothing. Also a man by the name of Dickson, he had three or 4 men hired and two or three black men hired; they worked all summer, and all they found was about two hundred dollars worth of mineral.

My partner and myself bought a prospect of Mr. Jones and went on to prove it, as it seemed likely to prove a valuable lead. A sheet about eight inches thick, lying flat under ground about four feet deep, was the first of our discoveries in the prospect we had purchased.

I had worked myself completely down and thought I would have a resting spell; and I hired a horse and went down to Galena, a good day's ride. Here I found the old *Josephine* and advertised for Fort Snelling. The thought struck me at once, "Here's a chance to go and see my wife and boy!"

It happened there was a man from our place, or diggin's, in town. I got him to ride the horse home again and I embarked on the old *Josephine* again, Capt. Clark, master. The old captain and myself had forgotten all our troubles of former times, and we sailed up to Fort Snelling very friendly together. On our way up the captain told me that when he got back to St. Louis, my brother had attacked him about the treatment he had shown me while I was on his boat. He said my brother had told him plainly that he, the captain, was chargeable with all the trouble and difficulty that had risen between us.

The captain acknowledged that when he got into a passion he would frequently say things that he ought not to say. He said that I was somewhat contrary and hard-headed, too, was the reason we could not get along together; and for himself he should say nothing about the matter, although I had once intended to shoot him, when the boat was frozen in at Galena. So there was an end to that affair.

After landing I went to the captain and asked what my fare was. He said he believed there was something due me from the boat "and we will say even." "So," said I, and we parted good friends again.

I went now in search of my old woman and boy. I found them with the old folks, where I had left them, at Mendota. They were all well

[5] This may have been Thomas McKnight, who in the fall of 1836 was a legislator living in Dubuque.

and there was an increase of family. A daughter [Lucy] had been added during my absence (now Mrs. Pettijohn). They had passed the winter very well, they informed me, and had not suffered for anything. They had been quite happy and comfortable, which was more than I could boast of.

I concluded to stop a while with them, so I stopped about two weeks. I told the old woman I must go again, as an opportunity was offered so that I could get a passage with Mr. [Alexis] Bailly. She opposed [it] and wanted I should stay with them. She said something might come about that we could live; if we did live poor that was nothing. She had got tired of living alone, and there were some traders that were always annoying her and telling her I would never come back, etc., etc.

[She] strongly opposed my going down the river again. I told her that I had some business in the mines that I must go and attend to. She said I had been hard at work all summer and had made nothing, and she did not see what use there was of working there for nothing, that I could stay with them and if I earned nothing I would be as well off, if not better [off], with my family than I would be roving about. So I agreed to go down and settle up my business and come back and live at Fort Snelling, poor or not, and run the risk of getting employment.

So I started with Mr. Bailly in a Mackinaw boat for Galena again. We were only 5 or 6 days going down. As soon as I landed I went right off to find my partner, Mr. Holliday. He was glad to see me; he said he wanted some help. I told him I could not stay, that I was going back to my family. This made him hold down his head, for I had always outdone him at digging and could dig as much in one day as he would in a day and a half.

"No, you can't go," he said. "I must; I cannot leave my family alone any longer." "Well, if you will, I will quit also so soon as I can get away." So we settled up our accounts and Mr. Holliday took all and was to pay all the debts, and he was to give me three hundred dollars if the property sold for enough to bring that amount.

Whilst I was absent Mr. Holliday had proved up the lead that we had bought of Mr. Jones and found that it did not much more than pay expenses. After taking off the top mineral the lead took a pitch into the rock in a seam or crevice about half an inch wide. Mr. Holliday worked the hard rock down 40 feet and the lead kept getting thinner all the way down; and at last the rock got so hard, the lead was only about as thick as a knife blade, and a great many tools [had been] worn out so Mr. Holliday abandoned the lead. Now he had nothing but a claim of wood land, and a good place for a furnace left, which he sold for $800 and paid off the debts of our co-partnership. He remained there all winter and until the next fall.

I left the mines and went up to Prairie du Chien with one Mr. Graham,[6] whom I found at Galena with a small keelboat. He was fitting it out to go into the pineries to cut pine logs to raft to St. Louis. We got up to Prairie du Chien. Mr. Brunet,[7] who was to assist Mr. Graham, informed him that the government had forbidden people to cut pine timber and that he could not go into the country. So that broke up the old gentleman's business and left him as poor as I was myself, and he had a large family of children to look after.

This Mr. Graham was a captain in the last war under one Col. [Robert] Dickson on the British side. These two officers took down a company of Sioux Indians as far as Sandusky, and they were at the battle when Col. Croghan defeated the British and drove them off.[8] The Sioux Indians and their officers were frightened almost to death when they saw the British falling by the hundreds. The Indians of all Nations that were there, of which there were a good many, secreted themselves the best they could by fences, ditches, and woods, etc., until the fighting was over. Then the Indians made off as fast as they could, and very glad they were to get off from the awful sight of so many dead and dying. The Indians said the sight was awful, and the Sioux and their officers made the best of their way home again, having been provisioned and clothed by the British at Michili-mackinac, or Mackinaw.

After I arrived at Prairie du Chien I looked around to see if there was any chance to get some employment in the Indian trade, but all the posts were supplied with clerks and interpreters. Mr. Brunet wanted me to go to Galena and sell some corn for him, and purchase some dry goods for him, as he had a number of men at work for him,

6 Probably Duncan Graham.

7 Jean Brunet, a trader at Prairie du Chien from the early 1820's on. His interest in the Galena lead mines began as early as 1822.

8 The attack on Fort Stephenson took place on August 2, 1813, when Colonel George Croghan distinguished himself in the defense of the fort. Many Sioux, Menominees, Winnebagos, and other Indian were present at the battle.

getting wood for a contract for the fort. He paid the hands partly in goods, so [I] went to work and filled up 200 or 300 bushels of corn and shipped it on the *Red River*, Capt. Throckmorton[9] master, and sailed for Galena again and back. Mr. Brunet was very well satisfied and sent me back again, and I done so well with the corn when I got back, he said I must go again. During my absence from the Prairie my wife [came] with her children and her father and mother with her, and I found them in their tent near Mr. Brunet's. I had been gone so long they said they had got lonesome and so came down to see what had become of me.

The boat was in a hurry to be off, so I hurried round and got my folks some provisions and some clothing and told them to go up to the foot of Lake Pepin and there wait for me. My father-in-law's brother lived there, where there was game and they could live much cheaper than at the Prairie.

I got into the steamboat and went down to Galena again and sold another lot of corn for Mr. Brunet. When I came back Mr. Brunet was well satisfied. This was the last trip. Mr. Brunet had given me a note to collect for him on a man by the name of Turney,[10] and told me to sue if he refused to pay. So I went and found the gentleman but he would not pay the note, so I sued him. But he had been elected to the Illinois legislature and [was] on his way there and the law could not stop him. So I left the case in the hands of an officer, to be attended to after he came back. He took his road and I, mine.

I loafed about Galena a few days with nothing to do. About this time one Mr. Kurcheval arrived there with a large lot of Indian goods. Mr. Hunt[11] from Detroit, a brother-in-law of Mrs. Snelling, was in charge. I went to Mr. Brunet and asked him to get a few of the

[9] Captain Joseph Throckmorton commanded steamboats on the upper Mississippi from 1828 to 1849 and continued his connection with the river trade until his death in 1872. (See William J. Petersen's discussion in *Palimpsest*, Vol. X, No. 4 [April 1929], 129–144.)

[10] This undoubtedly was John Turney, a native of Tennessee and a member of the Illinois House of Representatives (1828–1830) from the district in which Galena was located. A practicing attorney, he went to Galena in 1827. (Information from Clyde C. Walton, state historian, Illinois State Historical Library, in a letter of January 9, 1957.)

[11] Probably Benson Hunt, a brother of Mrs. (Abigail Hunt) Snelling who arrived in Galena with his wife and children in 1823 and was there for a number of years.

goods and I would go up to the foot of the lake [Pepin] and trade for the winter. So he went and made arrangements for five hundred dollars worth of cloths and blankets, and Mr. Brunet added some things more, which made me quite a little assortment for the trade.

So Mr. B. got two large canoes and 6 men and started me off. It [was] late in November [1828] and cold, and we had the hardest kind of work to get up, for the ice was running very thick before we reached our point for to winter. But we got up. The men took one canoe and started down through the running ice and got down before the river closed.

I took my goods and stored them in Mr. Graham's house and went out in search of my wife. I found [that] she and all the family had gone out hunting upon the Zumbro River, or Brushy River.* I found them one day's march with their uncle. They had killed some deer and elk and had lived very well and comfortable.

The next morning we took our luggage and started back to the place where we were to winter. We had heavy loads and were very tired when we got in, as we had to carry all on our heads with straps.

I had no house for myself and had to fix up our tent to live in through the winter. We put poles and hay all around the tent and made it tolerable comfortable. So by storing my goods in Mr. Graham's house, I had room enough. I boarded with Mr. Graham a few days until I found that an old Frenchman that he had was stealing my provisions and giving them to the opposition traders.

When we went in to breakfast I asked the old man if he had been giving my pork to the men of the opposition. He at first denied it, but I told him he need not deny it, for I had found out all about it from the men of the other house. He then acknowledged that he had taken some. Before all the table I turned to Mr. Graham and told him that I could not eat with a thief, and if he was determined to keep the old thief at the table, I could not eat with them. Mr. Graham said nothing, so I got up and left the table, and the next meal I had cooked and eat it in the tent.

Mr. Graham found he could do nothing where he was with a large family and concluded to move back to Fort Snelling again. In a few days 2 teams came for them and they moved back on the ice, and I moved into his house and passed the winter.

The opposition had got in a month before me and given all the Indians a credit and sent them off to hunt, so that I saw no Indians until they returned from their winter hunts. The moment the Indians arrived the trader went around and gathered up all the furs, and the Indians had nothing to trade, so I made no packs this winter.

In the spring [1829] I moved up to the head of the lake [Pepin] and lived in my tent amongst the Indians about a month and traded a few furs and sent them down to Mr. Brunet's. Whilst I was down at the foot of the lake in the winter, some teams arrived there from Prairie du Chien. A trader by the name of LaFramboise[12] was the man from the Minnesota River. In the evening they sent for me. The clerk of the opposition house [was] a half-breed by the name of Pierre Ortabis. He and Mr. LaFramboise [sent their] compliments for me to pass the evening with them and to play a few games at cards.

I went over all social, having been acquainted before. We sat down and commenced playing for amusement. After a little Mr. La-Framboise got up and went out and did not return. I sat and played until I got tired, and no Mr. LaFramboise came. I got up to go home, but Mr. Ortabis insisted on my staying longer, that Mr. LaFramboise would be in in a moment. I began to think that something was not right and started and went home.

I found all quiet and no person there but my wife and an old Frenchman that had come up from Prairie du Chien and had brought a load of provisions for me. I went to bed and went to sleep. The next morning my wife asked my why I had stayed so long. She said that trader, Mr. LaFramboise, had been over there all the evening annoying her. I started right over to Mr. Ortabis and found LaFramboise had started at daylight, expecting that I would be after him. So I tackled the other and he swore by all that was good that he knew nothing about the matter and that it was not a concerted plan of his. So I could do nothing, and having no fears of the chastity of my wife, the thing had to stop then. LaFramboise was one of the persons that my wife complained to me of as annoying her when she was alone, and thus opposed my leaving her alone any more.

In the [late] spring I moved up to Fort Snelling and got an old

---

[12] Joseph LaFramboise, a mixed-blood, had traded in the area for a decade or more.

house of the Indian agent[13] and moved into it and passed the summer loafing about. I [had] a few goods left and let one Duncan Campbell[14] have most of them to go and trade them at a profit. So he went off with the goods and traded a considerable lot of furs; he went off and sold them and kept all the proceeds, so I was left flat broke again.

In the fall [1829] Mr. Brunet sent up to see if I had any more furs, as he had to settle for the goods. I packed up what few I had and went down. While I was at Mr. Brunet's the fall before, I had left my papers that I had got of Mr. Holliday with him in part payment of the goods, and he had sent them down and collected the amount and what furs I had I could not pay up.

Whilst I was getting ready to go down to see Mr. Brunet, Mr. Holliday arrived with Mr. McKnight, before named, at Mr. Langham's, the sub-agent, on his way to Missouri. He wanted to know why I gave my papers to Mr. Brunet. "Did you not promise to keep them yourself?" I told him I had promised to keep them as long as I could, and that he had been so long making any returns from our lead business that I was obliged to let them go to live. "Well," said he, "there was not enough cleared to pay all, but I paid it and you are something in my debt." But I knew this could not be, for I knew the amount received for the wood claim would pay all debts and leave something besides. So I never troubled myself about paying him and he never troubled me more about the matter.

I set out for Prairie du Chien again and left my wife with her parents again. We had a cold, boisterous time of it going down. We went down in a large keelboat and it was late in November. The wind blew a gale sometimes, so the boat could not move, being worked by hand sweeps. Finally, a missionary, a Rev. Mr. [Alvan] Coe,* in a bark canoe [came along] and I got in with him and the man that Mr. Brunet had sent up after me. We went one day and had to lay to; the wind blew so hard we could do nothing with our canoe. After a while the old keelboat came driving along before the wind. We started for it and with much difficulty we got on board.

Mr. Coe would go with us. This was Saturday evening and Mr. Coe

[13] Major Lawrence Taliaferro (1794–1871), who was Indian agent at Mendota from 1819 until the fall of 1839.

[14] Duncan Campbell was a brother of Scott Campbell, the U.S. interpreter at St. Peter's for many years.

said he would not travel on Sunday. He went ashore and staid all night at a trader's and passed the Sabbath there. We floated on down but soon got blowed into some tree tops; it took us till near sundown to get off. We floated a short distance and tied up for the night. The next morning it was very cold but calm.

We were now near Prairie La Crosse, so named from the fact it was a fine prairie, below the mouth of Black River, Wisconsin, where the Indians used to go to play ball.[15] We went on very well until we got within about 30 miles of Prairie du Chien. We stopped for the night and there came up a heavy snow storm. The next day we had to work in the snow all day and finally got down to the Prairie.

I went to see my old friend, Mr. Brunet. He was glad to see me once more. I told him at once all my troubles and failure in trade. "Well," he said, "it can't be helped. The goods are paid for but you will owe me something." So I gave him my note for the balance, about $150, and he told me I could stay at his house until I could find some employment or a chance to go back again.

In a few days after, Mr. Brunet leased his tavern stand to a Frenchman that could neither read or write and they wanted me to stay and write or keep his books. So we went to work, but the business soon convinced me that it would not last long. In the first place, the proprietor was no manager; and another thing, there was no travel and no boarders and the rent had to be paid monthly. So the first month the thing failed and they made a new arrangement and took in a partner. Both of the proprietors had been soldiers and they did not agree long. The first one quit and hired himself to the last one as cook, and in fact he had done the cooking all the time. The other stuck it out till spring and came out about $200 in debt. I quit the clerk business, there was so much trouble amongst them, and waited for an opportunity to get back to Fort Snelling.

What to do I did not know. I was out of money and had no way of earning any; I had none to take back again, but I was determined to go if I begged my way home again.

The French are great people for balls. I went once in a while but did not enjoy myself with them, and I almost always went home before the balls were half over.

[15] The Indians were fond of playing a ball game called by the French la crosse a name later given to a city and a county in Wisconsin. ("Minnesota Geographic Names," *Minnesota Historical Collections*, XVII [1920], 239, 253.)

About the middle of the winter [1829–1830] an opportunity offered for me to go back by walking with some soldiers that were going up with the mail, and I got ready to start with the company. I went to Marsh,[16] an old acquaintance of mine in Prairie du Chien, and told him my circumstances. He took a new shirt and gave it to me, and off I went. Before I started I went to shake hands with the proprietors of the house. The one that had charge first took half a dollar and handed it to me saying the money was not his, it would be enough for one meal.

We went on very well until we got up about the middle of Lake Pepin. Here I got lame with the rheumatism and had to stop and rest frequently, but I got up to the head of Lake Pepin sometime after the rest of the party. Here we found a party of soldiers watching a boat load of provisions that had been frozen in in the fall. And about sundown two trains arrived from Fort Snelling to get a load of provisions. They stayed over one day to let [the teams] rest, and asked me to stay and go up with [them].

I was very glad to get a chance to rest. They had a good warm house and I fared very well and got over my lameness and started up with the teams. The mail had gone on the day before.

We had not gone more than 8 or 10 miles before in went one of the trains. Two spans of mules, 14 barrels of flour, sleigh, and all were afloat. The teamsters unhitched the forward horses of the foremost team, as they had gone over safe, and came back and hitched a chain around a mule's neck and pulled him out. And so they did to all of them and got them all out safe. Then the flour had to be got out, which was a cold, wet job; but by hard work all was safely landed on the solid ice and loaded up again. When the sleigh went down, the teamster and myself were both on the load and had barely time to escape before the load all rolled into the river.

We hitched up and went at a pretty smart trot in order to warm up the mules that were wet and cold, and by night they were all dry and well. The next morning we started early so we would get home that day, and near sundown we saw our old homes once more. And heartily glad I was to get back again where I could sit down and be quiet; even if I was poor and had nothing to do, I was with my family and at my home.

16 Probably John Marsh,* a bachelor who was sub-Indian agent at Prairie du Chien about this time.

SUPPLEMENT

The Zumbro River (page 119)

The Zumbro River empties on the west bank of the Mississippi a few miles south of the lower end of Lake Pepin. Its name is derived from the French river Des Embarras. The lower part of the river was obstructed by driftwood, and Forsyth in 1819 called it Driftwood River. Perhaps this fact also accounts for the name Brushy River used by Prescott. The driftwood hindered navigation by canoe and may have been the reason Prescott's group had to carry their luggage on their heads with straps. ("Minnesota Geographic Names," *Minnesota Historical Collections*, XVII [1920], 11.)

The Reverend Alvan Coe (page 121)

In 1829, the Reverend Alvan Coe was joined at the portage between the Fox and Wisconsin Rivers by the Reverend Jedediah D. Stevens, who had been appointed "to accompany him in a tour to the North Western Territory" in the interests of the missions. ("Accessions," *Minnesota History Bulletin*, Vol. IV, Nos. 1–2 [February–May 1921], 73.)

Coe was the secretary of the American Board of Commissioners for Foreign Missions, and the Reverend J. Dwight Stevens was his companion, leaving his own missionary work among the Indians near Mackinac. Upon their arrival at Fort Snelling, "they were welcomed by the Indian agent, Major Lawrence Taliaferro and the officers of the Fort, and upon Sunday, the 6th of September, 1829, also upon the following Sunday Dr. Coe held services in the Fort, preaching at each service, doubtless the first sermons delivered in this region of the Northwest. . . . After making some investigations in the region about Ft. Snelling and farther up the river, the ministers returned to Mackinaw, with the information they had gathered. How their report was received by the Board does not appear, but notwithstanding the encouragement given by the agent, more than five years passed before any representative of the Board reached this section of Minnesota." (Rev. Albert B. Marshall, *History of the First Presbyterian Church of Minneapolis, Minnesota, 1835–1910*, pp. 13–15.)

John Marsh (page 123 n.)

When the fifth regiment of U.S. Infantry came into the country in 1819, and established their headquarters at the mouth of the St.

Peter's River, they brought with them a man by the name of John Marsh, a graduate of some eastern college, as teacher of the post school at headquarters. He appeared to have a great fondness for the Sioux Indians, and was endowed with the faculty of acquiring languages with great facility; he soon learned the Sioux language. Getting tired of teaching an army school, he came down to Prairie du Chien in 1826.

(James H. Lockwood, "Early Times and Events in Wisconsin," *Minnesota Historical Collections*, II [1855], 169.)

VI

1829–1833

At Lake Calhoun

In the spring of the year [1829] the agent, Major L. Taliaferro, wanted to set some of the Indians to farming.* He selected Lake Calhoun for the place and told me he wanted me to go and stay there and take as many Indians as would go and settle down.[1] The agent was to furnish a team and a man to drive the oxen—two yoke. No Indians would go at first except my old father-in-law and another old man by the name of Mockpu-we-chastah, Man-of-the-Clouds.[2] [*My father-in-law was the first to venture out*].

We did not do much the first year; still we raised some corn. The Indian agent [*sent a soldier and a team of two yokes of cattle*] and furnished us with some provisions once in a while, and with my gun and fish line we made out to live. [*We plowed about a month, but there were few Indians that would venture out that year, as they were afraid of the Chippewas. . . . Some went to work with their hoes and dug small patches of ground to commence with. The first year we cut a large quantity of tamarack logs, with which to rebuild the council house . . . at Fort Snelling.*]

The next summer [1830] several families moved out to the lake [*and we had more applicants than we could supply places for*]. We had to plow about 80 acres that year in order that all might get a piece plowed. The teamster drove and I held the plow. We plowed until about the middle of June. We quit, for it was too late to plant after that time, and I had got tired of plowing, for it was hard work where the ground was so rooty. This season the Indians raised very good

[1] It appears from Taliaferro's diary that the Eatonville colony at Lake Calhoun started in 1829, and Prescott apparently was the chief white man at the site.
[2] More often called Cloud Man, or occasionally, Man-of-the-Sky.

126

corn, about enough to keep them through the winter [1830–1831]. But by spring the corn was nearly all eat up.

This spring [1830] I got into some trouble with my old mother-in-law. An Indian from Wabashaw's band whom she called her brother came up to see her; and when he started to go away, the old woman gave him a bag of rice. I opposed, saying that she had a large family and that she wanted the rice more than the man did. I told her not to give it away, but she persisted and said it was hers and she would give it to whom she pleased. I told her again she had a large family and she must not give away her food, but she still stuck to it.

I pulled out my knife and told them if any one touched the bag of rice I would cut it to pieces. They then found I was in earnest, and the man started off for home, no doubt thinking I was a very hard man. The old woman got mad and picked up some of her duds and my wife, and all started off down to the fort where the interpreter lived.

The old woman had played me a trick once before that I did not like, and I had not forgotten it. One day she was at my house and when she was starting off home my eldest boy [William] cried to go home with her, but I forbade him. The old woman came and picked him up and put him on her back and walked off. I stood and looked with my eyes full of vengeance, until she got out of sight, and said to myself, "You will not have that child long!" I was determined to send him below to school the first chance that offered. The next day the old woman returned in the afternoon with all the family.

Here we labored on all summer [1830], plowing land for the Indians. By this time we had quite an Indian town of about 250 souls. In the fall I went to the fort one day, and coming home, I got on to an ox cart that was going to the falls. Later I had occasion to get off as we were going along, and I stepped up by the fore end of the cart to get on again. The oxen started and the fore end of the cart struck me and pushed me over, and one wheel passed over my body and broke one rib for me. The men picked me up and took me to St. Anthony, where they had a party of soldiers sawing lumber for the fort. One of the soldiers started off for the doctor at the fort. As soon as we got up to the falls they came back with the assistant doctor. He examined me and said that one of my ribs was broken and that I had better go down to the fort.

What to do I did not know. My wife and children were at the lake [Calhoun] all alone. I wanted some one to go and tell them of my condition but no one could go, so she stayed there all alone with her children two nights, expecting me home every minute. As I did not come, towards the evening of.the third day she started out in search of me. She went first to Mr. Quinn, my old interpreter. Here she found out where I was and what had happened. She went right down to the fort and found me in the hospital in the fort, where the commanding officer and doctor agreed to let me stay until I should get well, which took 18 days.

After I got well I got a team and moved back again to the lake and found all little things safe, as the Indians were all hunting; none had been about. Here I sat down and passed the winter [1830–1831]. In the spring I went plowing for the Indians. Large numbers were added to our band or village this summer, so they numbered now about 300. They raised a large amount of corn and potatoes, and supplied the Indians with a great deal of corn on the Minnesota and Mississippi rivers.

Major Taliaferro made my father-in-law and Mockpu-we-chastah chiefs of the band and here the Indians made great progress in cultivating the soil; they always had a great plenty and had a large amount to sell to the traders.

In the month of March [1831] the agent sent out two men to stay a month, and wanted me to assist them to get out timber enough to rebuild a council house that had been burnt about six months before [August 14, 1830]. This council house that burned is where the missionaries used to preach as they happened to come along. Rev. Mr. Coe, sometime after I saw him, preached there to these words, "Do thyself no harm." He had heard of the dueling business and gave them a good moral lesson on the subject.

Mr. Coe came up to my place at Lake Calhoun and went over to the Chippewa country, and came near starving to death. Once he got lost and got out of provisions, but finally got into Fort Snelling and was saved. He was a man of great patience and perseverance, and traveled until his age and strength forbade his working in the missionary cause.

We went to work and cut tamarack logs, enough for the new council house, and carried them out of the swamp by hand, so the teams could get to them to haul them. There was a month's work of hard lifting, but we finished it all up completely and the new council house was built by the soldiers. It was never thoroughly finished and stood so until it was nearly rotten and ready to fall down.

In the fall of the year [1831] a new opposition started up, Mr. Howard and A. Bailly, the man that I had once been in partnership with. So the American Fur Company went around and hired all the interpreters they could get, so that the new company could not get good traders or interpreters, nor men that were acquainted with the Indians and trade. But Mr. Bailly had stolen a march on them and got some of the best of the traders before they knew what he was doing.

One evening quite late a man came to me from the American Fur Company and said Mr. Rolette[3] wanted to see me. So in the morning I went to see him. He said he wanted to hire me, that there was a strong opposition come in against him, and he would hire me for three years, and give me $400 a year, the same as he gave all his clerks. The object of his hiring for three years was to have enough clerks without running about and hiring them every year. I found them in the old storehouse up at Land's End.

So I hired out for three years at $400 a year and went right [to work]. The first thing we had to do was to go to Traverse des Sioux* to fix up things there to meet the opposition the best way we could. There I got news that my brother [Zachariah Wright] had left Messrs. Powell and gone home to New York state, and set up a drug store, and got married.

I got Mr. Rolette's canoe ready, and two men and myself took him up in 3 days and about 4 hours of the 4th day, a distance of about 150 miles by the river. I was tired almost out when we got up. Mr. Rolette was one of the greatest cowards on the water I ever saw. He kept his pocket handkerchief tied in a hole in the side of the canoe all the time. I told him I could not swim a rod but I was not afraid, for the canoe was large and heavy, which made such hard work for three of us to go up in so short a time. It generally takes loaded boats and canoes 5 days to go from Fort Snelling to Traverse des Sioux.

We landed Mr. Rolette and started back. Mr. Rolette went on up to Lac qui Parle and Lake Traverse, making arrangements to oppose the new opposition.

[3] Joseph Rolette* (d. 1841), one of the most prominent traders of the Northwest.

The 2nd day we got down with our canoe and went to work giving credits to the Indians. The Indians [got] more goods this year from the [American Fur] company than they had got in the three former years, for they got everything they asked for; even large quantities of liquor was given them.[4]

After all the Indians were outfitted I took an outfit and went over beyond Cannon River to a place called the Bittern's Nest, a large lake on one of the branches of the Blue Earth River.[5] Mr. A. Faribault[6] was wintering here for the opposition. He had got there long before me and built and was in a comfortable house when I got there. He had given the Indians all a credit and started them off again, so when I got there, there was not an Indian to be seen.

I went to work to build. It commenced raining the next day after we got there, and I never saw it rain harder in the summer than it rained then, although it was late in November [1831]. I built a little house for a storehouse, one for my men, and then one for myself. We had to make mud chimneys, which was very difficult, for the snow had fallen nearly a foot deep and it was very cold. We had to heat all our water to make our chimneys with. We set up 4 poles, then would tie sticks across about a foot apart, then take mortar and some long grass and make slabs about 2 feet long, and lay it over the cross piece and bring the two ends together at the bottom. Then we stuck them together and so go on until we go round the square, leaving a space in front for a fireplace. We make chimneys narrow and burn our wood endwise, and we make a very hot fire in this way. We generally have very warm houses, as we place the chimney in one corner of the room, fronting the whole room. This makes more room in the house when the rooms are small. We build our chimneys from 10 to 14 feet high, all of mud and hay or grass, with the four poles to hold it up until it gets dry, when the poles generally burn out and the chimney stands by itself. I have used one chimney for 3 years with a little repairing.

There I passed the winter [1831–1832] doing all I could to prevent the opposition from making anything. Sold goods for anything we

[4] The use of liquor in the fur trade was an old, established custom, though Major Taliaferro was at this time doing his utmost to curb the practice.*

[5] The Blue Earth River has a number of branches, and it is now impossible to locate Bittern's Nest Lake.

[6] Alexander Faribault,* the son of Jean Baptiste Faribault.

could, if it was about half price only of the value of the goods we would sell, to keep them from going to the opposition; and, of course, they had to sell at the same rates or they could not get any trade.

In the winter the Indians at Traverse des Sioux, about 30 miles west of us,[7] had had a drunken frolic and had killed one. The murderer had fled. All at once an Indian came into my house [painted] as black as black could be made, and made the Indian women, when they saw him, run away. I made some inquiries about the fuss; they told me that was the murderer, and all were afraid of him. I said nothing to him but gave him some supper and he laid down and went to sleep; but at daylight he was off, fearful that some of the relatives might be after him.

An Indian when he commits a murder paints himself all black, and puts on the meanest old clothes that he can get, and goes that way until the troubles are settled, either by presents or the murderer is killed by some of the murdered person's relatives. There is now and then a case of murder that is done unbeknown to anybody, which is never known, but this does not often happen.

Here we passed the winter annoying each other as we could. When we could not do anything else we used to induce each other's men to run off, and we would do all the mischief we could to injure the trade for each other.

In the spring [1832] we took out our packs, but my opponent got most of the trade, as he had got into the country long before me, and got all the good hunters and, of course, made the best trade. The company sent me back to pass the summer and be ready for the business next fall, so I went off alone and left my family. As I had no provisions, I did not want to take my family out there to half starve, so they went and stayed with the old folks until I should return.

So I went to my old wintering ground and planted some potatoes to have for the winter, for I had passed the winter before on bread and meat, which is not very healthy living. Whilst I was out there we heard of the defeat of the Fox and Sauk Indians at Bad Axe.[8] The

7 If Traverse des Sioux was "about thirty miles west" of Bittern's Nest Lake, Prescott must have been wintering at Cannon Lake, where Alexander Faribault had an establishment about this time. If so, he was not on a branch of the Blue Earth River, but rather of the Cannon River.

8 The Bad Axe Battle occurred on August 1–2, 1832, near the end of the Black Hawk War (1830–1832), the final Indian conflict on the northwestern frontier until the Sioux Uprising of August, 1862, in Minnesota.

Sioux that were about got up a great scalp dance in honor of the great victory gained by the whites and Sioux Indians.

We had no provisions, and all we had to live on was a few fish that we caught in a small net that we had. We boiled them in water and eat them with a little salt. That was all that we had for two months.

One day as I was sitting outdoors hunting fleas, of which all the Indian traders' houses are alive with, lo and behold, who should present himself before me but the Indian that I had the fuss with when I first went to trade on the St. Peter's River. Old grudges apparently had worn away and he was quite friendly. I gave him some turtle's eggs and fish and he made a meal and went off; I was glad to see his back, for I never liked him after our first trouble, when he threatened to kill me.

At the end of two months I started in to see what was going on with the traders. On the way I had to cross a stream that took the horse up to his back. I got wet and had to travel all day in wet clothes; as it was misting, my clothes did not dry on me, and I laid down at night in wet clothes. I had an Indian with me for a guide. He made a good fire and roasted a sandhill crane that I had killed during the day. Every now and then we would hear the whistle of a buck deer. It would [come] out of the bushes, see the fire, and start off whistling and blowing at a wonderful rate.

In the morning I felt somewhat unwell, but traveled on and got in to our depot at Land's End. I found Mr. [LaBathe],[9] a Sioux half-breed, in charge. Mr. LaBathe could neither read nor write. He was a good trader and kept his accounts by figures, or representations, such as animals and birds, according to the name of the Indian. If it was a bird, the shape of the bird was made for the man's name, and colored according to the name expressed. And all the things that an Indian gets is marked in the same way, charged by making characters. An old Frenchman at Traverse des Sioux by the name of Le Blanc kept his accounts in the same way, as he cannot read nor write, but can make figures.* He kept his accounts very correct.

My family were off on a hunting expedition. The 2nd day after I

[9] Probably François La Bathe, a prominent trader of the period. Like Prescott, La Bathe was killed by Indians on the first day of the outbreak in August, 1862. (Henry H. Sibley, "Reminiscences of the Early Days of Minnesota," *Minnesota Historical Collections*, III [1870–1880], 248.)

arrived I was taken sick with fever and ague and had to go to taking medicine. I staid about a week and started back with a one-horse cart, some goods, and a little provisions. The first night we had a very heavy shower and I had no tent and had to get under my cart and protect myself the best I could. I was afraid of the ague again, but I got home to my wintering place without getting sick. We started late in the morning and we met Mr. Bailly, who had come from Hastings that morning. He told me he thought the two companies would be one very soon again.

So, in about a month I was sent for and [told] to abandon my post. You may be assured I was glad to get out of that lonesome place and get back to Land's End again. I was not long in packing up. The Indians, as soon as they learned I was going to leave, turned in to stealing my potatoes, of which I had some very fine ones, and in three nights they had about finished them.

When I got back to my old stamping ground, Land's End, I learned that Messrs. Howard would not furnish Mr. Bailly with any more goods and had not made one dollar profit, and the only way they made both ends meet was by counting the remainder of old stock on hand and to put it at cost. This is not often done, for what goods remain over are generally more or less damaged. But to get rid of Mr. Bailly they took all at cost and told him to go. After sending that amount of goods, $30,000 worth, into the country, and not making one dollar profit, they would not embark any more in the Indian trade.

This news made the Indians hang their heads again, for they knew they would have to pay for the feast they had [had] for the last year. So a number of small posts were broken up and some new ones pushed farther into the Indian Country. And who should go was the question, for the new trading posts were far out in the prairies and in a country where there was little game, where there were no buffalo.

Well, I was called upon to go to one and Mr. LaFramboise was ordered to go to another, and Mr. Bailly, to keep him quiet and from inducing other oppositions coming into the country, was made chief clerk for the Minnesota River. Mendota was made the main depot for the whole Minnesota trade.

I was ordered to prepare for Crooked River, or Big Sioux,* a tributary of the Missouri; and Mr. LaFramboise was ordered to the same river, only some considerable distance higher up. The object of [wintering at] these posts in this forlorn and barren country was that it was reported that large quantities of beaver were to be found in the Big Sioux and its tributaries.

I went to work getting my equipment ready. A part of the route was by water to Traverse des Sioux and from thence in one-horse carts. Mr. Bailly fixed everything to suit himself—goods and provisions—and we all shipped in a mackinaw boat[10] for Traverse des Sioux, men, women and children, and Indians—some by land and some by water in canoes. For the Indians that accompanied us for to trap beaver we had to take along a large quantity of corn to feed them through the winter; otherwise they would not go. They knew the country and were afraid of starvation.

The third day out it commenced raining and we had a tremendous storm, and all at once a little before sundown the wind changed from the southeast to west and blew a gale for an hour or two. It was very cold and it actually froze ice, and the next morning there was not a leaf hardly but what was frozen stiff, and all the gardens spoiled— this in the morning of September 1st, [1832].[11]

We moved on the next morning and in two days more we got up to the Traverse and found our carts and horses all ready. But the horses were poor things, and some of them had been worked but very little. One of them we had to throw him to get the harness on, and when he found he was overcome he set up a squealing more like a hog than anything else, and gave over struggling and lay quiet until we got the harness on, and in fact was quite gentle after that.

We got all things ready, loaded our carts, 8 in number. I had one cart for myself and family, and we went off all in good spirits, and Mr. Bailly returned home from here and took charge of the whole concern, Indians, and men, and goods.

There were about one hundred Indians—men, women, and children. The first day we got on very well and the 2d day went to the crossing of the Minnesota River and found the river fordable, and next day got all over and reloaded, ready for a start in the morning. We had two Frenchmen, hunters, and I got an Indian to go as guide

[10] A mackinaw* was a flat-bottomed boat pointed at both ends, sometimes forty to fifty feet long with a twelve-foot beam and three- to four-foot depth of hold.

[11] Although Prescott's manuscript gives the year as 1831, the trip took place after he had heard the news of the Bad Axe Battle of August, 1832.

and hunter both, and one of his brothers and a cousin of his went along.

We went on very well, although we had very heavy loads and the horses' shoulders began to get sore, and we had some trouble in getting the horses started, from the soreness of their shoulders. We worked along until we got upon a branch of the Cottonwood River.

Our hunter found elk tracks and went in search of them. In a little while we heard a gun and in a few minutes another, and shortly after a call. We halted and our hunter came up and said he had killed an elk. The men all raised a shout of joy, for they had been living on corn meal, ground by hand.

We had taken along a corn mill for that purpose, and when we would camp our corn mill had to be set up regular every night to grind corn for the men's supper and for the next day—not sifted, and a very little grease to season their mush. After eating of this corn mush the stomach eventually revolts at the sight of it and some of the men cannot live on it; and I will assure you they were glad to see venison once more.

I sent a man and horse after the elk. They were gone about an hour and came back with the whole buck elk on the horse. It was just as much as the horse could pack and, in fact, it staggered with the weight of the load. We put the meat into the carts and went on to a large lake where we found some good dry wood, and camped and staid one day to dry our meat.[12]

And such feasting you seldom will see. We got our meat dried a little and started on, and in two days we got to what is called the Big Clump of Woods.* It is [like] an island is the cause of there being timber, for the fire could not get to it. This shows plainly that fire has been the cause of the most of the prairies, as I have noticed in many other places in this country that where fire could not get to a piece of land, there is very large and thrifty timber.

This point is the head of the River Des Moines.[13] It is a large, grassy lake and a great place for muskrat and water fowl, consequently a great place for Indians, as there is no timber for a long distance to the south and west.

[12] The Indians preserved meat by cutting it into thin strips and exposing it to the sun and air, usually on scaffolds.

[13] The Des Moines River is a continuation of Beaver Creek; thus it rises some fifteen miles from where Prescott thought it did.

At this place I halted and hung my grindstone and ground my axes, and almost made up my mind to winter here. But on further reflection I thought it would be better to go to the place where I was ordered, whether I made anything or not, as I knew the man that I had to deal with was a kind of self-conceited character, and if I should fail of making a good trade all the blame would be attached to me.

The next morning I ordered the teams to be got up and harnessed, and ordered each cart to take on a good stick or two of dry wood, for we had two nights to sleep without woods. And on we moved again through the wild, open prairie.

Once in a while we would pass a buffalo trail from 6 to 8 inches deep—old ranges—but the animals we had not the pleasure of so much as seeing one.

We camped on the head of a little stream [14] running south towards the Missouri. We were now fairly over the great coteau, the great and renowned ridge that divides the waters of the Minnesota and Missouri. This ridge we could see two days before we reached it.[15] It looked like a blue cloud on the horizon, stretching as far as the eye could reach southeast and northwest. This ridge is from thirty to forty miles wide, and in the mountain or ridge the rivulets of the Missouri and Minnesota take their rise in a great many lakes that are on the highest part of this ridge.

The land is generally very uneven all over the length and breadth of it and [is] a good place for wild fowl and [musk]rats. Here we discovered a change in the color of the stone. Wherever we saw any [they] were of a reddish cast and had the appearance of granite.

The next morning we moved off in search of water, for where we camped water was scarce and the horses could not get enough. About noon we arrived at the famous place called the Pipestone quarry.* Here we found water but no wood, and we camped and dug pipestone one whole day. We got out a considerable quantity, but a good deal of it was scaly and full of seams. So we got only about 20 good pipes after working the rock all day. We put in two blasts of powder, but it did not have much effect.

This quarry was discovered by the Indians, but how and when we

[14] Probably the headwaters of Rock River.

[15] The crest of the Coteau des Prairies sustains an altitude of 1,800 to 1,900 feet, about 700 feet higher than the altitude thirty miles to the east.

never have learnt. It is on the head of a little spring branch.[16] In fact, a part of the stream takes its rise from under the same ledge that forms the quarry. Where it was first discovered appears to be near the top of the ground. It runs south and lies flat between two layers of solid rock that looks like granite.

The farther you go south the deeper it gets, also east. It runs under the ledge that covers the quarry. The north end of the diggings was about 2 feet deep and about ten feet wide; and instead of working eastward and under the bank or ledge, they have dug south.

When I was there the diggings were about 100 yards long, and at the south end the diggings are about ten feet deep. The pipestone is about a foot thick, but in seams from $\frac{1}{4}$ to 3 inches thick; in the deep part of the quarry there is more clay and the pipestone is speckled. Otherwise it has pale, white spots, and some has deeper red spots. And some is a pure red and smooth as marble, and fire does not crack it.

We got out a considerable [number of] scaly pieces, of which we made some very pretty flat pipes. The Indians have labored here very hard with hoes and axes, the only tools they have except large stones which they use for breaking the rock, as the Fox and Sacks did in mining for lead, with this difference—the Fox and Sacs used to make fire on the rock, and when it was red-hot, they would dash on water. This would crack the rock for some distance around, and in this way they discovered some very large bodies of mineral.

But the Sioux used no fire and could not conveniently if they wanted to, for there is no wood nearer than half a day's travel. The Sioux clean off the dirt, then get stones as large as two Indians can lift and throw them down as hard as they can, and in this way break or crack the rock so they can get their hoes and axes into the cracks and pry out piece after piece. It is very laborious and tedious and costs them considerable in the way of axes and hoes for all they get.

At this place there is a story, as related by the Indians, that a young warrior gained his lady love by performing a feat which many an Indian shrinks from with a terrible dread. A few rods east of the pipe quarry is a perpendicular rock with a crevice in it. It is 3 or 4 feet wide; and some 6 or 8 feet from the crevice stands a lone rock about

[16] Now known as Pipestone Creek.

12 feet high about 3 or 4 feet wide at the top, and below it all around is lying sharp and ugly, cragged rocks.

A number of Indians had gathered there to dig pipes, and amongst them was a love couple. The young warrior had courted the lass for a long time, but she did not care much about marrying. So she took a plan to try his sincerity as to whether he loved her or not.

So she told him she had heard that young men had leaped from the main rock to the one standing alone. The young man remonstrated and said that he did not believe that anybody had performed the feat and lived, but some of the old Indians were called and questioned and said it was a fact that young men had leaped across and back. And their statements were confirmed by their pointing out a quantity of arrows and balls there that they could see from the main rock.

It is a frightful looking [jump]; the lone rock is about 12 feet high and small at the top. In jumping across, if he should lose his balance or slip and go on and fall amongst the sharp and craggy rocks below, a fearful death would be the consequence in case a foot should slip, it being only one step across at the top.

The young man saw by what was on the top of the rock [that] some persons had been on top of the rock and they would of got there by jumping over, for there was no timber there to lay over to walk on.

When the young man saw that the feat had been performed it gave him courage, and he got his medicine out and prayed to the great god of the rocks, Tunkanshe, to give him strength and courage and dexterity enough to take him safely over and back.

After his ceremony was over he stripped himself and stepped back a few paces and ran up, but stopped. The Indians all shouted. Then a large number made the prairie ring again—"Coward," and "no girl!"—"You do not love her!" and so on rang in his ears.

This made him resolve either to die or succeed. So the second time he made the leap, and went with so much force that he came near going clear over, for there was nothing to hold on to; and all he could do was to jump and stand right where he struck.

When he got onto the rock he found that there had been several over before him, for every one that jumps over leaves some memorial of the feat performed. Most of what he found were arrows and some balls.

After he was over he found no difficulty in jumping back. He claimed his prize and was married in love, as the young woman now believed him, as he had gone through such a dangerous feat for to get her.

At the quarry we found a six-pound cannon ball that Indians had brought there from the Missouri to break the rock in quarrying for pipes. This cannon ball, the Indians informed us, was one that had been fired at the Arikaras at the time of war with that tribe on the Missouri River.*

After we had worked the pipestone quarry until we were tired, we made preparations to be off, as our Indians were getting alarmed for fear of their enemies,[17] although I never heard of any of them ever being killed at the pipestone quarry.

In half a day we went from the quarry to the Big Sioux River, a tributary of the Missouri. We camped and looked about for a wintering place, and the next day we found a place and camped there and went to chopping and rolling up log houses.[18] We put up some 70 or 80 feet in length, and partitioned off as was wanted for rooms.

The Indians found there was no game, and they all started off [southward] for the Missouri and to the Omaha village,[19] and there they passed the winter and made no hunts. One or two lodges came in from the prairies and trapped beaver about two weeks and caught some 8 or 10. They had some dried buffalo meat and several otter skins.

Whilst they were there a courtship started up within the camp of prairie Indians, and the young man got his friends to purchase the girl he had been courting. But the offering was rather a small affair,

[17] The Sacs and Foxes, the enemies feared most by the Sioux in that region. At the quarry peace traditionally prevailed even among hostile groups.

[18] The distance from the quarry to the Big Sioux is about twelve miles due west. The river makes a big bend at the point where Prescott struck it. It is impossible to locate the exact site of Prescott's log houses, since all traces have been destroyed by flood or fire. La Framboise probably left the main group at the quarry or on the Big Sioux and wintered farther up the valley.

[19] The nearest point on the Missouri was about 95 miles distant. If the Indians followed down the Big Sioux River to the Missouri, as they probably did, the distance was about 110 miles. The Omahas, a Siouan people related to the Sioux, or Dakota, Indians, had long had a village on the west bank of the Missouri about opposite present-day Sioux City.

being 2 guns and a few blankets and some trinkets. They were taken to the lodge of the parents and laid down, and their errand was made known.

But the father and mother looked upon the offering with disdain and, without any further ceremony, told the messengers to carry them off. So they picked up their duds and off they went—ashamed, as they said. The young man took offense at this, or at the treatment his messengers had received from the old folks.

He took his gun and went out and shot one of the old man's horses. This raised the old man's pluck a little, and he started after the youngster with a short gun in one hand and a war club stuck in his belt. On one hand the old man had but two fingers,* but he was a brave old fellow and went to the lodge where the young man lived and raised up the door.

The young man saw the old man from the opposite side of the lodge and mistrusted what the old man was after. He made a dive and under the bottom of the lodge he went. Before the old man could get around, the youngster was off, dodging about amongst the trees so the old man could not get a shot at his intended mark. The Indians got round the old man and held him until his rage was passed off a little, and he went off home to his lodge again.

The young man stayed away all day, and at night came home to his lodge again. But the old man was on the lookout for him and went back again. Although the young man had cut a hole in the lodge to look out from, the old man crawled up on them without being noticed and raised the door again. The fellow inside dived out and took to the woods again. The old man let go at him, but it was dark and he missed.

The Indians took the old man home and in a short time the young man came back again and took his gun. He sent word to the old man and told him that if he did not quit his attacks on him, he would go and kill the old man and take his girl and all he had and go off with [them]. This frightened them, and the old man quit with the loss of a horse. In a few days he moved off to hunt in the prairies, and we were all peace and quietness again.

We went on with our building and got into winter quarters some time in December [1832]. We got along about living very well until the ice made; then we had hard times. All the fresh game that I could get was some hawks that were living about the stream. They were fat and very good, only the name of them would naturally make a person spleeny. I used to shoot them and put them on a spit before the fire and roast them, and they were very good to a hungry appetite.

My men used to shoot wolves for their fresh meat and, once in a while, a fat skunk. The skunks, I could eat some of it; but the wolves, I could not eat a mouthful of them. They were awful strong, far stronger than the skunk meat.

All at once we saw a team coming a long distance off in the prairie. Who could it be? was the word, as we were not expecting any visitors. And who should arrive but Mr. William Brown, one of the old clerks of the American Fur Company. The company had put [him] in with Mr. Bailly to look after things a little, for the company never liked Mr. B., as he had given them the slip once before and got up an opposition that made them lose all their profits the year before, and something more along with it.

Mr. Brown said he had come over to see what we were doing and what our prospects were for trade, etc. Mr. Brown ordered me to follow up the Indians that had gone to the Missouri and try to bring or induce them to come back and hunt beaver; and if they would come back, he, Mr. Brown, would insure them plenty of corn.

I started with a cart and two men and one horse and a small supply of provisions. The first day we started, one of my men killed a small deer, and a large buck got away. We camped at the falls of the Big Sioux.[20] Here the river is about 20 yards wide, but shoal and rapids are just below the falls of the Big Sioux. The falls are about ten feet and fall through so many broken rocks and crevices that you cannot see much water about the falls when the water is low.

In the morning we pursued our journey on down the river and kept constantly going all day. And as the sun was going down we crossed the Big Sioux below the forks [Rock River] and camped, tired and hungry; and our deer meat served us well, for we had but a small amount of provisions.

I found that we could not overtake the Indians, for, from appearances, they had not stopped only to camp, and had pushed forward

20 Prescott is the first white man on record to have visited the site of Sioux Falls. (C. Stanley Stevenson, "Expeditions into Dakota," *South Dakota Historical Collections*, IX [1918], 347–368.) The falls, a notable geographic feature, were said to be the largest in the Northwest, next to the Falls of St. Anthony.

to the Missouri, which was two days' more travel in the direction that we were going, that is, to the Omaha village.

So I concluded to turn back, for I knew the Indians would not leave the Omahas, where there was plenty of corn, deer, and some other vegetables; whereas at our wintering ground there was nothing but musty corn, and no grease to eat with it; and the men complained of its having or leaving a burning sensation in the stomach, as it was only coarsely ground and not sifted.

I turned back next morning and came back to the falls and camped. The next day we were early at home. Mr. Brown started back to Fort Snelling again, with a poor prospect ahead for a successful trade in that quarter. The Frenchman that came out with us to hunt left also, as there [were] but few beaver, and they all turned their attention to hunting [musk]rats.

I forgot to mention one circumstance; at Big Sioux River we had a son born, named Hiram Prescott, 21st December, [1832].[21]

About the middle of winter a band of Sisseton Sioux arrived almost starved, and I had to turn in [to] feed them on two considerations. One was [that] if I did not give them some corn they would kill my horses and eat them, and then I could not get away from there in the spring for want of teams in case they should kill and eat my horses. And another consideration was [that] this was the party that took me prisoner and saved my life when I was in the Chippewa country [December, 1824].

The old chief, Limping Devil, told me: "Do you recollect," says he, "the time when the Indians found you in the woods, and robbed you, and wanted to kill you, and I saved your life? Now, I want you to help me," he said. I told him I was willing to go as far as [I] could, but he must recollect that I had a good many people to feed, and that he must not think of my feeding all my provisions out to them. The old fellow looked surly and did not say much.

I had a bushel of corn ground and made two large kettles of mush, and sent for all the men and filled their stomachs. I told the men to take the balance of the mush and take it home to their children. So they all had a feast the first day. The next day I fed them again. Then I let them wait a day or two, but the old chief came again and said

21 Prescott gives 1831 as the date of his son Hiram's birth; however, it must have been 1832, between two known events mentioned by Prescott, the Bad Axe Battle of August 1–2, 1832, and the time of shooting stars, November 12–13, 1833.

they were starving. I told him to move, for he would starve us all to death. "Where can I go?" he said. "You see there is nothing but grass, and now and then a clump of trees along the river."

The band held on for about two weeks, and I had to cook a large kettle of mush for them every day in order to save my horses. The object of my cooking for them was that all might get a share, and by grinding the corn make it go further. Finally, the weather moderated and they started, and you may be assured I was glad to see them off, for they were a rough set of customers. The weather kept on moderate and the Big Sioux River broke up and early in March [1833] the wild fowl made their appearance and to the joy of us all, for we had been penned up there, as you may call it, five months, in a land basin, and destitute of most all game of any kind.

I had sent over to the heads of the Vermillion River, a tributary of the Missouri, in search of buffalo, but none was to be found. We saw none nor eat any all winter, except a little that I got from the old man who wanted to kill the Indian for shooting his horse, and that was dry and hard, and I had to pay two prices for it, or a cloth blanket for 2 pieces of meat.

When the Big Sioux broke up, the water rose so high that we had to move out of our house and go and camp on the prairie, for the water came into the corner of my house, and I [was] fearful we would get flooded out entirely, and I moved beforehand.

But we had a severe time out in the open prairie. A northwester set in and blew a gale, and it got very cold and snowed some. We were so cold that we could not sleep, and the wind blew so that we could not cook. We stayed two days and I found the river would not rise any more. I went back to my house and tapped a few of the soft maples and made a little sugar. We had been out for a month.

The fall [of water] came, so we began to kill some [game] and began to live a little more like white people again. And in a few days our Indians came straggling along from the Omaha village on the Missouri—no furs or game, and starving. They had given all their powder and lead to the Omahas to feed them through the winter. Some of the Sioux had [had] a keg of powder each, and in fact, they were [the] best fitted for a hunt of any Indians that I had ever seen fitted out. And it all amounted to next to nothing, for they did not pay one-fourth of their credits.

And what was worse, we had to let them have more powder for

the spring hunt, or else they could not hunt in the spring. So we supplied them with powder again, and they started for the Minnesota River and to hunt as they went along. As there was no beaver of any amount, the Indians went hunting muskrats.

In the latter part of April Mr. Brown came over again to see if he could induce the Indians to hunt beaver, but it was no use. There was no beaver, with the attention of so many Indians, and, in fact, they could not live, so many of them, where game was so scarce. I wrote Mr. Bailly that the Rock of St. Helena was a preferable point to the one he had sent me to.

After Mr. Brown arrived, we moved our quarters to a point called the [Medary] Forks of the upper Big Sioux with the expectation of getting some fish, but we got disappointed. After remaining a few days, half-fed, we pulled up stakes, as the Indians had all left and there was no trade, and no Indians to be seen or heard of.

One of the hands, while hunting the horses to get them ready to start, came across a skunk and made war upon it at once for to have a feast, for the men were all hungry. The dog made the first attack and got the first shot from the skunk's battery of musk, which sent him off howling. The man then tackled the skunk and he got a shot, but the skunk got a blow from the butt end of his whip, which leveled Mr. Skunk. But the man and dog came home completely used up in the eyes. Neither of them could hardly see, and their eyes were terribly inflamed and were fiery red—and such another smell! We could not bear them about the camp and kept them at a distance for two days.

We got all packed up and started for home once more. The first day we went to the Pipestone Quarry and camped, and made fire with wood that we brought with us from the Big Sioux. There we stopped one day and dug pipes, but we did not get many. It was very difficult to break the rock, and we had no tools fit for the business.

So we set out for home as fast as possible. It set in to raining and we had a storm of three days, which made it very disagreeable traveling, for we were in the water from morning until night. Sometimes we mired down crossing streams made by the snow and rain, and we had to depend upon our guns for a living. We frequently killed geese that were setting, and then would eat the eggs when they had young ones in them. And we killed a good many of the little prairie plovers as we walked along by the side of our teams.

After much fatigue and misery we got back to the Minnesota River again. We had taken the precaution [in the fall] to bring a bark canoe and hide it so we could cross without much trouble. From here we went to Swan Lake. Here we eat up the last mouthful we had, but the next day we got in to Traverse des Sioux. When we got to Traverse des Sioux we had a job to do to get our furs in order. A great many of them had got wet and we spent 3 or 4 days in drying them. We then took a boat for Fort Snelling, or Mendota, where the company's post was found.

SUPPLEMENT

The Indian Colony at Lake Calhoun (page 126)

Evidently Prescott wanted to complete his stories of his experiences at Galena, Prairie du Chien, Lake Pepin, and Fort Snelling before starting on a new topic, his farming activities at Lake Calhoun, six and one-half miles northwest of Fort Snelling, the headquarters of the Indian agent, Taliaferro.

In so doing, his manuscript seems to imply that these activities began in 1830, whereas the date was undoubtedly 1829. Taliaferro's diary (MS, Minnesota State Historical Society) states that the Indian colony at Lake Calhoun started in 1829 and that Prescott was employed, apparently as the chief white man at the site, "to superintend at $10.00 per month."

Of this project, James B. Rhoads wrote:

Believing as he did that the Indian must be civilized before he could be Christianized, Taliaferro had in 1828 [*sic*] persuaded a few Sioux families to cease their nomadic life and settle down at Lake Calhoun in the neighborhood of Cloudman's village to learn agriculture. This settlement he called Eatonville, for Secretary of War John H. Eaton. Writing to him in 1830 to appeal for funds for his "little colony of agriculturalists," Taliaferro described its progress. "During the summer of last year," he said, "three men were employed for the purpose of collecting materials for a log village, and also for a house for the protection of the property belonging to the Indians generally who might submit to become cultivators of the soil." He went on to tell the secretary that "six or eight hundred dollars would mature what has happily been begun."

(James B. Rhoads, "The Fort Snelling Area in 1835, A Contemporary Map," *Minnesota History*, Vol. XXXV, No. 1 [March 1956], 22–29.)

Earlier in his manuscript, Prescott wrote that he spent the summer of 1829 "loafing about." Apparently, he was using his time to persuade various Indian families and bands to settle at Lake Calhoun. The "loafing about" included some plowing, which would not have taken much time.

Evidently Prescott was employed only for the growing season, for in the fall and winter, as he notes, he engaged in other activities.

Joseph Rolette (page 129 n.)

A Canadian by birth, Joseph Rolette was of French extraction. About 1804 he went to Prairie du Chien, where he entered business with Murdoch Cameron, an old Indian trader who usually resided at Lac qui Parle. Although his headquarters were at Prairie du Chien, Rolette occasionally wintered at or in the vicinity of Lake Pepin. In 1836 Henry H. Sibley formed a copartnership with Rolette in the American Fur Company.

Traverse des Sioux (page 129)

Traverse des Sioux (Crossing of the Sioux) was a ford of the Minnesota River much used by Indians and traders from the Fort Snelling area on their way to the upper Minnesota Valley and the Red River Valley. Long's expedition in 1823 called it "the Crescent," referring to the big bend in the river at that point near modern St. Peter. Soon thereafter it received its French name from the Sioux name "Oiyuwege," which means "the place of the crossing; the ford." (Minnesota Geographic Names," *Minnesota Historical Collections*, XVII [1920], 373–374.)

Taliaferro's Policy in Regard to the Whiskey Traffic (page 130 n.)

Some of his journal entries of this period show how Taliaferro was trying to handle the whiskey problem. When on July 4, 1831, Joseph Renville and Louis Provencalle, traders at Traverse des Sioux and Lac qui Parle, reached his agency from Prairie du Chien, Taliaferro wrote, "Sent to see & examine their Boats—& to detain all whiskey, over a certain Quantity." On July 5, before the traders departed for their posts, he allowed Renville 34½ gallons of whiskey "for the use of his Boat hands." He allowed Renville's son a 33½-gallon barrel "for his outfit to River De Roche." For Provencalle's outfit he allowed a 34½-gallon barrel, and "one barrel of whiskey to A Culbertson for A Baillys outfit at Entry of St Peters, for men Cuting Hay &c."

On July 12, 1831, the Agent recorded:

H. Mooers departed this day for his Post at Lac qui Parle Alowed him One Barrel and 10 gallons of whiskey for his men and outfit.

Narcis Franier—One Barrel—and one other Barrel for Post at Cheyanne fork of Red River—3 bls 10 gals. Some ten or 15 gallons was in a Barrel.

Old Faribault & others made great Talk about [Mooers'] haveing been permited to pass with 4 Bls whiskey without any knowledge of the circumstances—This is however an Indian Trader like propensity—and unworthy of notice.

Taliaferro reported on August 23, 1831: "Indians hot in pursuit of whiskey—one trader complains that another gives a great deal & so another states that the other trader gives six Barrels—and so we go.—The Indians are pushed to complain of these things to the Agent —all to urge the Agent to alow the articles to be used." (Taliaferro's Journal, Vol. 12, pp. 22, 26, 49.)

Alexander Faribault (page 130 n.)

Alexander Faribault was born at Prairie du Chien on June 22, 1806. On October 4, 1822, he was granted a license to trade on the Minnesota River. He began trading at the Bois Plume, frequently spelled "Bois Plaine," on the Cannon River in 1826 or 1827. In 1826–1827 he was a clerk at Traverse des Sioux. By 1828 he was already located on the Cannon River, his home for many years. ("Alexander Faribault," *Minnesota History*, Vol. VIII, No. 2 [June 1927], 177– 180; Grace Lee Nute, "Posts in the Minnesota Fur-Trading Area, 1660–1885," *Minnesota History Bulletin*, Vol. XI, No. 4 [December 1930], 382.)

Le Blanc (page 132)

Stephen Return Riggs wrote of a visit in 1837 as follows:

At Traverse des Sioux . . . we made the acquaintance of a somewhat remarkable French trader, by name Louis Provencalle, but commonly called Le Blanc. . . . He was an old voyager, who could neither read nor write, but, by a certain force of character, he had risen to the honorable position of trader. He kept his accounts with his Indian debtors by a system of hieroglyphics.

(*Mary and I: Forty Years with the Sioux*, introd. by Rev. S. C. Bartlett [Boston: Congregational Sunday-School and Publishing Society, 1888], p. 49.)

Crooked River (page 133)

The French called the Big Sioux "la Rivière Croche," meaning "the Crooked River." The Sioux called it the Tchankasndata, meaning "the Thickly Wooded River," although this name seems to have been applied only to the lower two-thirds of the river. The name Calumet River was also used for the Big Sioux, doubtless because of its proximity at the Big Bend, near Flandreau, to Pipestone Quarry, where the stone for peace pipes, or calumets, was obtained.

Manipulation of a Mackinaw Boat (page 134 n.)

"The oarsmen, four in number, were bestowed in the bow, and the steersmen on a high perch in the stern, while the cargo was piled up in the space between them. The current was the main reliance for propulsion. The cargo capacity was about fifteen tons, the rate of progress seventy-five to one hundred miles per day, and the cost about two dollars per day. . . . The boats were cheaply made and were intended only for downstream navigation, being abandoned at St. Louis." (*Minnesota Historical Collections*, I [1850–1856], 34.) Prescott was using his boat for upstream transportation, and it took him five days to go the sixty or so miles from Mendota to Traverse des Sioux.

Big Clump of Woods (page 135)

When Joseph La Framboise had a post there in the middle 1830's, the place was called "Grand Lisière" by the French, while the English-speaking people called it the "Oasis" or the "Great Oasis." The French sometimes used the expression "Bois Cache" ("Lost Timber") for the place. The Sioux called these woods "Tchan-na tambe," "hidden or lost woods." It is located between the lakes, now drained, in Lowville township, Murray County, Minnesota.

Pipestone Quarry (page 136)

Pipestone Quarry is known as an important site in aboriginal geography and lore. Though it is not shown on any map earlier than 1703, records indicate that as early as 1637 Indians living far from the quarry treasured the pipes made from the stone found there. George Catlin visited the quarry in 1835 and is usually credited, erroneously, with being the first white man to do so. The pipestone is called catlinite after him.

The Battle with the Arikaras (page 139)

On June 2, 1823, the Arikaras killed thirteen white traders and wounded ten others of General W. H. Ashley's party which was ascending the Missouri River. Colonel Henry Leavenworth led a large force of soldiers and Sioux allies against them and drove them from the region. The artillery fire played a large part in the battle, which took place on August 10, 1823. This was the first battle between Indians and soldiers west of the Mississippi. (Hiram M. Chittenden, *The American Fur Trade of the Far West* [New York: Harper, 1902], II, 584–600.)

The Indian Custom of Self-Mutilation (page 140)

The loss of three fingers may have been due not to an accident, but to mourning for a deceased relative. It was the custom of the Indian men to gash their bodies, cut off fingers or toes, or otherwise mutilate themselves in mourning. The pain, they said, made them forget their grief. (Samuel W. Pond, "The Dakotas or Sioux in Minnesota as They Were in 1834," *Minnesota Historical Collections*, XII [1908], 482, 484.)

VII

1833–1836

In the Fort Snelling Area

We found all well. Mr. Bailly did not feel so well, for our trade had not been very successful. We all turned in and went to making packs and summed up quite a number after all was in, for some of the posts had made very good returns. In all, they made between 3 and 4 hundred packs.

Mr. Brown and Mr. Bailly could not agree, so they dissolved; and Mr. Brown left the country, went to Milwaukee, and settled down there, and Mr. Bailly continued the trade. So Mr. Bailly went down to Prairie du Chien to get his supply of goods for another winter's business and left me in charge. He left with me a brother of Mr. Rolette,[1] a drunken crazy fellow. He had been an officer during the last war but had been dismissed for some of his wild acts. When Mr. Bailly left, he left part of a cask of port wine in his cellar. This man found it and went to drinking and he kept crazy for about a week; and of all the wicked men I never heard his equal. Finally, I got a man to get into the cellar and pull out the tap and let the balance of the wine run out. Then we got peace in the house once more.

I promised to send my eldest boy to school. Major Grooms, the sub-agent, had informed me that the government had a free school what was called the Choctaw Academy [in Kentucky], and that if I would send my boy there he would take him there with pleasure, as he was going to take two of Mr. Bailly's boys. All that we had to do was to furnish them clothes and pay their expenses there otherwise, going to the place or academy.

---

[1] Laurence Rolette, a brother of the noted trader Joseph Rolette, was also in the fur trade for many years. ("The Fur-Trade in Wisconsin, 1812–1825," ed. Reuben Gold Thwaites, *Wisconsin Historical Collections*, II [1911], 196.)

So I agreed to send [him] and got the boy ready and embarked him in the canoe along with Mr. Bailly's boys, and off they started. All at once I heard a cry behind me. I looked around and saw my old mother-in-law a-trying to stab herself. She had an old dull knife and did not effect her purpose before I got to her and took the knife from her and threw it away.

In the evening the old woman took a canoe and followed on down the river and went to the place where Major Grooms was camped. She took my boy and walked off with him and brought him back again. This made a fuss all round in our family. My wife she got mad and went off, and I said to myself that my son should not be raised amongst the Indians, for the old woman had perfect control of him when she was about. She thought more of him than of any of her own children; and as she had scorned me two or three times before by carrying away my child in opposition to my wish and was making a perfect Indian of him, I had determined that she should not have the control of him, and was determined to send him off the first opportunity that offered, for the old woman had made me repent the day that I had ever taken her daughter.

One of my children [Harriet] took sick and my wife in her mad fit, because I scolded them for bringing the boy back, had kept away for two weeks. Finally, the child got so sick that she was compelled to come back and get the child some medicine. She did not come into the house to stop but lived in her lodge some distance from the house with her mother where they had the Indians conjuring over the sick child. This was the old woman's work again, and I was tried to the quick to see my children treated in this manner.

Still they thought they were right and, no doubt, thought they were doing for the best. But still they would not put any confidence in what I told them about doctoring or the raising of our children. Dr. Jarvis was very kind and came over from the fort several times to see my child; he finally told me the child could not live, and medicine would do no good, as the child had the dropsy in the head, and he stopped visiting [us].

When I told the Indians the doctor's opinion about the disease of my child, they ridiculed the idea and laid the child's complaint to some other Indians as having the power of necromancy to bring in disease when they got offended at each other. The child died on [the] 8th of December, [1833]. A few nights before, we saw a singular phenomenon in the sky which appeared to be a shower of stars falling from the heavens [November 12–13, 1833].

The Indians had a great crying spell after my child died. I asked them why they did not cure it, as they had laughed at what I told them about the disease. They held down their heads and made no reply. So I got my child up to the burying [place] to bury it. Mr. Rolette was reading a prayer at the grave and a parcel of half-breeds, Roman Catholics, were standing off a little distance and laughing at us, as they never had seen a funeral in that form before, and of a Protestant nature.

In a few days Mr. Bailly arrived with his goods and all was busy in making up outfits for the winter trade. I was to remain for interpreter for Mr. Bailly for the winter. My family had no house room about the fort, so we had to go to Land's End and stop, and I had to walk up and down every day, a distance of 2½ miles, making five miles a day to go to and from my work.

This I had to do because Mr. Bailly had no accommodation about him, and a miserable, revengeful wife. Mrs. Bailly,[2] a half-breed, and my wife, a full-blood, had got into some trouble about one of our little girls. Mrs. Bailly wanted one to live with her and help nurse the children, and my wife let Lucy go. She had not been there long before she got a whipping. Mrs. B. was remarkably fond of whipping other people's children, so my wife took her daughter away. This offended Mrs. B. and it was so arranged that I could not have a house for my family, and [this] was the cause of my traveling to Land's End and back every day.

And whilst I am speaking about the whipping business—Mrs. Bailly had a little black child raised in the family and a young Sioux girl. Those two children, I actually believe, would get from 25 to 50 lashes a day and sometimes more, every day almost. I frequently would leave the house to get away from the miserable crying of those children when she was cowhiding them. I felt the reproach and the trouble and misery I had for trifling revenge, but I stuck to my work all winter, going back and forth, and finally winter ended.

I got a house after Mrs. Bailly had gone to Prairie du Chien, and I got the use of her kitchen for myself and family. Mr. Bailly went

---

[2] About 1825 Alexis Bailly married Lucy Faribault, described as a daughter of Alexander Faribault, but more likely his sister, both being children of Jean Baptiste Faribault. (*Minnesota Historical Collections*, III [1870–1880], 319.)

below and left me in charge again. This summer [1834] brought about another opposition in the person of Mr. B. F. Baker, the gentleman that I brought up the Mississippi when I first came up to trade with the Indians.

This summer the cholera raged throughout the world, and a great many people died on the Mississippi. A party of Canadians were coming up the Mississippi—there were some 40 or 50—and the cholera got amongst them when they were between Prairie du Chien and Lake Pepin. And when they got to the Grand Encampment, about ten miles below Lake Pepin, they commenced dying, but they were out in the open healthy air, and but few of them died. They worked their way up to Fort Snelling, where they got medicines from the doctor of the fort.

About this time the traders up at the Little Rapids had got out with the Indians on account of high prices for goods;[3] as there had been no opposition for 3 years the Indians had to pay for the past good times they had when there was an opposition, for then they got goods cheap. The Indians of Little Rapids were mostly rovers in the prairie and followed the buffalo for a living, and they had suffered a good deal for the want of ammunition. The traders would not give them powder on credit, and when they sold anything, charged a very great price, and the Indians were drove into desperation.

They shot and severely wounded a man by the name of [La Bathe], but as he did not die, there was nothing done about it. They fled to the Missouri, and that was the last of it. This gave the other Indians encouragement, and one time [1833] one of them stabbed old Mr. Faribault in the back, but the old gentleman recovered.[4] The Indian ran off to the Missouri and nothing was done about it. Mr. Faribault had refused to let the Indian have a credit; and [the Indian] out with

---

[3] Little Rapids is up the Minnesota River about thirty-four miles in a direct line from Fort Snelling toward the southwest. The Indians were probably Wahpetons.

[4] "[Jean Baptiste Faribault] narrowly escaped death in 1833 at his station, at the hands of the treacherous Sioux Indian, who became enraged because he could not procure some articles he desired on credit, which Mr. Faribault did have in his store. Without saying a word, the savage drew his knife and stabbed Mr. F. in the back . . . the wound was a serious one, the knife having penetrated the lungs, and a long time elapsed before Mr. F. was considered out of danger." (Henry H Sibley, "Memoir of Jean Baptiste Faribault," *Minnesota Historical Collections*, III [1870–1880], 178.)

his knife and gave him a dig in the back. But it all passed off without any further trouble.

The summer [1834] passed off without any particular incident. Mr. Bailly arrived from below with his winter supply and brought the old note that my brother and I had given to settle up our old co-partnership business: first, Bailly and Prescott, and again, Brunet and Prescott. I paid them all up in full, $280, and stood clear of the world once more.

I thought of starting my boy [William Alexander] off to school again, as Major Grooms was about starting for the East. So I got my boy ready again and put him in the canoe and sent him off to the Choctaw Academy, but this time my family did not make any visible signs of opposition, but I was told the old grandmother took on terribly about it.

In the fall my time was out and I went over to Mr. Baker and asked him if he would trust me with some goods to trade up at Traverse des Sioux. He was very glad to get me and we made our arrangement. I went back to Mr. Bailly and told him my time was up and I wanted a settlement. After his wife came back I had been sleeping in their sitting room, with a sick child; I had to give it medicine in the night several times. It was damp and cold in the lodge to which we had moved after Mrs. Bailly came back, so I had asked Mr. Bailly's permission to sleep in the sitting room on the floor, but to be off early in the morning [and] out of their way.

But this did not suit the Madam and she ordered otherwise, and we had to sleep in our lodge with our sick child. But thanks be to Providence, my son still lives, but she has gone to her long home.

Mr. Bailly asked me why I went to the opposition to get employment. I told him he had made me no offer, so I had accepted the first opportunity to get employment. "Well," said he, "if I will give you employment, will you stay with me?" I said yes, knowing that he could not employ me. Otherwise I should have said no; the company had more clerks than they knew how to employ. I knew I was the first one to let go; therefore I made my arrangements with Mr. Baker without saying anything to Mr. Bailly. But Mr. Bailly made no proposition, so I went off over to Mr. Baker's and bade the American Fur Company good-bye forever.

Mr. Rolette came up in a few days and he gave me an order on Mr.

Mirie, the sutler at the fort, for the balance of my pay, which was about $130. I purchased some goods and got a little money and got clear of them. I went to work and got my equipment ready for the winter trade, and myself and Mr. H. Mooers,[5] who was getting goods at the same place, put our goods all into one boat and started off for a new business on our own account. I stopped and built on the bottom on the low land opposite Traverse des Sioux.

Mr. Le Blanc, an old Frenchman that I have before mentioned, that could neither read or write, was trading for the American Fur Company on the opposite side of the river. He had been there several years and had good hewed log houses, both warm and comfortable, and they were built far from the river where the spring freshets could not reach him.

But some of the old man's clerks got caught once in the bottom opposite his house. They were over there one day hunting ducks. The bottom was all overflowed, about fifteen miles long and from one to two miles wide. This whole bottom was under water and these two men that were hunting ducks, Messrs. Faribault and D. Campbell were the persons, they capsized their little hunting canoe. There was no land that they could reach and they climbed a tree, and then stood all night calling for help.

One Indian heard them and started in a little hunting canoe to go to them, but the wind was blowing very hard and the swells ran very high and upset the Indian and he drowned. The next day the Indians, about ten o'clock, got over to them and relieved them of a most distressing situation, not only by the position they had to be in all night but their clothes were all wet. The night was very cold and they had to keep on the move all night to keep from freezing. They said they were sick for a week after the occurrence.

Here I passed the winter [1834–1835] and made a very good trade and cleared about one thousand dollars. I made a large black walnut canoe in the spring, and in two trips I got all my furs down. I went down and passed the summer in traveling; I went out with a

5 Hazen P. Mooers (1789–1858), like Prescott, was a native of New York and had long experience in the fur trade. He spent many years at a station on the Sheyenne River of present southeastern North Dakota before going to the boundary lakes of Big Stone and Traverse. He later had charge of the American Fur Company post at Lake Traverse, where he married Gray Cloud, a half-blood.

surveying party to run a boundary line between the Sioux and Chippewa Indians, according to treaty stipulations.[6]

I was hired to go as interpreter for the troops and Mr. D. Campbell went as interpreter for the surveying party. Mr. J. Johnson[7] was to go as interpreter for the Chippewa language, but did not join us until we got near the end of our journey. The party was under the charge of Major Bean.[8] He once had been a lieutenant in the army and an agent for the Missouri Indians, but by some move had got out of them all and had now taken this contract to survey the boundary line between the two Nations.

I started up [June 18, 1835] in a Mackinaw boat with a party of soldiers, a sergeant, and a lieutenant; another party had gone up by land, and we all arrived at Sauk Rapids together, or all in the same day. The first river above this point was called Little Watab, or the river where they get the tamarack roots to sew canoes with. We had some hard pulling to get our big Mackinaw over the rapids, and in fact, we had to put on two yokes of oxen to pull the boat through the strongest part of the rapids.

Finally we got all over and went and camped where the line was to cross the river. We got the wagons, carts, and all the other things ready for the tramp, and the next day we crossed the river. The soldiers camped but the surveyors were not ready, but crossed the next day and took their latitude and the next day we got under way and made about ten miles up the Sauk River and camped. Here we had to change our course and go west in order to strike the head of Watab River, which was one of the points on the line.

So off we started right into the brush, which was so thick that we could not see 5 rods ahead. The teams and wagons, and even the

[6] At the Treaty of Prairie du Chien, August 19, 1825, the Sioux and Chippewas agreed upon a dividing line* between their respective countries which the Indians solemnly promised would never be crossed by either tribe except on a peaceful mission. This agreement had been broken several times since 1825.

[7] Perhaps the Reverend John Johnson (1812–1902), an Ottawa by birth who had been adopted by the Chippewas and was educated in a Methodist mission school at Jacksonville, Illinois. He later worked among the Chippewas as a Methodist minister. (Stephen R. Riggs, "Protestant Missions in the Northwest," *Minnesota Historical Collections*, VI [1894], 137, 141, 161, 164–166; "Minnesota Biographies," *Minnesota Historical Collections*, XIV [1912], 208.)

[8] Major Jonathan L. Bean, a native of Rhode Island. He graduated from West Point in 1818 and in 1830 was a sub-Indian agent with headquarters at Fort Lookout on the Missouri in present-day South Dakota.

carts could not get along, and we all turned in and went to cutting a road. We all worked hard all [day], and at night went back where we started from in the morning and camped.

After we had got our suppers and the surveyor looked over his day's work, he asked how far we thought we had come that day. Some said 5, some 6, some ten miles, and so on. "Well," said the surveyor, "we just made one mile." Everybody looked astonished and could hardly be made to believe that that was the case. Well, the contractor said, that never would do for him, for he would be ruined if he did not get along faster than that.

In the morning he ordered the surveyors to take two mules and pack them, with two men to lead them, and go through the woods while the main party went around by the Sauk River and the prairie, and in that way we got along very well for 4 or 5 days; then we came to the woods again. Here there was no chance to go around, so we left all the wagons and carts and left 2 men to take care of them at a large lake, where they caught a large amount of fish.

We packed all the horses and mules and followed the surveyor through brush and swamps from morning till night, and in fact, we were wet all day long. One night we camped on the headwater of Long Prairie River, where there was a lake with an island about 300 or 400 yards from shore, on which we could discover a large quantity of fowl but could not distinguish what they were. So some of the soldiers volunteered to swim over to them, and over they went, four or five of them, and found a roost of cormorants and they knocked down about 100 of the young. They tied them together and dragged them to the lake and put them in the water. They walked and pulled their game after them until they could no longer touch bottom, then they began to swim and finally reached the shore. They said they found it very hard work, for there was considerable grass in the lake, which impeded their progress.

As soon as they landed they all set to work picking their birds. They made a great stew out of them, but they tasted so fishy that nobody relished them.

When the surveyors came in they reported they had seen some Indians on the opposite side of the lake. We all went to bed as usual, and the next morning the men went out to look for their horses. They had not been gone long before they returned and reported one mule dead and another badly stabbed. There was a fuss in the camp, and we expected to be attacked. We got ready to fend off [the attackers] the best we could, and all sallied out to see if we could find the depredators, but nothing was to be found but the horses. So the contractor had the other mule shot to put it out of its misery.

We got ready and started as soon as possible and left the mules for the Indians to eat. We learnt about a year later it was the Chippewas. They took us to be Sioux Indians [which] was the reason they killed the mules. But I doubt this statement, for our tents were plain to be seen which are so different from the make of Sioux lodge they could not be mistaken. I believe it was nothing but wanton mischief that made them stab the mules. [This act] embarrassed the contractor a good deal, because by loading his other animals very heavy made all their backs sore.

We went on without seeing any Indians. The woods were so dense that some one most every day got lost. I amongst the rest one day got lost and probably should have been troubled very much to get back or forward, as I had got off the track, and did think I was lost for some time. After a while I gave a whoop, but no answer came, and again, but no answer. Now I found that I was lost and fired off my gun, but there was no answer.

Now, I thought, the thing was up, and a thousand plans were in my head all in a moment, and which was the best? I stood a few moments but heard nothing. I fired my gun again, and shortly after, I heard a gun a long way off. I fired again and heard two more [shots], and made off in that direction. After a while I fired again and got an answer close by, and in this way we got together again; and after that I stuck pretty close to the party.

The contractor, Major Bean, complained and said I had made him lose nearly a whole day. We went on and camped; we found the next morning that we had got into a swamp and there was no way of crossing. We had to go round about 15 miles to get back where we left in the morning, or opposite. The width of the swamp was only about 50 yards, but [it was] so deep that we could not wade or ford it.

We took our course again and went to the edge of the prairie the next day, and crossed the Chippewa River on the prairie, about two days' travel from Lac qui Parle. We turned our course for Otter Tail Lake, nearly due north, and got in amongst some lakes, and where to go we did not know. We hunted about three days for a place that we could get between the lakes. Whilst we were in this quandry Mr. Johnson came up with two Chippewa Indians. All were glad to see them, for we were at a standstill and knew not where to go. So the Chippewas soon put us right, and in two days we were at Otter Tail Lake.

The most northern point of the lake is ten miles long and [is] one clear sheet of water and [has] a plenty of fish. From this point we came back down to the outlet of the lake and took our course down the river. The first day we got lost. We treed 2 young bears; the men all had sport in shooting with their pistols at the little bears, and then again a great feast of the meat.

Lieut. Storer,[9] who had command of the soldiers, sent a note to Major Bean, the contractor, notifying him that he could not go any farther. He gave for his excuse that the soldiers were out of shoes and clothes, and that the rations were low, and for that cause the troops could not proceed any farther. They wrote back and forth half the night, and in the morning Lieut. Storer ordered the command to pack up and return. I will assure you the party were all well pleased, for we were all tired, ragged, and glad to get off.

But Major Bean said it would ruin him, for the government would not pay him for what he had done. Lieut. Storer said he did not hinder him from going on. The major insisted that Storer was ordered to go through to the end of the line. "Yes," said Lieut. Storer, "but my men cannot go barefoot and without food." And he gave the order to march, and off we all started. In about half an hour the surveyors caught up with us. Major Bean had thought it was not well to go alone with his party, so he followed on after us and ran his correction line as he went.

From that time they [Major Bean and Lieut. Storer] did not speak to each other, and they had not spoken to each other for about a week before they arrived at this place about three miles west of Otter Tail Lake in the water of the river that runs out of that lake but is called the South Fork of Red River* and runs down by Lord Selkirk's settlement in the North.

We made our [way] back as fast as we could. Lieut. Storer had got

9 William H. Storer (d. 1878), of Maine and New York, was graduated from the U.S. Military Academy in 1828. In November, 1839, he resigned from the service. (Francis B. Heitman, *Historical Register and Dictionary of the U.S. Army* [Washington: G.P.O., 1903], p. 930.)

out of all patience. He had been lately married to one of Mr. Rolette's daughters, of Prairie du Chien. She was quite unwell when we left and Lieut. Storer was very anxious to get back on her account. We got back to the Mississippi and the Lieutenant took his boat and left the party to finish up the survey by themselves, as there was no further danger of being molested by the Indians. In 8 hours we ran down to the falls and footed it down to the fort.

Here ended another expedition that was of no benefit to the government or to the Indians. The Indians destroyed all the land-marks they could find, and in a few years a treaty was made that made the lines and boundaries of no use or necessity to either party.

I got my winter's supply of goods and went up with Mr. Mooers again in his boat, but I had to go for the boat first from Fort Snelling to a place called the Little Rock up on the Minnesota. I had first to go in a canoe to Traverse des Sioux, then I footed it from there two days by land, making in all about 6 or 7 days' hard work to get a boat, and then five days rowing to get back. And then I had to row back to Traverse des Sioux again.

I unloaded my boat and moved into my old house of last winter and went to work. I gave my Indians some credit and they went off and killed enough furs to pay their first credit and took more for the winter. This made me short of goods and I had to send for more to Mr. Baker at Camp Coldwater, near Fort Snelling, the old Summer Encampment of the troops when they first moved up to build the fort.

I had but one man, so I put him into a canoe and sent him off with an order for what [was] wanted, and to hire a man to help up with the canoe and load. The man went down and got his load, and the first night they camped near the fort. There they made a plan to steal the goods and run off, so they took the heavy things and hid them in a manure heap about the fort stables. Amongst the things hid were three Indian guns, some axes, and a corn mill. The dry goods they sold about amongst the soldiers for a little or nothing, and put off down the river.

Mr. Baker did not hear of it for 2 weeks. He immediately started a man up to me with a few more goods to inform me of what had transpired. I had been waiting very anxious for my man for nearly three weeks, never dreaming of his having run off, for he had a squaw and she was living in a lodge near by my house. I thought certainly he would come back to her again, but he was too much of the old

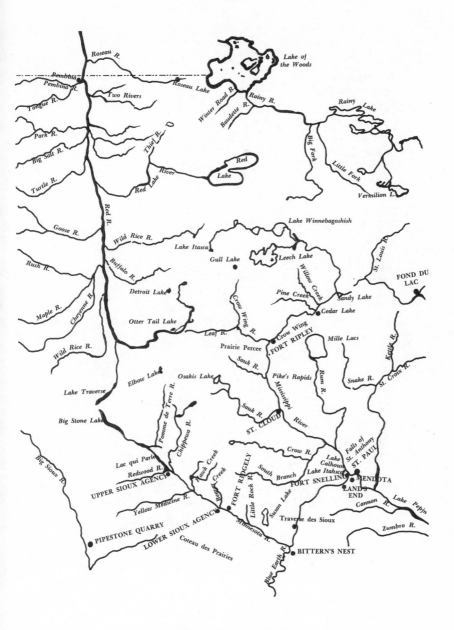

The Upper Mississippi Area

soldier for us all, as he had been an old soldier in the army. He had learned many bad tricks and this was one of them, stealing.

I supposed all the time that he was sick, or some accident had happened him, when all the time he was in Prairie du Chien living on what he had stolen from me. I got Mr. Baker to advertise him and offered a reward of $25.* He was apprehended and put into prison and kept there for three months, but I did not go to prosecute the case and he was set at liberty. He threatened vengeance for false imprisonment, but he never tried it and left the country after having made me lose $350.

This made a big hole in my profits, for the price of furs had gone down very much. Muskrats declined 300 per cent, or rats that were worth the year before forty cents were now worth only ten cents.[10]

So I concluded to pass the winter alone, and went to chopping my own wood for the winter. This I found pretty hard, for I had never chopped much, but in a few days my hands got hardened and the blisters all healed up, and in one month I had wood enough for the winter chopped.

About this time my wife and the old folk, my wife's father and mother with a sick daughter, arrived from below to pass the winter [1835–1836]. A few days after we received a letter from the Choctaw Academy stating that my son [William Alexander] was dead. This set the old folks wailing at a terrible rate, and if one of their own children had died they could not, and did not, take on so much, as was proved a few days after when their daughter died.

My son, it appears from the letter we got, died of bilious pleurisy; the old folks' daughter, of abscess in the side, internal. I never heard such wailing and weeping. The woods fairly resounded for miles around from the bellowing of the old man and woman at the death of my son.

I felt bad at the thought of the circumstances, the trouble, and the cause of my sending him off, but I thought of the Great Ruler of the Heavens and the Earth, and that the Lord had taken what was

10 The average price of skins during the period from 1815 to 1830 was given by Indian Agent Dougherty as twenty cents for muskrats, thirty-three cents for deer, twenty-five cents for raccoons, three dollars for otters, four dollars for beavers, and three dollars for buffaloes. (Hiram M. Chittenden, *The American Fur Trade of the Far West* [New York: Harper, 1902], I, 7–8.)

His own. And I thought probably my son had been saved from some other calamity and that God had foreseen this and had taken him home before some great trouble overtook him. I bore up with the affliction better than those that have no hope, believing that some day I should see my son again in peace. But my poor Indian relations had no hope and, therefore, could not be comforted, and mourned at a terrible rate for more than a year after the death of my son.

I learned the situation that my son had been in at the Choctaw Academy. Major Grooms had spoken of the institution in most glowing terms, and said he was very glad to get the chance to send his sons to the academy, and told me it would be a good place for my son. The following is what I was told by Mr. Bailly's boys that went to the same place at the same time, that the children got only one meal a day, and if they got anything more they had to go and beg it of the cook. Sometimes they would give the boys a little, and sometimes not. They would have to go from noon until the next morning before they could get anything to eat.

They were only half clothed and, in fact, they said the Indian children amongst the wild savages were better cared for than they were. When I heard of this my blood run through my veins first cold, then hot, with revenge at the old Major Grooms who had told me that all about the Choctaw Academy was so nice and pleasant, and that the children were so well cared for. If I could have got my eyes on him, nothing could have kept me off of him.

My son, whilst he was sick, had no nursing at all, and when he would cry for water, the old brute of a Negro woman would whip him for crying for water and food. I never shall forgive myself for sending my boy off to school amongst strangers. But the old woman was the cause; she always would vex me by taking the boy and carrying him home with her. I told her she never should have him, and in retaliation for my rashness to keep my son from the old woman, he is gone from both of us. And many is the hour I have passed in sorrowing over the miserable death of my poor boy, away amongst strangers and but little better treated than the brute beast.

O, shame on a government that would have an institution of that kind, and have no person to oversee the business and see that the children did not suffer! But death relieved him from suffering, and God in His wisdom took him on purpose to take him out of misery and brutal treatment; and [he] is now better off we hope than his persecutors. And may God be praised for His goodness and wisdom for delivering my child from tyrannical hands.

And I do not say anything more about Major Grooms, only I hope the Lord will reward him according to his deeds in deceiving me in the manner he did, in getting my child off to school where there was neither regulation nor food, a poor bed, and nothing but Negro shanties to live in. And for this the government paid Mr. Johnson $25,000 a year—a complete game of swindling at the expense of poor, innocent, and suffering children. The thought of the thing is enough to chill any one's blood, and I must draw the veil to relieve my mind from the subject.

The old folks had not been there long before their daughter died very suddenly. The abscess broke inwardly and she died instantly, but the old folks did not make half the mourning over her that they did over the death of my son.

The sudden death of this young girl set me to reflecting about my future state and what would become of me if I should die suddenly and without repentance. I should lose my right to the promises of God of eternal life, and be barred from enjoying that bliss offered to all that repent and turn unto the Lord. The two deaths, so close one upon the other, made me reflect seriously. The longer I went the more I thought on the subject and commenced praying. And I went and finally made up my mind to join the church, and I found no peace until I did make up my mind to do something.

I kept on at my work through the winter [1835–1836], hauling wood and trading, and at last spring came and I commenced making my packs. It commenced thawing and raining; the water commenced rising and rose so much that it came all around my house. I was afraid of being flooded out of my house, and I moved all my packs and put them on a scaffold outdoors. But the weather set in cold, the water fell again and staid low, and we got down in safety, myself and my wife alone.

SUPPLEMENT

Boundary Between the Nations (page 156 n.)

The boundary agreed on stretched in a general southeast direction from the junction of Goose Creek, a North Dakota streamlet, with the Red River of the North to a point on the St. Croix about eight miles below Osceola, Wisconsin. It passed east of Fergus Falls, west of Alexandria, and crossed the Mississippi between St. Cloud and Sauk Rapids. Prolonged into Wisconsin, it continued to a point on the Chippewa River just below Eau Claire, thence eastward to the Black River, which it followed to its junction with the Mississippi. It was not till 1835, after repeated requests by the Indians, that any part of this line was run out, and then the savages pulled up the stakes as fast as they were driven. Its tardy establishment was without material effect.

(William W. Folwell, *A History of Minnesota* [St. Paul: Minnesota Historical Society, 1918], I, 147.)

Red River of the North (page 159)

The Red River was known in 1848 as the Otter Tail River from this lake to its junction with the Red Lake at Grand Forks. Present usage by many of the older white people retains the name Otter Tail for the river above the lake of this name and indeed occasionally it is still called Otter Tail River along its portion continuing below this lake to the axis of the Red River Valley at Breckenridge and Wahpeton, where it receives the Bois des Sioux River and turns from a westward to a northward course. ("Minnesota Geographic Names," *Minnesota Historical Collections*, XVII [1920], 390–391.)

Advertising for Fugitives (page 161)

Advertising for runaway thieves, apprentices, slaves, etc., was a common practice at this time. Usually it was done in newspapers or by handwritten notices posted at a few of the larger towns on the Mississippi River.

VIII

1837–1853

At the Indian Councils

[Prescott makes no mention of his activities in the winter and spring of 1836–1837. It could well be that, as John H. Stevens reported, Prescott was then traveling through Texas and the South (see Appendix C).—*Ed. note.*]

We got our outfit ready. We set out in our old boat and I had Rev. Mr. [Stephen Return] Riggs and lady in camping with me.* We went into the Little Rapids and camped over the Sabbath. Here I was tempted all day long by the Indians to trade. I told them it was the Great Spirit's day of rest and to pray, and I could not work nor trade. This was a new thing to them and [they] could not understand anything about the object or principle of the Sabbath, but I kept them until next morning, when I traded them furs, and went on with my missionary family and got up to my wintering ground the 5th day.

Rev. R. S. Riggs was missionary for the Sioux and was stationed at Lac qui Parle, where Dr. T. S. Williamson had lived several [two] years. They were changing posts that they might be equal partakers of the privations of an Indian life and manners and customs.

And speaking about the missions, when I was going up the river a few years before with Mr. Bailly, the trader, I took out of my stuff some tracts and went to reading one day as we were going up in the boat. Mr. Bailly looked at me and asked me what I was reading. I told him, "Some tracts." He commenced swearing and said, "Do you want to sink my boat?" I said, "No." "Well," he said, "if you go to reading those papers on my boat I am sure she will sink before we get up." Mr. Bailly is a Roman Catholic by creed but in spirit is an infidel.

I [had] passed the summer [1837] out at Lake Harriet where the Missionaries lived—Messrs. S. and G. H. Pond and Mr. Stevens.* The Messrs. Pond had lived already 2 years alone before Mr. Stevens came up there, but after Mr. Stevens came they all joined together for a year or two and kept a missionary school, etc.

I built a small house out at the lake also, and during the summer I joined the church and lived happy and comfortable under the influence of religion. I wrote my brother[1] at Vienna, State of New York, of what I had done.

He wrote that he thought I would, or had, sold my all for a pew in Heaven, or that the religious people had persuaded me to join them to get something from me, and he thought the whole was a chimera and that I had better leave them. I think that was about the amount of what he wrote me, but his advice did not jar me in the least. I stuck to the work of prayer, and believe I never shall be sorry for the step I took in joining the church. Repentance and faith had got [a] fast hold upon me, and I was determined to live by it. I never have seen the time yet but what I could say I wanted more of the love of God and a better or greater desire to serve Him and my Saviour.

It kept me pretty busy all the fall to get my work done in time. This season the Indians had been to Washington and made a treaty* and sold all their lands on the east side of the Mississippi,* and returned home the fore [part] of November.[2] One old chief got crazy and jumped overboard and was lost. In this treaty the Indians gave the traders $110,000 and the half-breeds, $90,000.

I made my way up to my old winter ground. I made good returns, but the furs were worth nothing of any account, and I lost money. And Mr. [B. F.] Baker lost so much that he had to suspend business, for he was so much in debt that the Messrs. Powell would not trust him any more.

I had been quite sick in the winter [1837–1838] and I wrote down and got Mr. Samuel Pond to come up and keep house for me whilst

[1] Probably Zachariah Wright Prescott.

[2] "The home trip was successfully accomplished, arriving at Fort Snelling on November 10th. . . . On the way up the river the boiler of the steamboat, the Rolla, exploded, and one of the Dakotas was killed." (Doane Robinson, "A History of the Sioux Indians," South Dakota Historical Collections, II [1904], 184.)

I should go down and see the doctor.[3] So Mr. Pond came up and I went down and staid a month and came back.* Mr. Pond went up to Lac qui Parle to see Dr. Williamson's family. He suffered very much going up, he told me. Still the Indians do not appreciate the missionaries' sufferings to try to teach them how to live like white men. All the Indians appear to care for is something to eat, and religion and farming is the last things in their minds. And there is a plenty of white men to keep them in ignorance, and use all their influence to thwart the moral and civilizing of the Indians.

About this time some Chippewas came down with some trade to get some goods at Mr. Baker's store. The Sioux had been out hunting somewhere up north of the Minnesota River and the Chippewas had come across them and killed some of them. The Sioux were determined to have their revenge, and now was their chance. They hid themselves in the bushes near the houses toward sunset, and as one of them [the Chippewas] was going from one house to the other, 4 or 5 in number fired on him and killed him, and then ran up to scalp him.

The [Chippewa] chief, Hole-in-the-Day, heard the fuss and ran out and just as he got out the Sioux were in the act of scalping the Chippewa. The chief fired his ball [which] struck one of the Sioux in the mouth, knocked out three teeth, and came out at the back part of the lower jaw. He was supposed to be mortally wounded, but he got away and ran to Mud Lake, a distance of two miles, in about 15 or 20 minutes' time.

Here was a great commotion again in the whole community. The soldiers were ordered out after the Sioux. The Sioux and Chippewa half-breeds were barricading their houses and all kinds of preparations were made for war. The soldiers returned but could not find the depredator. The Chippewa, as [he] was supposed [to be], was found to be a Coutire or Cut-ear from some of the tribes about Mackinaw, a half-civilized, peaceable nation. [He] had married a Pillager Chippewa* woman and lived by boating and voyaging for the traders.

[3] It seems probable that it was Dr. John Emerson who cared for Prescott at this time. He had been appointed post physician in 1836 and was there as late as 1840. Until 1838 he had with him the celebrated slave Dred Scott. (Samuel W. Pond, "Two Missionaries in the Sioux Country," *Minnesota History*, Vol. XXI, No. 2 [June 1940], 165 n.)

The government officers took the body and buried it in the graveyard near the fort. The Sioux [became] so enraged to think the whites showed so much respect to their enemies that they went in the night and dug open the grave and cut a hole through the coffin and shot the dead body full of arrows and went off and left the grave in that situation. They [the soldiers] sent out and had another hunt from the fort for the mischief makers, but could find nothing; they had all fled to the upper country.

So the thing [was] passed over by the whites. But the spirit of revenge, which never slumbers in the breast of the Indian, was not composed, and [they awaited] only an opportunity to get satisfaction, which offered one year after. But a dreadful calamity followed upon the heels of the continuance of this revengeful spirit, which I shall relate in its proper time in this work.

I bought Mr. Baker out and he agreed to furnish me with goods,[4] and [I] passed the summer [1838] and made a little at trade. Mr. [Baker], having given up the Indian trade, went into the sutling business and commenced a large sawmill at a place called Taylor's Falls* on the St. Croix [River] and spent some 4 or 5 thousand dollars and was taken sick. And the trouble about his business being very much embarrassed, he went to St. Louis and died of consumption [November 2, 1839].

This broke up all his business, and all his traders were left out of of employment again. I lived in his house during the winter [1838–1839], and towards Spring I had one offer from the officers of the fort to go down to the St. Croix and take charge of a claim they had taken up for a town site. They agreed to furnish me with one thousand dollars to build a house and store with, and give me one-eighth of all the land and buildings.[5] I had nothing to do, so I accepted their offer and went to work.

I got the body of my house up and went home to see my family.

4 Prescott evidently took over Benjamin F. Baker's store at Cold Spring, or Cold Water, about a mile up the Mississippi from Fort Snelling.

Samuel W. Pond states that in the summer of 1838, Prescott and others "applied for the appointment of farmer for the Lake Calhoun band, but the Agent [Taliaferro] refused to give it to them and offered it to me. I at first told him I could not take it, but ... I consented to hold the appointment...." ("Two Missionaries in the Sioux Country," ed. Theodore C. Blegen, *Minnesota History*, Vol. XXI, No. 2 [June 1940], 163.)

5 The town that grew up there is now Prescott, Wisconsin.

While I was gone a man by the name of C. D. Foote, a carpenter of the St. Croix Mill Company, came and jumped my claim. I went to law with him about the right, etc. The case* was fought before J. R. Brown, Esq., Justice, who lived on what is called Gray Cloud Island,* and had a whisky shop up near Fort Snelling, where he kept a man by the name of [Menck],[6] an Englishman, to peddle the whisky for him. This establishment was an eyesore to the officers, for the soldiers used to go there and get whisky and get drunk and make a great deal of trouble for them.

And the Indians used to go there and get whisky and kick up a fuss. This was the cause of the citizens all being drove off from the reserve—J. R. Brown's whisky shop—for none others kept any but him, and to get rid of him the commanding officer had orders to move all persons off that were not there by authority of law, that is, Indian traders under a license. And it is very likely if Mr. Brown had not established a whisky shop in the vicinity of the fort, that the citizens never would have been drove off from the reserve by the military, for this liquor traffic gave the officers a great deal of trouble.*

One day the Indians went over to the whisky shop and broke all the kegs and poured out the whisky. This was all charged upon the Indian agent [Taliaferro], and a warrant was procured from Dubuque for his apprehension. And one night about midnight the sheriff and the man Menck came to Major Taliaferro's room and were admitted, and they took hold of the agent and held him down to his bed for sometime. They extorted some promises from him and kept him in until morning, when the major's servant went to the fort and told the commanding officer. He sent an officer to enquire into the matter, and found that a sheriff and Mr. [Menck] had seized the agent with a warrant for getting the Indians to break up [Menck's] liquor establishment.

The commanding officer sent a guard out and had the sheriff and Mr. [Menck] marched off over the river, and forbid [them] to put their feet on this side of the river again. This made a great talk about the military disregarding the civil law and aiding to take prisoners from the custody of the sheriff. But it blew over, and after a while another one tried the whisky trade again by the name of McDonald, a Frenchman. He came in the fort one day and was taken and put in the guardhouse and kept there a month, and was not let out until

[6] Henry C. Menck, or Mencke, although Prescott wrote his name as Minck.

he promised not to bring any more whisky there to sell to the soldiers.

He promised to do so, and this put a stop to whisky selling to the soldiers, but in about a month after, a sheriff appeared there and took the commanding officer for imprisoning a peaceable citizen, etc. But the officer ordered the sheriff out of the fort again, and he went off without any prisoner; and that case went by the board, and the whisky trade was stopped for a time.

But the people that had been drove off the reserve at the point of the bayonet had commenced anew below the line of the reserve, now St. Paul. The traffic commenced anew and increased up to the present time. St. Paul would have been somewhere about where Fort Snelling is if the citizens could have remained where they commenced settling, for the first settlements were all about the fort.

I must now go on with my lawsuit in which Jos. R. Brown was the Justice of Peace. I sued Foote before Brown. [In] the first trial the jury could not agree and a new trial was ordered, and [again] the jury could not agree. I found that every influence possible was working against me. The Justice would like to see my claim taken from me because the officers had an interest [in it] and, in fact, owned near the whole.

Brown felt sore about the whisky shop being broken up, for it [was] a source of quite a little income to him, and he would like to see the officers injured in return, if he could do anything to injure them. Here it is supposed he done all he could to get a jury that would decide against me, but my proof was too strong, and the work showed too much for any just jury to decide against me. But there were enough always to make a split [jury] and keep me in expense, which had now come to over $200. I told Foote to take half the claim, and we settled upon that. This the officers did not like, but it was the best I could do, and so it stood.

Mr. Brown after this went up to the head of the Lake St. Croix and took up a town site and lived on Gray Cloud Island himself. He built a large house at the upper end of Stillwater and made arrangements for a District Court to be held there. But [on] the appointed day Mr. Brown was absent; the judge came and found no preparations and nothing to eat. The judge went off scolding Mr. J. R. Brown, [who] had been appointed clerk of the court and was not to be found, and [there was] no court, of course.

Mr. Brown had left his first wife, a Sioux half-breed, Miss Ellen Dickson, and married a Chippewa half-breed. He got a divorce from her on the flimsy excuse that he wanted to go to trade with the Sioux Indians and he was afraid they would kill his wife. He took her along and he got [a] divorce and went and married a Sioux half-breed,[7] whom he lives with up to this time, and as many more as he likes.

During the summer [1839] a large number of Chippewas came down to visit the Sioux by invitation of the Sioux. The Chippewas stayed near two weeks, feasting and counciling with the Sioux Indians. There were judged to be about 1000 Chippewas—men, women, and children. As they were leaving, two Pillagers, relatives of the man that was killed by the Sioux the summer before, went out to Lake Calhoun to see if they could get a scalp. They said the Sioux owed them one.

They went and placed themselves in a trail that led from Lake Calhoun to [a] shack half a mile south of Lake Harriet, or a mile and a half south of Lake Calhoun, and hid themselves in the bushes. After a while an Indian came along. He was Neka (the Badger), one of the best Indians in the Lake Calhoun band. As he passed, they, the two Chippewa Pillagers, shot him and took his scalp and made off.*

The news spread in half a day all over the country, and the next morning the Sioux to the number of about 300 were off on a war excursion. They traveled all day and all night, and just at daylight they came up with the Chippewas. A part had gone by Rice River and some by the Mississippi and some by the St. Croix. Those that went by Rice River were mostly Mille Lacs Indians and were going to make a portage into Rum River.

They had just crossed a lake and was carrying their canoes and baggage across the portage when the [Sioux] attacked them and killed of men, women, and children, 60-odd persons. The Chippewas were surprised and could not account for the conduct of the Sioux,

[7] Ellen Dickson was the daughter of the early fur trader Robert Dickson. It is possible that her "mother was the sister of The Beaver, also known by his Indian name, Shoppa, the most notable chief of the Cuthead band of Yanktonais." ("Records of Fort Tecumseh," *South Dakota Historical Collections*, IX [1918], 100 n.)

Brown's Chippewa half-blood wife was a Miss McCoy or McKay. His third and more permanent wife was Susan Freniere.

as they had parted all in friendship only two days before. The
Chippewas fought bravely to save their children, and the Sioux lost
fifteen of their braves.

The party that went by St. Croix, Little Crow's band followed
them and attacked them [at] about the same time as the battle on
Rice Creek. They killed about 20 Chippewas, so that in about one
hour's time there was one hundred Chippewas and Sioux slain for
the mischief of two [Pillager] Chippewas.

If the two Chippewas had notified the others, they would have
been on their guard and got out of the way; but as they knew
nothing of what had taken place, they were traveling along very
unconcerned, thinking of no danger until they heard the war whoop,
and the next thing a discharge of guns and the shrieking of the
women and children. The Chippewas fired and retreated and
saved a large part of their women and children.

The next morning the Sioux arrived with their scalps and danced
a while, and went off home to their villages to spend a month in
dancing the scalp dance.

The Chippewas that went by the Mississippi got off without being
attacked by the Sioux. The ones that deserved chastisement the most
of any were the ones that got off with a whole skin, for there is no
doubt but [that] the two men that killed the Sioux went and joined
that camp, and probably had the scalp at the time the innocent ones
were selling their lives at a dear rate.

After my arrangement with Foote, I went on to work and finished
my house at the mouth of the St. Croix. There was no business then
at that point. There was one little boat that done all the business;
[it was] called the *Rock River*.[8] This boat run from Galena to the
fort once a week and then did not get enough to pay her expenses. I
frequently piloted the boat from St. Croix to Fort Snelling. I made
a little farm, but there was no market for anything and nothing to be
made.

Mr. Foote, after our settlement, left a man to live in his part of
the claim, but the St. Croix Mill Company discharged him [Foote],
saying they had not hired him to go about stealing other people's
claims, and they were afraid to trust him for fear he would play
them a trick. He went off and left his man there for six months. I
was on the watch all the time to get an opportunity to jump my claim

8 Count Haraszthy, a Hungarian exile, was the captain of the *Rock River*.

back again, so sometime after the six months were up, the man went off one day to see if he could sell the claim to get his pay.

Whilst he was gone I took my axe and a witness and went [and] marked the claim over in my name, and put a padlock on top of his and left it. So the next day he came home and found he was fastened out. He talked pretty strong about it for a while and threatened to break the lock, etc. I told him we had a penitentiary for people that broke locks. This did not suit [him] very well and he stopped his threats, and a friend of his advised him to compromise the matter. He [said] all he wanted was his pay for the time he had been there. I told him I would give him $60; he agreed to take it and moved off, and I was once more left in quiet possession of my claim. But I was making nothing and had spent about all that I brought with me, and was now about flat broke again.

[Although Prescott gives no account of his activities during the period 1841–1842, he was evidently at Prescott, Wisconsin, farming and holding down his claim.—*Ed. note.*]

The winter of 1842–43 was one of the severest winters I ever saw. The snow fell first about a foot and a half [deep], and went off mostly and fell again over a foot, and mostly went off again. And in February [snow] fell again, near two feet, again making in all nearly four feet of snow. I lost some 70 hogs and pigs for the want of feed. My crops had been small and tight.

My cattle got through the winter, for there was a plenty of rushes and the cattle could get the tops of them, and on the islands there was brush and trees. So I saved my cattle; that was all I had left in the spring of 1843. I farmed a little.

I had taken into my house two Swiss missionaries.* They got their wood of me and I sold some wood to the steamboats. In this way I dragged the summer through. Messrs. Gavin and Dentan gave me one hundred dollars for house rent and wood from their mission society [funds].

During the summer we had a lawsuit brought on by a man from Galena by the name of Waddle against Henry Jackson of St. Paul.[9] I was the only Justice of the Peace near about, and they brought the

9 Henry Jackson arrived in Minnesota in 1842 and established the first general store in St. Paul.

case before me. The first was to replevy a lot of goods that Waddle said Henry Jackson had obtained of him by false pretenses, so I issued a writ of replevin and off we started in the old *Rock River* steamboat. And such another crowd of river blacklegs I never saw.

We got up to St. Paul and the party having the writ went up to Mr. Jackson's store and found it fastened. They demanded admittance, but [the] word was no. The party outside threatened to break the door down, and they all got [out] their pistols and bowie knives and flourished them a while, and swore enough to sink a boat if there had been any weight in the oaths. But the party inside thought it was best to let them in and the writ was served.

The goods [were] boxed up and put under my charge. The day for the trial came on and the suit was quashed, or non-suited. Mr. Jackson got the goods back again, and Mr. Waddle went off, with his finger in his mouth, back to Galena and took to drinking and died, as he had run through a good store of goods and wasted them all.

St. Paul about this time was a den of card players and a place for the soldiers to go to get liquor, and they used to have some high times amongst the blacklegs in those days. In the fall of 1843 I received a letter from Col. Bruce, the Indian agent,[10] offering me the interpreter's berth, as he had discharged his old interpreter. I went and accepted the office and came down and made arrangements to move my family. I got a man by the name of Joseph Montjeau to move into my house and gave him all he could raise from the farm, and one-half of the cattle.

I moved up and settled down in one of the old stone houses near the fort, September, 1843, and entered upon the duties of interpreter for the government. A contract was written out and signed, and I was sworn into office. Here I commenced another kind of life and my hands were full of business all the time, in writing, interpreting, and looking after the farmers and the wants of the Indians.

About every month the Indians would get up some excuse to counsel with the agent or the commanding officer, and the wind-up would be a begging for some provisions, or a charge for cutting

[10] Amos J. Bruce succeeded Major L. Taliaferro and was the U.S. Indian agent at St. Peter's from 1839 to 1848.

timber on their lands, or fire wood. Sometimes the commanding officer would give them a few rations and they would go off satisfied for a while until they would get hungry for bread; [then] they would come again.

After the great battle when the Sioux killed so many of the Chippewas [1839], Major Taliaferro advised them to move from Lake Calhoun, as he thought the Chippewas would come down and kill the whole band of them. But the real cause of getting them removed was to get them farther off from the settlements, for most every [day] there were complaints brought against the Indians for killing cattle, and they were constantly hanging about the fort and the officers complained of their being a nuisance to the fort.

The Indians said they were not afraid of the Chippewas. The agent kept advising them to move from the lake down to the river and then they would be more secure from the Chippewas. [He] finally got them started and they moved to the Minnesota [River] and mixed up with the bands (most of them) that lived on the Minnesota, but still this did not get them out of the way of the Chippewas, for they would come down in their bark canoes, land above the falls, leave their canoes, and cross over to the road that leads from the fort to the village, and shoot down one or two and run off. And in most every path that was traveled, the Chippewas would waylay them.

They [the Chippewas] came down [1842] in large numbers and attacked Little Crow's village.[11] The Sioux were all drunk; they rushed over the river to attack the Chippewas, some with guns, some with lances, some with knives only. The main body were hid in the long grass and two or three of the Chippewas went out to the village. The main part was on the west side of the river. (Little Crow's band was the one attacked.) The first [Chippewa] braves that went out found a woman, the wife of a Canadian, hoeing corn; they shot her and gave the war whoop, and ran up to scalp her. The Frenchman ran to her relief, but by this time three or four more Chippewas got up, and some of them kept the Frenchman off whilst the other took the scalp and went off shouting.

At the same time some other Chippewas attacked a lodge and killed a woman and child. The Indian had two wives; one was with

[11] The battle, fought in June, 1842, was known as the Battle of Kaposia. Kaposia was a village of Little Crow IV, also known as Big Thunder.

him in a white man's house nearby where his other wife was killed, but the man had no gun and dared not venture out. The Chippewas went off rejoicing back to the main party.

Shortly after, the Sioux got over and rushed on to the Chippewas, a large number being secreted in the grass. The Sioux did not see them until they got close to them. The Chippewas rose from their ambush, fired, and wounded and killed fifteen the first shot, then took [to] their heels and ran off. A few Sioux that were not hurt followed on after them and killed five of them.

Their [the Chippewas'] timidity made them lose the honor of the day, for if they had stood their ground, in a few minutes they could have killed all the [Sioux] men, and then they could have went and killed their women. But they were too big cowards and made off, the Sioux following. The Sioux were only five in number that kept up the chase for about five miles, when they killed the last Chippewa that was to be found.

There were in all 280 Chippewas, and only 30 men of the Sioux, and half of them were shot down [at] the first fire of the Chippewas. Some [of the Sioux] were old men and had only knives and did not follow [the Chippewas].

This left Little Crow's village in a pitiful state. The dying and wounded were all with the dead brought in and laid out in their own lodges, and a great day of lamentation and mourning it was! The doctor came down from the fort and some troops were sent down, but the Chippewas were all off, out of the soldiers' reach, and they went home as they came. Little Crow felt that he had received a chastisement that he had deserved, for he had been in the habit of going or sending out two or three war parties every summer and killing some of the Chippewas. This blow cooled him down; he never went to war again.

I had not been in my new office long before an order came from Washington for the agent and commanding officers to make an effort to stop the whisky traffic, which had grown to such an alarming extent that every few nights an Indian would be killed or frozen to death. I had to be out sometimes every night, sometimes once a week, watching the Indians with a party of soldiers.

We caught a great many and broke their kegs. One night we took seven kegs and the Indians with them. The next morning the commanding officer sent for me. I went down to the fort; Capt.

Backus[12] was in command. He came along laughing. "Ah," he said, "you have been running the mail again, have you?" "Yes sir." "What luck had you?" "Seven kegs," I said. "My! You have got enough for the whole fort. We must go and look at it."

So he told some soldiers to take the 7 kegs to the top of the hill outside the fort, and ordered the Indians to be brought out. He took an axe along in his hand. Several persons had gathered round and Captain Backus told the Indians if they did not stop running whisky into the Indian country he would punish them worse than breaking their kegs. He handed me the axe and told me to go to work. I took the axe and knocked in the seven heads of the kegs and [the whiskey] made a stream half way down the hill towards the river by the fort. The Indians looked very solemn. They had come a long distance to get whisky to trade for horses,[13] and had lost a considerable amount by the operation, but this put a stop to the trade for the winter; but in the spring they commenced again in canoes.

I was sent with Lieut. Hall and a party of soldiers to watch them and seize them if possible, and if they would not stop, to fire a ball close to them and see if that would bring them to. Presently along came a canoe. I hailed them in Indian, but no reply, and again I hailed [with] no reply; but they paddled off as fast as possible. Lieut. Hall took [his] musket and fired, and the water spattered all over the Indians, but no stop. He fired again, but no stop to Mr. Indian, and they got off.

Lieut. Hall went and reported that he could not bring them to, and two canoes had got past him. [The] captain ordered him to load with fine shot. He done so and we went back again. We had not been there long before another canoe came along. We hailed again but no stop. Lieut. Hall fired; one Indian fell over but the other paddled across to the [far] shore, and they ran off before the [Lieutenant] could load again. So we gave it up.

Their canoes had passed [us] and we did not catch one of them, but one of the Indians got a charge of shot that laid him up for a

[12] Captain Electus Backus (d. 1862) was born in New York. He graduated from the U.S. Military Academy in 1824 and was thrice commandant at Fort Snelling during the period 1843 through 1845.

[13] The Sioux of the plains had many times more horses than the Sioux near Snelling. Thus horses were less expensive to buy toward the west, and whisky was at this time a medium of exchange.

while. The commanding officer told them if they did not stop running whisky by there in the night, he would put a boat there and a party of men with orders to fire on all that were passing after night. This stopped the business for a while, but the next winter they commenced again. Captain Backus had been ordered away and Captain Eastman[14] was in command.

Captain Eastman was always ready, and whenever I would notify him of any whisky having been smuggled past, he would always have a sleigh and team, a party of men, and an officer, and we would go in pursuit. But the Indians had got too smart for us, and frequently when we would overtake them they would have it hid before we could get to them.

Some nights I have traveled nearly all night to catch an Indian with a keg of whisky, so determined we were to break up the traffic. And I may say that Capt. Backus and Major Eastman did more for the benefit of the Sioux, so far as stopping liquor from going into the Indian country [is concerned], than any other two officers that commanded Fort Snelling.

[*The evil effects of whiskey-traders is immense.* . . . *The Indians complain bitterly of the white people settling down on the lines with large quantities of whiskey. They say they believe it is done on purpose to ruin them, and they have often in council called the attention of the President to this fact, and hoped their great father would take pity on them, and stop the white people from bringing the spirit-water so near their settlements. Some of these whiskey-shops are within a half mile of Indian Camps; in fact, all they have to do is to cross the Mississippi, and they can get it by barrels full.*

The existing laws have very little practical effect on the Indians or the white people. . . . *The late law respecting the whiskey-trade the Indians say is all humbug, and can avail nothing. The most contemptible of the whiskey-traders laugh at the law, and sell as much, if not more, than if there was no law on the subject; because there is no one to enforce it. The late law of making Indian testimony lawful in the Indian country, is also of no effect at all, because the Indians go to the ceded land for the whiskey. The whiskey traders are very careful about*

[14] Captain Seth Eastman (d. 1875) was commandant at Fort Snelling four times between 1841 and 1848. Born in Maine, he graduated from the U.S. Military Academy in 1829, and was breveted brigadier general in 1866. He is, however, perhaps best known as an artist.

*crossing the Mississippi with whiskey; when they do so, it is at a time
when no person can see them. In fact, it is almost impossible to get any
testimony against them, under the now existing laws. The Indians came
and reported the white people for selling whiskey to Indians on the
ceded lands, and they were told that their testimony was good only
in their own country. They laughed, and said such laws were of no
use.*

*Keep up the intercourse law, or else forbid the Indians from passing
over into the ceded country, and be sure to punish any of them who pass
over the boundary.*

*There is but a small quantity of alcoholic drink carried into the Indian
country by white men. It is done mostly by the Indians themselves.
Some of the Indians travel as many as four hundred miles, and come
into the ceded territory where the whiskey-traders are, and get whole
barrels of whiskey, and carry it off to the Sisseton country.*][15]

One Sunday morning some Indians were returning home from the
agency, going upon a gallop. All at once a shot from behind them
brought them down—the rider and horse. Each received a buck shot
in the head. The second shot missed and the second Indian and
horse got clear. The Chippewas ran up and took the scalp [of the
fallen Indian] and ran off. The Indian that escaped stood and looked
on, having no gun, until the Chippewas went off, when he came back
and reported [the affair], and in about an hour a hundred Indians had
assembled. Some went in pursuit, [but] returned and said they could
not find anything, for the Chippewas had made tracks fast with
their scalp.

They brought in the dead body and laid it down at my door, and
here all the Indians, the commanding officer, and we had a long and
tedious council. The Indians wanted to know if he was a-going to
allow the Chippewas to come and kill the Sioux in sight of his fort,
and spill their blood and they could get no satisfaction.

The commanding officer, Capt. Backus, asked them if they had
forgot how many Chippewa women and children they had murdered
a few summers before. He told them the Chippewas could not forget

15 In 1847 Prescott answered a questionnaire drawn up by the Indian Bureau
in which he gave his opinion of the liquor trade. His answers have been incorporated above, in the italicized passage. (Henry R. Schoolcraft, *Information
Respecting the History, Condition and Prospects of the Indian Tribes of the United
States* [Philadelphia: Lippincott, Grambo, 1851–1857], II, 188–190, 192.)

such a butchery in a short time and were now and then getting a small part of satisfaction.

The Sioux got mad and clamorous for blood, and said it was their [the Chippewas'] own fault. The Chippewas would come down in large parties and make peace with the Sioux, and when they were unsuspecting the Chippewas would, some few of them, leave the main body and waylay a Sioux and kill him and run off, as [they said] was the case when so many of the Chippewas were killed, and if they [the Sioux] could have had the chance they would have done the same thing.

"They kill all they can, and so do we kill all we can as opportunity offers. But this thing of allowing them to come right under the guns of your fort and spilling our blood, you ought to be ashamed of it!"

Captain Backus told them they had done the same thing, reminding them of the time they had fired upon a camp of Chippewas camped on the flat below the fort. "Yes," said the Sioux, "and we paid pretty dearly for it. Three of our young men were taken up and shot by the Chippewas, by order of Col. Snelling, and none of them [the Chippewas had] died." The commanding officer said, "If none of them died, you tried to kill all you could by firing into the whole camp!"

This made the Sioux mad, for they began to see that the commanding officer was not a-going to help them in the matter. The relations [of the dead man] were all around, bawling and crying and making the most awful lamentations, and cutting themselves at a terrible rate.

They [the Sioux] hung on and told the commanding officer that a camp of Chippewas was encamped below the falls, the same ones that had got three of their young men shot a few years before. The chief [was] Hole-in-the-Day, they said, [and the Sioux] would go and kill the whole of them [the Chippewas] if the commanding officer did not do something about the affair. The commanding officer told them if they went up there he would take his cannon and go up to their village and batter everything down, and kill everything that came in his way.

This cooled them down a little and they began to talk a little more reasonable. The commanding officer told them if they would take their dead man and go off home quiet and peaceable, that he would send for Hole-in-the-Day and have them all to meet at the fort the next morning; and if there were any of his [Hole-in-the-Day's] party that had been in the party that killed the Sioux, that he would take them and keep them in prison and let their Great Father, the President, decide how the matter should be settled.

So they went off, and the next morning they were all there betimes. The Chippewas had come down the evening before and camped near the fort for fear of some treacherous move on the part of the Sioux. They [the soldiers] were all paraded in front of the fort so as to be handy, if the Sioux did pounce on the Chippewas, to give them a shot from the fort.

The commanding officer asked the Chippewas if any of them had been with the party that killed the Sioux the day before. They replied that they knew nothing about it and that it must have been some strange Indians from the upper country. The [Sioux] said they lied, and pointed out two or three that they suspected of the murder, and told Hole-in-the-Day that if he did not leave two hostages with the captain until the real murderers could be found, that they would make war upon him, for they knew, they said, that he must have knowledge of what had taken place.

So Hole-in-the-Day told them, to satisfy them, that he had nothing to do with the affair, [that] he would leave two young men. The commanding officer was glad to get rid of them and their trouble. It so happened that Hole-in-the-Day, in selecting the two young men to remain as hostages, left one that was a relative of the actual murderer. But it was found out that it was two Pillagers from Leech Lake that had done the mischief, unbeknown to anybody, and ran off safe. A demand was made for them, but they put off for the Red River of the North to the British possessions, and there remained. The two hostages were kept in Fort Snelling about two years and a half, and when they were let out they both had the consumption and died shortly after.

So ended that murdering scrape, but still the Sioux were not satisfied, because they could not wash their own hands in their enemies' blood. The first chance they got [they] killed some more Chippewas. The commanding officer and the Indian agent, Col. A. J. Bruce, called a grand council of peace of both Sioux and Chippewas. They assembled at the appointed time and each party had loud and large complaints to make. Both parties demanded damages for murder and for breaking a peace that had been made some years before [1843], in which treaty* it was stipulated there should be perpetual peace kept between the two tribes or nations, and in case of murder by either party, the murderers were to be given up and be dealt with as the President of the United States should direct; but in case the murderer should flee to some unknown country, where [he] could not be apprehended, then the tribe or nation to which he belonged were to pay a sum in goods or money, as the parties could agree upon, and the agents [were] to assist in the arrangements of their difficulties.

In this great council the Indians could do nothing themselves, and each party chose some of their friends [among] the whites to decide for them. So there were three [whites] for the Sioux and three for the Chippewas.* The whites went off by themselves and came back and reported that they could not agree upon anything that would be acceptable to either party. Finally, their troubles were partially settled by leaving it to the President to settle for them; but the President took no notice of the affair for a long time.

[Meanwhile] they got to killing on both sides again. The Sioux commenced [it]. The agent told them they must pay the Chippewas something to stop the Chippewas from coming to war on them, and probably causing the Sioux to lose a good many of their people because of the misdeed of one man. After much talk and twisting about, the Sioux agreed to give one half of the annuity goods of the band that committed the murder, which amounted to about one thousand dollars from Little Six's band.

The powder and lead had arrived and that was turned over to the Chippewas, but the [annuity] goods were not all arrived and that part was left [to be turned over]. All happened very well, for the Chippewas came to make war and killed one Sioux and ran off, and this settled the matter again. The goods were returned to the Sioux, and this was the last of the treaty of peace. They have from that time to this kept up their killing whenever they could get a chance.

The country was now filling up very fast and all the good locations were taken up. The whites were encroaching upon the Indian lands and marking and taking up claims, which gave a great deal of trouble to the government; and the Indians killed some whites and frequently killed cattle. To get the difficulties settled, the government thought best to make a treaty and purchase all the lands* and put them upon a reservation. [This] would put an end to Indian hostilities amongst the Sioux.

The treaty was made by Governor [Alexander] Ramsey and Mr. Luke Lea, commissioner of Indian affairs, commissioners to make the treaties. In the summer of 1851 all things were got in readiness and the commissioners proceeded to Traverse des Sioux to make a treaty, with the Sissetons first. Here the commissioners labored a month before they could get the Sioux to sign a treaty. The Sioux stuck out for more money and more goods. The commissioners had made two or three alterations in the treaty for them and had come to a standstill point. Finally, after much patience and waiting, the Sisseton and Wahpeton Sioux signed the treaty at Traverse des Sioux [July 23, 1851].

The commissioners then proceeded to Mendota to make a treaty with the lower Sioux, or Mdewakanton and Wahpekute Sioux. The commissioners labored there about a month and finally succeeded in making another treaty.[16] These two treaties took from the Mdewakanton, Wahpekute, and Sisseton Sioux the last prop under their feet, except their reservation, and all they had left to depend upon is their annuities for fifty years, when their annuities are to end, except a perpetual annuity of $5,000 per annum for life only remains for the lower Sioux.

In making this treaty there was a great deal of private interest brought to bear upon the Indians and commissioners. The Wahpekutes were brought in by the traders for a large share of the annuities, although they were not a large band. The other bands opposed this move, and very justly, too, I think. Private interest worked its point, and the Wahpekute were to pay their traders $100,000, of which Mr. Alex Faribault got $50,000, if I recollect right, and Mr. Sibley about $25,000, and the balance was divided in small sums to smaller demands. A large amount had been set apart for the removal of these Indians to their reservations: $100,000 for the Mdewakantons, $20,000 for the Wahpekutes. It was a long and tedious piece of work for the commissioners to get all things to suit the traders and Indians.

The treaty was sent on to Washington to be ratified by the Senate. This body thought the best way to make the Indians more obedient and dependent upon the government was to take all their lands from them, and let them have the use of the reservation for a term of

16 In actuality, the treaty was signed on Pilot Knob, Mendota, on August 5, 1851, thirteen days after the earlier treaty.

years. [The Senate] sent the treaty back and stated that the Sioux must relinquish their right to the reservations also, and then the government would ratify their treaty, provided they signed the amendment at their own expense and the same rates of the lands [prevailed as stated] in the first treaty.*

The Indians opposed this at the start and said at once, "Are we not to have a place for the sole of a foot? What can our Great Father mean?" [They said] that the President and Senate wanted actually to run them off out of the country and starve them to death and [they] said right up and down they would not sign the treaty. Again the Governor called them together on a certain day. Before that day a number of chiefs and braves came over to the agency and talked with Major McLean,[17] the agent, and asked his advice in the case.

The agent told them he had nothing to say on the subject. The Indians told him the traders and the government wanted to ruin them and starve them to death. The agent told them to do as they pleased as the land was theirs; they were the best judges how to act in the case. They went away dissatisfied, saying they had no friends.

In the evening some of them came back again and asked me privately what I thought of their case. I told them I could say nothing only what the agent told me to say, or the Governor and the Indians, and I was bound by oath to repeat what they said and [what] the government officers [said] and nothing more. They hung their heads and said half the time they could not get any person to repeat exactly what they said, and advantages were taken of them in their councils.

I had not interpreted much at the councils for the treaty. The Indians thought that their claims had not been fairly stated or they would have been better dealt [with] by the commissioners. They asked me if I would interpret exactly what they wanted to say to the Governor in regard to signing the Senate's amendment to their

[17] Major Nathaniel McLean (1787–1871), Sioux agent at Fort Snelling from 1849 through 1853. He was said to have had the interests of the Sioux at heart and to have opposed the "traders' paper." (William W. Folwell, *A History of Minnesota* [St. Paul: Minnesota Historical Society, 1921–1930], I, 283–284, 289.)

The "traders' paper" set forth the alleged indebtedness of the Indians for unpaid credits they had received in past years. By signing the "paper" the Indian chiefs acknowledged the indebtedness. Many later claimed that they were not fully informed of what they had signed.

treaty. I told them I was bound to tell the Governor all they said, and all the Indians said, "Now, can we depend upon you?" "Yes," I said. "Well," they said, "we will not sign the treaty and we want you to say so for us," and they went on with a long string of excuses for not signing.

I told them there was no use of bringing in all those long stories, but if they were determined not to sign, just to say so and be done with it in as few words as possible, for they had been quite saucy about it and said it was some device to ruin them. I told them it would do no good, but make the business look worse, if they were turbulent and saucy about it. They finally agreed to say nothing, only to say that they had concluded to not sign the treaty, and [they] went off home.

So the next day was the time [for the meeting with the Governor] and quite a number of the Indians came in and some of the traders, for the traders were anxious to see how the thing would turn [out], as there were some $400,000 or $500,000 to be paid out to traders, half-breeds, and so on.

The Governor told them that their Great Father and council had seen fit to alter their treaty a little, and [he] wanted the Sioux, his red children, to let him, the President, and council have all their lands without any reserve, only that the President would permit them to cultivate the lands within the boundaries of the reserve for a time of years. The Indians asked how long they could use the land. The Governor told them the President had not determined how long they should occupy the land, but thought as long as they wanted to use it but he was [not] certain on that point.

Old Bad Hail, their orator, got up and said, "Father, we fear that our Great Father at Washington wishes to drive us to some country to starve us to death, and we cannot sign the treaty as our Great Father wishes." Another got up and said the same, and so it went round the circle, and all the chiefs said the same thing and sat down. The Governor said he was sorry that [they] could not agree to do as their Great Father wished them [to do], and said he thought their Great Father wanted to do the best for his red children, and [he] knew that their Great Father did not wish to take advantage of them. The Indians said but little and got up and walked off.

Here was now a great hubbub! The treaty broken up! No room for immigration! No money for the traders (the worst part of the business) and none for the half-breeds! A large sum was to be paid according to these treaties. The traders all got together and had a council to see what was to be done. "We are all ruined," they said, "if these treaties are not signed!"

After they had refused to sign for Governor Ramsey, Good Road, an old, treacherous, lying fellow, went over to Mr. Sibley's one day and told them that I was leagued with the Indians to defeat the treaty, and that the Indians were generally displeased with the traders for charging them so much on their old accounts. In the two treaties about $375,000 was to go to the traders alone.

The Indians told me the Governor was very much displeased because he did not succeed in getting the treaty re-signed, and said if he knew for certain that I had advised the Indians to not sign the treaty he would remove me from office. But I never heard anything more about the matter until Mr. H. M. Rice[18] sent for me one day.

I went to St. Paul and saw Mr. Rice. He informed me that he was employed to try to get the Sioux to sign the treaty, and he wanted me for an interpreter and said he had got the agent's consent to my being absent from the agency during the time required to get the Indians together and council, etc. So I agreed to undertake the task, although [it was] a very tedious and unpleasant one.

Mr. Rice told me there would not a trader come near nor interfere in the business at all, for they [had] found that the Indians were [at] outs with the traders, and they could do nothing with them; therefore they had to get disinterested persons to work for them, so the Indians would not see through the operations.

And now, how was this great work to be performed? The government were not to pay any part of the expense, so the following plan was adopted: to pay the expense of assembling the Indians, and presents, and runners, physicians, etc., [the money was] to be taken out of the removal fund. An appropriation of something over $200,000[19] had been reserved for the removal of the Indians, [the sum] to be taken out of their own monies.

[18] Henry Mower Rice (1816–1894) arrived at Fort Snelling in 1839 and was for many years an agent of the Chouteau Fur Company. He was later a territorial delegate to Congress and a senator from Minnesota. He aided in negotiating several Indian treaties. ("Henry Mower Rice," *Minnesota Historical Collections*, IX [1898–1900], 654–658; "Minnesota Biographies," *Minnesota Historical Collections*, XIV [1912], 638.)

[19] The exact amount was $275,000.

Mr. Rice and myself went to work sending for the Indians all over the country, a few of the principal men, and a chief or head man of the different bands. In five or six days they began to come in and we commenced feeding them. We fed them like gluttons, and I assure you the way they used up the beef and melons was wonderful! But some had moved to their fall hunts and it was a long time before we got them all together.

Mr. Rice commenced giving them presents. Some he gave horses, some saddles. Burning Earth [20] got a silver mounted Spanish saddle worth 30 or 40 dollars. Some got fine coats. After feeding and waiting upon them for 15 days we got them all together, and the great question was put [to] them by Mr. Rice about signing the amendment to the treaty, with all the explanations as to the results and the cause of the Senate's wishing to claim the whole country.

The Indians went off by themselves and they talked the matter over for three days and still had not come to anything definite. One chief was wanting; Wabasha had not arrived. He arrived at the last hour and he had to hear [the matter] all over again, which kept us another day and a night. Finally, I went to Wabasha alone by himself. He told me he meant to sign the treaty but did not care about hurrying the matter, as he wanted to understand all about the result. By so doing he kept us to the last moment, and even when they went out to have their last council Wabasha would not give his views to the Indians in general until I went out where they were and told him we had been [here] some twenty days, and we were tired of dragging along when they could make up their minds in a few minutes if they chose.

The Indians all said that they had made up their minds to follow Wabasha, and "Which way he goes, we follow." Finally, Wabasha came out and said that the Indians had accused him of doing everything by himself, but now [that] he had their assent to do as he pleased he should sign the treaty. That was all that was wanted, and off we all started for Governor Ramsey's office to sign the treaty.

When we got up there we had another long parley. The lower Sioux demanded that they should have a new or a change of blacksmiths; this was agreed to. Then they asked for their reservation to be made on Lake Hokah Mump, the head of one of the tributaries

[20] Burning Earth was probably Who Sets the Earth on Fire, a Mdewakanton Sioux of Wabasha's village.

188   PHILANDER PRESCOTT

of the Blue Earth River. The Governor studied some time to get an answer to this request. Finally, [he] said he would write to their Great Father at Washington and tell him their request, and in the meantime he wanted them to sign this paper as he had some medals to distribute.

Well, then the upper Sioux demanded $5,000 in money to sign. The Governor told them their Great Father had given a great deal of money and he thought that if he asked for more they would not get it, and they better not ask for any. So, after pulling back and forth until late in the afternoon, they commenced signing, Wabasha first, I believe.[21]

After all was done then came the medals. This made quite a competition and a good many went away dissatisfied. I think we were all truly happy to bring the business to a close, for we had labored night and day for about 20 days. I never worked more assiduously than in this case. I was determined that if there was any possibility of getting them to sign I would do it, for this reason: they had circulated a lie about me in relation to my being a party to breaking up the first council, or their not signing the treaty when the Governor first proposed it to them.

When the Sioux found out how the thing had been managed, they were terrible wrathy at me and Mr. Rice; and the [fact that the] whole expense had been paid out of their funds made them feel still more hostile than ever, the whole expense being about $25,000 to $30,000 out of their removal fund. I got for my services a kind of a suit of clothes from Mr. Rice. Mr. Rice was to have $10,000, but from whom I do not know, but I think Mr. Dousman had a hand in the matter; and I think Mr. Rice got no money but a turn on some old account that Mr. Rice thought he ought not to pay. And I think probably Mr. Dousman made Mr. Rice pay for some of the horses.*

So that Mr. Rice had all our work for nothing, in a manner, and the traders reaped all the benefits, for they got all the money, except what Mr. Tyler[22] got for assisting the business along in Washington;

[21] On September 4, 1852, forty-five chiefs and headmen signed at St. Paul, on behalf of the lower bands, the formula of assent. Four days later twenty-seven chiefs and headmen of the upper bands took the same action at St. Paul. (Folwell, *A History of Minnesota*, I, 294.)

[22] Hugh Tyler of Pennsylvania was a professional negotiator of Indian treaties —for a consideration. (*Minnesotian*, July 10, 1852.)

fifteen per cent was his demand, and he got it, which amounted to some $50,000 for him and his party.

After the treaty business was all over, Mr. Rice and myself were both taken sick. Mr. Rice had a pulmonary complaint and came near dying; I had typhoid fever and I was very low for a time. The Indians said it was a judgment upon us, and some of them wished we would die. Good Road,[23] in particular, said he wished I would die. He was taken sick a short time after, and died himself in a few days. The news came one day that Mr. Rice was dead. An Indian whoop of joy went up from the mouths and hearts of some people that lived not far from me, but the alarm, happily, was a false one.

We both lived and are still working for the good of mankind. And the immigrants found a place to settle down on the finest country in the West; whereas, with one word, the treaty could have all been blowed to the winds, and the traders would have got no money, nor the people any lands on the west side of the Mississippi to settle upon.

In the fall, in September following [1852], I had been down with Major McLean to Wabasha at the lower end of the lake [Pepin] to pay off Wabasha's band. It rained and thundered most of the time we were there, and the lightning one night struck an Indian lodge and killed a man and wife; a child was at the breast but was not hurt. The fluid [lightning] apparently had went into their mouths. The electricity went along the ground to another lodge and wounded 6 or 7 more, and then run along to another lodge and wounded some more. So, in all, there were thirteen wounded and killed by one flash of electricity. Wabasha would hardly speak to me; he was still displeased about the signing of the treaty the fall before.

As I have not much to add to my narrative until the Indians commenced to move [1853] to their new homes,* I shall write something about their history and events and their probable destiny, so far as forty years of experience amongst them will permit, having only their tradition for proof, which does not extend far back.

[23] Good Road was an important Mdewakanton chief whose village was located eight miles from Fort Snelling on the south side of the Minnesota River. He had signed the treaties of 1837 and 1851.

SUPPLEMENT

On Board Prescott's Mackinaw Boat (page 165)

With the month of September came the time of our departure for Lac-qui Parle. . . . Then we had our household goods packed up and put on board Mr. Prescott's Mackinaw boat, to be carried up to Traverse des Sioux. Mr. Prescott was a white man with a Dakota wife, and had been for years engaged in the fur trade. He had on board his winter outfit. Mary and I took passage with him and his family, and spent a week of new life on what was then called the Saint Peter's River. The days were very enjoyable, and the nights were quite comfortable, for we had the advantages of Mr. Prescott's tent and conveniences for camp life. His propelling force was the muscles of five Frenchmen, who worked the oars and the poles, sometimes paddling and sometimes pushing, and often, in the upper part of the voyage, wading to find the best channel over a sand-bar. But they enjoyed their work, and sang songs by the way.

(Stephen Return Riggs, *Mary and I: Forty Years With the Sioux*, introd. by S. C. Bartlett [Boston: Congregational Sunday-School and Publishing Company, 1888], 46–47.)

On September 2, 1837, Mrs. Mary Riggs wrote:

We have just breakfasted on board our Mackinaw, and so far on our way have had cause for thankfulness that God so overruled events, even though some attendant circumstances were unpleasant. It is also a great comfort that we have so good accommodations and Sabbath-keeping company. You recollect my mentioning the marriage of Mr. and Mrs. Prescott, and of his uniting with the church at Lake Harriet, in the summer.

Perhaps you may feel some curiosity respecting our appearance and that of our barge. Fancy a large boat of forty feet in length, and perhaps eight in width in the middle, capable of carrying five tons, and manned by five men, four at the oars and a steersman at the stern. Near the centre are our sleeping accommodations nicely rolled up, on which we sit, and breakfast and dine on bread, cold ham, wild fowl, etc. We have tea and coffee for breakfast and supper. Mrs. Prescott does not pitch and strike the tent, as the Indian women usually do; but it is because the boatmen can do it, and her husband does not require as much of her as an Indian man. They accommodate us in their tent, which is similar to a soldier's tent, just large enough for two beds. Here we take our supper, sitting on or by the matting made by some of these western Indians, and then, after worship, lie down to rest. [*Ibid.,* pp. 47–48.]

The Mission School at Lake Harriet (page 166)

The two Pond brothers arrived in Minnesota on May 6, 1834 and spent that fall and the following winter in their rude log cabin on Lake Calhoun. On May 30, 1835, the Reverend Jedediah D. Stevens, his wife, and a niece arrived and the Ponds helped them to establish a mission and school at Lake Harriet, just south of Lake Calhoun, where they all resided for a time. In the spring of 1836, Gideon Pond left to join the mission at Lac qui Parle, up the Minnesota River. Soon thereafter Samuel Pond returned to his native Connecticut to study theology. On March 4, 1837, he was ordained a Congregational minister and again went west to Lake Harriet, where he kept his residence in 1838 and 1839, though absent for considerable periods. "In July 1839, Stevens was appointed farmer to Wabasha's band . . . and resigned from the Lake Harriet mission, of which Samuel Pond then took charge." (William W. Folwell, *A History of Minnesota* [St. Paul: Minnesota Historical Society, 1921–1930], I, 184–195.)

The Sioux Delegation to Washington (page 166)

Little Crow, Redwing, Wapasha, and Etuzepah were among the delegates, who numbered thirty-five in all. They made a prosperous trip and Secretary of War Poinsett introduced them to the President. General Sibley, Alexis Bailly, Joseph La Framboise, Francois La Bathe, the Farebaults [Faribaults] and others were on hand to protect the interests of the traders. The treaty finally agreed upon was signed in Dr. Laurie's church at Washington on September 29, 1837, and was reasonably satisfactory to all parties concerned.

(Doane Robinson, "A History of the Sioux Indians," *South Dakota Historical Collections*, II, [1904], 182.)

Cession of Indian Lands (page 166)

By the year 1837 many conditions called for the cession of these lands. The forest, the water power, the mines of lead and other ores aroused the desires of speculators. Settlers were thronging to Wisconsin, and it was felt that if the land could be purchased and the Indians removed, the people would be safe from any attacks, and the Indians would be removed from the contaminating influence of many of the undesirable whites. There were also the traders who for years past had given credit to many worthless Indians who had never brought back from the hunt furs sufficient to pay for the goods advanced them; and they hoped that in the payment for the lands certain sums would be reserved for the liquidation of these debts.

(Marcus L. Hansen, *Old Fort Snelling, 1819–1858* [Iowa City: Iowa State Historical Society, 1918], 178–179.)

Samuel Pond Tends Store for Prescott (page 167)

Pond's narrative indicates that he was at Prescott's post from about February 1 to April 10, 1838. He wrote that he had been with an Indian party late in 1837, and continued:

I returned to the Lake in January, but soon received a letter from Mr. Prescott who was sick at Traverse des Sioux with no one to take care of him, so I went up about the first of February. Taking care of Mr. Prescott a while, and then of his store while he was brought down to the Fort. There I found myself among the most degraded Indians I had seen, and Mr. Prescott left a Canadian with me who was more disagreeable than the savages so that I was glad to call occasionally on M. Le Blanc whose manners were always exceedingly polite, and his conversation always amusing.

About the middle of April, I left The Traverse on foot with Eagle Head a chief and his son . . . to go to Lac Qui Parle. [Pond, "Two Missionaries in the Sioux Country," pp. 161–162.]

Pillager Chippewas (page 167)

The Pillager Chippewas were those living at Leech Lake. They received the name, it is related, from the circumstance that soon after the conquest of Canada they robbed a certain trader named Berti of the arms and ammunition which he was planning to sell to their greatest enemies, the Sioux. ("A Description of Northern Minnesota by a Fur-Trader in 1807," ed. Grace Lee Nute, *Minnesota History Bulletin*, Vol. V, No. 1 [February 1923], 39 n.)

Taylor's Falls (page 168)

Baker "probably lived at Fort Snelling but made occasional trips up to Taylor's Falls, at the head of the Dalles on the St. Croix

River. The village is said to have been named for Jesse Taylor, who came in 1838, and Joshua L. Taylor, to whom the former sold his claim in 1846." ("Minnesota Geographic Names," *Minnesota Historical Collections*, XVII [1920], 110.)

Prescott's Lawsuit (page 169)

The first jury trial ever held in the valley was at Marine in 1840, with Joseph R. Brown as justice, Philander Prescott, plaintiff, and C. D. Foote, defendant. The accusation was for jumping a land claim at Prescott. During the trial the court adjourned to allow the jury to visit the claim and obtain the facts in the case. The jury failed to agree, but the case was compromised by Prescott's allowing Foote eighty acres of the claim. (William H. C. Folsom, "History of Lumbering in the St. Croix Valley, with Biographic Sketches," *Minnesota Historical Collections*, IX [1898–1900], 298–299.)

Gray Cloud Island (page 169)

Gray Cloud Island was named for Gray Cloud, the Indian half-blood wife of Hazen P. Mooers. It was in the Mississippi River above Hastings, about twenty miles from Fort Snelling. Brown, who is said to have raised the first wheat in Minnesota on the island in 1831, and Mooers were associated at the island in trading and farming in 1838 and 1839. ("Minnesota Geographic Names," p. 552.)

Settlers on Land Under Military Jurisdiction (page 169)

"Until 1837, when the treaties were made, there were no lands in Minnesota open to settlement. Nevertheless, several hundred whites had illegally settled on land in the Fort Snelling area. Some of these were Swiss from the Selkirk colony, others were an odd collection of white and half-breed employees and mere hangers-on. . . . On July 26, 1838, the white settlers within the area reserved were told that they were residing on land under military jurisdiction and they were forbidden to cut any more timber or erect buildings or other improvements." (Folwell, *A History of Minnesota*, I, 219.)

In October, 1839, according to Neill (*The History of Minnesota from the Earliest French Explorations to the Present Time* [4th ed.; Minneapolis: Minn. Hist. Co., 1882]):

The impudent conduct of the whiskey sellers between the Fort and the site of the present city of St. Paul, was made known to the

War Department, but that very month Mr. Poinsett, then Secretary
... directed the U.S. Marshal of Wisconsin to remove all intruders
on the land recently reserved for military purposes opposite to
the post, on the east side of the river; and should they delay
beyond a reasonable time, he was authorized to call upon the
commander of the post for aid. All winter was given to the
squatters to prepare, and the next spring there being a disposition
to further procrastinate, on the 6th of May, 1840, the troops were
called out, and the cabins destroyed to prevent reoccupation.

The squatters then retreated to the nearest point below the
military reserve, and there they became the inglorious founders of a
hamlet . . . St. Paul . . . capital of Minnesota, which has emerged
from the groggeries of "certain lewd fellows of the baser sort."

The Murder of Neka (page 171)

In 1873 Gideon H. Pond described the Sioux' reaction to Neka's
murder:

The village was a cluster of summer huts, constructed of small
poles and barks of trees, the summer home of four or five hundred
savage souls, surrounded by their gardens of corn and squashes.
It was an Indian village. The five hundred had swarmed out into
and around the shores of the lakes. Men, women, and children
were all engaged in hunting, chopping, fishing, swimming,
playing, singing, yelling, whooping, and wailing. The air was full
of all sorts of savage sounds, frightful to one unaccustomed to
them. . . .

Suddenly, like a peal of thunder when no cloud is visible, here,
there, everywhere, awoke the startling alarm whoop, "Hoo, hoo,
hoo!" Blankets were thrown in the air, men, women and children
ran—they ran for life. Terror sat on every face—mothers grasped
their little ones. All around was crying, wailing, shrieking, storming,
and scolding. Men vowed vengeance, whooped defiance, and
dropped bullets into their gun-barrels. The excitement was
intense and universal. "The Chippewas! The Chippewas have
surrounded us—we shall all be butchered!" [John H. Stevens,
*Personal Recollections of Minnesota and Its People and Early
History of Minneapolis*, pp. 398–399.]

Two Swiss Missionaries Among Sioux (page 173)

The two Swiss missionaries were the Reverend Daniel Gavin and the
Reverend Samuel Dentan. In 1834 the Société des missions de
Lausanne sent these two young men to work among the Sioux, one

locating at Red Wing's village, and the other at Trempeleau. Later they were united at Red Wing's village, on the west side of Lake Pepin. In the course of time the mission there was abandoned for one at St. Peter's, and that in turn, for one on the St. Croix River. (*Minnesota History*, XXI, 27, 159–160, 165, 167; *Minnesota Historical Collections*, III, 117; VI, 134–135.)

Treaty of 1843 (page 181)

On August 2, 1843, a great gathering of the two nations was held at the fort, where a treaty of peace was drawn up under the auspices of the civil and military authorities. During the first year it was kept inviolate, except for two or three individual cases of outrage. (Hansen, *Old Fort Snelling*, p. 131.)

Conferees Ask Governor to Enforce Treaty (page 182)

While both Neill and Prescott give the number of conferees as six, Folwell says: " Upon the suggestion of Governor Ramsey four white men were appointed, with the acquiescence of the Indians to ascertain what new agreement, if any, could be made. At an adjourned council late in the day the conferees reported that the parties cared for no new stipulations but were disposed to leave it to the governor to enforce the existing treaty according to his discretion. On the following morning the proceedings were concluded with a love feast by the hostile chiefs, much to the pleasure of the governor, who gave each party an ox." (Folwell, *A History of Minnesota*, I, 259.)

Indian Lands Ceded Under the Treaties of 1851 (page 182)

The instructions to the commissioners suggested that they try to obtain what they actually were later able to secure, namely the tract of land lying between the Mississippi River and the Big Sioux River in what is now eastern South Dakota. The northern boundary was the Sioux-Chippewa line of 1825, which Prescott had helped to survey in 1835, and the southern boundary was to include all land in northern Iowa still claimed by the Sioux. (Folwell, *A History of Minnesota*, I, 272.)

Ratification of the Treaties of 1851 (page 184)

The ratification of the 1851 treaties was finally obtained on June 23, 1852. Several amendments had been added. "One cut the half-breed provision out of the treaty of Mendota; the others cancelled the two reservations on the Minnesota River, authorized the President to select for the Sioux suitable homes outside the ceded territory, and gave him large discretion in making such selection. The reservation lands were to be taken over by the government at ten cents per acre and the value was to be added to the trust funds. An addition of eight thousand dollars, it was estimated, would thus be made to the cash annuities." (Folwell, *A History of Minnesota*, I, 290–291.)

The awful massacre in August, 1862, led to the passage of an act February 16, 1863, whereby all the rights and claims of the Sioux under these treaties, not consummated, were abrogated and annulled, the reservations decreed to be sold, and the Sioux themselves to be deported forever beyond the confines of their ancient home. (Thomas Hughes, "The Treaty of Traverse des Sioux in 1851," *Minnesota Historical Collections*, Vol. X, Pt. 1 [1905], 116.)

Dousman's Contract with Rice (page 188)

Folwell notes that Hercules L. Dousman, "when testifying as a witness before the investigating commission, refused to answer a direct question regarding the contract with Rice. When it came to payment, Dousman brought out a note for five thousand dollars, then past due, which Rice had made as his subscription to the building of the steam-boat *Nominee*." (*A History of Minnesota*, I, 283 n.)

Mdewakantons Moved to Redwood Agency (page 189)

It was not till September, 1853, that the Mdewakanton could be collected at Little Crow's village, whence they moved on leisurely, some in canoes and some on foot to the Redwood Agency located by the agent near Fort Ridgely. The Wahpekute were equally tardy. . . . The bands of the upper Sioux on Lac qui Parle, Big Stone Lake, and Lake Traverse were already on or near their reserve. The bands which had lived about the Traverse des Sioux and Little Rapids, now Carver, moved reluctantly to their designated places on the lower margin of the upper reservation. . . . By the close of the year 1853 the 'Suland' was nearly empty of Indians."

(Folwell, *A History of Minnesota*, I, 353–354.)

IX

Sioux Lore

As the first travelers in the country could not speak the language, they, of course, could get no history from the oldest Indians that probably [would] have given some insight into their native country, from whence they came, etc. But so far as I have been able to understand them, they seem to think they have lived here, near about the center of the earth, from time immemorial, but by what power of authority, they do not know or understand. They claim to have occupied the country far north and west of this [present] Sioux country, and that they have not relinquished or given up any territory, only as it became destitute of game and was not worth spilling their blood for.

As they have been at war with most all the surrounding nations, it is a wonder they have not become extinct, or been swallowed up by some other nation and lost their [identity]. The Assiniboines and Omahas are supposed to have been tribes of the Sioux, but by quarrels and family broils they separated and have been so long apart that their language has become so changed that they have to have interpreters now to understand each other. And frequently [they] make war upon each other in the Missouri country. Now the Sioux nation extends to the Rocky Mountains, and other nations are making way for them constantly and receding farther west; and was it not for the whites and treaties that secured to other nations from invasions upon their rights, the Sioux in a few years would have reached the Pacific in another century.

The general supposition is that they crossed the Strait from the northern part of Russia where the Esquimaux are now found and live, apparently contented, as they can roam all over those polar

197

regions. Why could the Sioux not do the same, and continue their march by degrees until they found game enough to subsist upon, where they made a stand and have fought many bloody battles. Their marks and traces of their war parties were visible at the Lake of the Woods and Rainy Lake when the British traders first went to that country.

I was told of a scene that took place somewhere not far from the Lake of the Woods, at a place called the Warpath (or *chemin de guerre*), where a party of Sioux had been to war. They had attacked and killed a whole family of Chippewas except one young woman that had, by her dexterity, got away from them. The young woman had the name of being a great runner and at the ball plays [lacrosse] always would win for the side she was chosen on.

The Sioux saw her making off and some of the swiftest men started in pursuit. She saw them coming but paid no attention to them. They thought they were a-going to have an easy prey. She let them come until they were within arrow shot, when she started off, beckoning to the Sioux to come on. They now in turn put down as hard as they could, the Chippewa girl all the time beckoning to them to come on. At last the Sioux burst out all a-laughing and stopped and gave the whoop [of] joy. They made signs to her to go and probably would not of touched her if she had come to them, as they are generous in such cases.

They speak of many bloody battles [near] Devils Lake or Minnewaukan, Spirit Lake; and speak of whole parties having been cut off except a man or two [able] to escape.

Although they are cruel and savage in war, still there are instances where they have been merciful and spared the life of a part, [or] of a few, of their prisoners. There are now some Chippewas amongst the Sioux that were taken prisoners when they were children; also some from the Missouri I found that had been taken prisoners, and had families and were as much Sioux at heart as their own people.

On the plains the Sioux have seen so much misery by starvation and snow storms that they have done some terrible deeds that have been handed down to posterity, deeds that are of the brute nature more than human. One [such deed] I have heard related frequently by old Indians [is] about a camp of Yanktons traveling in pursuit of buffalo, and necessity compelled them to travel faster than they had been traveling; but they had a number of old people with them that clogged their march and they could not overtake the buffalo. One family that had no horse said they could not pack an old man they had any longer, and they were going to leave him on the prairie to perish.

The [other] Indians disapproved of this way of getting rid of the old man and held a council [on] what to do with the old man. So they agreed that the old man should be set up as a mark to be shot at, or otherwise [they] called him a Chippewa, and he was to have a gun given him and [was] to be placed behind a little mound and was to defend himself the best he could. There was about twenty young-sters who were picked out, with bows and arrows and some had guns, and they were to attack the old man the same as an enemy.

This pleased the old man, for he said it was an awful thing to sit down in a large open prairie and linger along for a number of days, and [finally] die a most miserable death of starvation, or be torn to pieces alive by the wolves. "Yes," said the old man, "I had much rather die in the way you have appointed." So, accordingly, the old man was fixed up in the best position by his relatives for defense that they could place him [in], and the youngsters received the signal for attack.

They commenced their war whoops, and so did the old man. The youngsters every now and then would let go a volley of arrows, but [they] were too far off to do much, and kept advancing on the old man. The old man urged them on, too, to combat, shouting all the time. Whilst the youngsters every now and then some would run almost up to the old man and aim, then their hearts would fail them and the old man would bring his gun down to fire. The boys would jump away and run off, and come back to the charge again. At last an accidental shot brought the old man down. As he could not see well, the boys had all the advantage. The old man was taken and buried according to the Indian custom, and the party proceeded on their hunts.

Suicide is not of frequent occurrence, and when [it] does take place [it] is more frequent amongst the women than with the men. In 40 years I have heard of only two or three cases amongst the men, and about a dozen amongst the women. The women have much more cause for such acts than the men, and those that take place amongst the women are caused by forced marriages or abuse of their husbands.

I know of two cases where two young women hung themselves

within a few days of each other. An Indian had applied to the father for one of them and the father gave his consent, but when it came to the girl's ears she ran off. She was sent for and brought back and was asked her reasons for disobeying the wish of her father, who was a chief and a great man and would be made ashamed. The girl said [the young man] was an inferior person, that he could not talk he stuttered so much, and had had two or three wives already and that she had no love for him.

But the old chief said his words must be law and told his daughter that she must go and live with the man of his choice. She rose up silently and went out. After a while some inquiries was made about the girl, but no person had seen her. Some search was made and she was found hanging to a tree that was leaning over the river only a few rods from the house or lodge. A great lamentation was made and the old chief got a great reprimand from the mother for his interference in the marriage of her daughter. And a few days after, a cousin of the same girl hung herself for the same kind of offense. The Maiden Rock on the east bank of Lake Pepin was named for a tragedy of the same cause and polygamy. This kind of life would suit the Mormons.

Many people think the Indians live a happy life; the men do in comparison to the women. I have known instances where 2 or 3 sisters, or as many as 4, have lived something like a peaceable life [as wives of the same man]; but even if they were sisters I have known them to have their jars on account of jealousies.

Their customs are a law amongst themselves. As for having anything like laws of force, or officers to enforce any of their old customs, they have nothing regular. [In] any quarrel or dispute arising in a family where a man has 3 or 4 wives no one interferes unless some one of the relative females will volunteer to help or keep the parties separate, so they cannot injure each other severely. A man having three wives, the one that has the first son is looked upon as the legal heir; as for the girls, they are all respected alike, of or in the family.

The Mandans are supposed to be a branch of the Sioux, and the way they got separated was a quarrel about polygamy.

I have known the women to quarrel until they would drive the husband to desperation, and he would turn in and thrash them all, if he did not get worsted and get a flogging himself. I have known that to take place where the women would all turn in and whip the man, for many of them are very strong, owing to their constant labor, chopping, carrying wood and heavy burdens.

The [Aurora] Borealis is looked upon as a sign of war in some country, and the Indians say, when one appears when they are returning with scalps, [it] is a sign of the old woman's being pleased with them. The shooting up of the Borealis is a sign for them to dance. The Borealis is here called an old woman, the goddess of war, and when it appears the old people urge the young to dance and play. They say the old woman is looking down to see them dance.

Then they turn in and dance round the scalp with renewed energy, and songs of the victorious burst forth, and the woods and wilderness echo to a distance of four or five miles. I have heard them [that distance] in a calm evening. The words are few in their songs, but the chorus is never ending. The words they use are something similar to the following: "The spirits have given us a large fat scalp. The spirits took pity on our distress. We found him in a fine bark canoe. We found them in the midst of a scalp dance. My father's spirit has come back again."

Such are about the sentences that are used in the scalp dance. The men sing the words first; then the women rehearse the same words, and the whole assemblage, both men and women, join in a chorus to the words. For instance: "My father's spirit has come back again. Ah-ta-nag-hree-tah-wa-hen-dee. He-yo-ha-yah-ha-he-ya-ha-hah-ha-he-ya-ha-yah-ha," and a long string of nothing but a chorus something similar. Still they appear to have a tune to every set of words, and the words are seldom ever longer than the specimens as above, and some not so long even.

Their games at chance are singular, what few they have. It would be better if they had none at all, for like the white man in expectation to win more, [he] loses all. I have known Indians to sit down and play away everything he possessed of any value, even to his wife, which in this case there was no harm, only the character of immorals, for the Indian had two or three wives, and probably the woman was better provided for by getting a single man than to have to live with two or three in the same lodge, in want and misery half the lifetime.

Card playing was but little known when I first came amongst the Dakotas. Their games were games of their own adoption. [One was] the plum stone [game]; 5 or 7 plum stones are scraped clean and several devices burned on them; some represent buffalo, some turtles, some deer, and so on. The characters represent so much [for each kind], and they are put into a wooden bowl. The gamblers all gather round and sit down in a ring. They commence by taking the bowl and hoisting it about 4 or 6 inches from the ground, and let it down suddenly and pretty hard, so that the plum stones turn over, sometimes half a dozen times, and sometimes jump over the dish, and counts on the outside of the dish as well as the inside from 7 to 21 as the parties agree before commencing. Sometimes they make a game in one throw, sometimes in three, and quite a number of blanks.

I have known of horses, guns, large kettles, and traps [to be] bet by the men, who play by themselves most always, and the women by themselves. The women bet their earbobs, finger rings, and such like trinkets.

[In] the game called the mockasin game they have three mockasins. They all assemble in a lodge in the evening, from 5 to 20 of them, all men. Three mockasins are placed in the center and they choose sides [of] equal numbers. They have a little ball that they hide in one of the mockasins and one man is to find the ball. If he points to the ball the first time, he loses; but if he points to it or finds it the second time, he wins and is allowed to keep his place until he loses, when they change sides. It is something similar to thimble playing, only they are in parties and quite a number on a side.

Such a noise as they keep up all the time the man is hiding the ball, by singing and rattling sticks together! It is almost deafening to be in the lodge where they are. When one wins, what a shout [is heard]. But if the opposite party wins by the other's losing by guessing where the ball is the first time, then there comes a shout from the winning party. As long as one party guesses where the ball is after it is hid so long, they can hold the time of guessing.

They bet very high on this game for Indians, for they bet their all, sometimes horses, guns, traps, etc., all their means of living. They play all night and I have known them to keep it up for three days and their women were suffering for want of food.

Ball play [lacrosse] in the forepart of summer is another game that is played by large parties from fifty to one hundred on a side. This is a hard work game, for there is a great deal of hard running to be done in order to win and some medicine man is employed to make the ball, as it is supposed that the medicine man can do something by his witchcraft to make the ball win. [The ball] is about as large as a large hen egg, perfectly round, and stuffed with earth in it. It is quite heavy and when they throw it, it goes a long distance. I have seen it strike a man that stood about ten yards off, and the blow from the force of the ball almost killed him. The Indian was picked up for dead but came to in a little while, but did not get over it for some time.

This ball play is a hard game; they use all sorts of harsh means to get the ball from each other. I have seen them catch an Indian running with the ball by the hair and throw him two rods, and probably half a dozen others would fall over him whilst they would be pulling and hauling for the ball. I have seen them take their ball sticks and slip them between other players' legs when they were going like horses and pitch them [the players] headlong and three or four on top of them, and hurt each other very badly sometimes.

Upon the whole it is a game of hard work and subjects them to injury, for they get so excited when there is large bets that they do not look to see what they do. They rush ahead at the risk of life and limb to get the ball and throw it as far as they can. It's amazing to see how far they can throw the ball by their little sticks made of hickory, about two feet and a half long, with a round bow at one end. A small leather string passes three times across the bow, by there being as many holes burnt through the bow, and [it] is sometimes in the shape of a bird's nest.

They pick the ball up with this [bow end] and throw it, or run with it as long as they can, until some[one] overtakes them or runs before them and meets them. Then they throw [it] and then another takes it and runs or throws the ball, and keep it a-going until they get it over the [goal] line, which is about ¼ of a mile each way. When one party gets the ball over the line one way, they turn and go the other way next time, and if they or the party that gets it over two in three times, they win, or the best in three wins.

Indians are accused of cannibalism, but the Sioux have no such inclination. But they have eat human flesh, many of them, they say to make them brave. Therefore, when they kill an enemy they sometimes take out the heart and cut it into small pieces about as large as they can easily swallow, and the young warriors are compelled to swallow a piece of his enemy's heart. This, they say, makes them brave, and if they refuse to swallow a piece, he is called a coward. I [have] heard them say it went mightily against the will to get a piece down.

Their amusements are common and some of them are rather of a vulgar order. The fish dance or feast is a dirty practice, therefore is not often got up. If a man dreams about seeing fish in the night and has much other trouble in [his] dream, the dreamer must give a feast to the fish gods, or he must give a fish dance to appease the spirits of the fish to keep them from getting angry for his dream the night before.

If the man has nothing to make a good feast of, he makes a dance in the following order. He goes out in the morning looking for fish, and the first one that he gets he brings it in. A lodge is pitched and a brush fence [is built] on two sides, leaving a lane about ten feet wide, and closed at the end by brush also, except for a small doorway for the dancers to enter. The fish that they have killed in [the] morning is painted sometimes red, sometimes blue, and not cleaned at all. Scales, guts, head, and tail is staked down to the ground, and some painted down from a swan is placed in little bunches all around the fish, a peace offering also, and in the brush fence all around the place where the party is to dance.

The dancers are represented as some kind of bird or animal, as one man will represent himself as an owl, another a loon, another a crow, another a fish hawk, and so on. Every man that dances must adopt some kind of fowl, or beast of prey, [such as] a bear, wolf, fox, panther, wildcat, and so on. And each one has a little nest in the brush fence; and the bear, wolf, and so on have little holes in the ground under the brush fence.

When all things are ready the old man appointed to sing will commence his song. After a while you will see the fowls and animals approaching from some place where they have been hid, [each] trying to represent the animals he represents, and all apparently shy of each other. The old man keeps rattling the gourd shell and drum, making all kinds of noises until he gets all his band of birds and animals, and gets them seated each one opposite to his nest.

The old man commences singing for them to dance, and up they jump, making all kinds of noises. In fact, every one makes a noise like the fowl or animal he represents, and in the dance he tries to represent his character. It makes much amusement for the bystanders, of which there are many, to witness their comical operations.

After they have danced a while the given signal is made for them to commence eating their feast of raw fish. First one will approach and turn off and leave it, with squall or screech, and move on round. Another will come up and do the same and hobble off round to the tunes of the old man's music. By and [by] one will make a grab [at the fish] with his mouth, and he may succeed in getting a piece; if not, he will move on round and another will try to bite off a piece.

And so they keep a-going until they all get a piece off and stored away in their nests if they possibly can. But sometimes they do not succeed the first time and a halt is made by the old drummer. Then they set down and take a smoke, and while they are smoking someone will try to steal the other's piece of fish. The owner discovers him and a great fuss is raised by the owner making a hideous noise to try and frighten the thief off, and the other [does] the same, and [he] probably will be a wolf and the other a crow. So the crow will squawk and the wolf howl, snap and snarl, and cut up wonderfully.

And whilst the others on the opposite side are looking on, some are stealing on the other side. Here another quarrel commences, and so on until nearly all get to quarreling about their bits of fish [that] they have hid away, to the great amusement of the bystanders, some acting the wolf, some a hawk, and so on.

All at once the old man starts his drum again and they all start for a dance, some trying to fly, some croaking, some barking like a wolf, and so on, but all the time watching their nests for fear of being robbed. By and by a signal is given for them to pitch into the fish again, and [a] regular dog-pull and hauling takes place, as they are not allowed to touch the fish with their hands. Only they can hold a little stick in their hands to keep the fish down with whilst they bite a piece off.

The fish has to be completely used up in this way—head, guts, skin—and, in fact, everything has to be eaten up raw. The struggle for a piece by the different kinds of animals and fowls represented is great, [especially] for the last piece. Finally, one gets it and goes round the ring with it in his mouth, the others after him, making noises, pulling and hauling this way and that, until finally he swallows it raw, like all the rest have done. The old drummer [then] makes a little speech of praise for bravery in eating the fish up clean in its raw

state. He [says] he thinks the spirits are satisfied and the family will
be able to sleep in peace hereafter, and the dance is ended.

In their wars there is considerable ceremony used by the war chief,
and he is quite an arbitrary officer at times. He lays all the plans of
attack and makes all laws regulating all the transactions of the trip.
There is no regular war chief; any person that loses a relation by
death, either in sickness or in battle, can get up a war party, if they
have influence enough to raise a party. Some try to get up war parties
but the [other] Indians do not put any confidence in their powers of
spiritual discernings and will not go with them. Sometimes [this]
breaks up the party. And [in] all these war parties the man that
makes up the party never asks or invites a single person to go with
him; it is all done on a volunteer score. The man that makes the party
commences his songs to the gods of power and war, which is the
rocks first and the earth, 2nd. The war chief keeps up his war [songs
and prayers] for about six nights, sometimes very secret, for sometimes the band in general do not wish to go to war at that time for
various reasons.

However, the man is obstinate and is determined to go, and keeps
up his night songs and prayer. And all that wish to go come in and
join in the ceremonies. When the warrior, or war chief, thinks he has
force enough, and has found out by his dreams and magical works
about the point where he will find the enemy, [he] tells the [others]
that on such a day, or in so many nights, he will start.

At the appointed time, off he goes; and after he gets about 2 or 3
miles from the camp, he sits down, lights his pipe, and smokes to
Tunkanshe, the large boulders of rocks, and asks the Spirit of the
Rocks to give him success in killing some of his enemies and not
getting any of his own party killed.

After a while the party begins to assemble, and inquiries are made
to learn if all are there that they know are coming, then they all start
off. Every night the war chief invokes his spirits of war and asks for
direction in the right path to pursue to find the enemy off their guard
and most accessible. So they go on for two or three days, hunting
along until they get within the enemy's country, when spies are
arranged [for]. One man has to take the war pipe and go some
distance ahead of the party.

Orders are given that hunting and firing must be stopped, and if any of the party breaks the order by firing a gun, the party take him and break his gun and cut his blanket for him, to all [of] which he never says a word in opposition to the fulfilling [of] their customs of law.

The man that goes ahead with the war pipe, if he sees any signs of the enemy, returns to the party and makes known what he has seen or heard. Then he is relieved and another is sent ahead, and probably by this time they are in the enemy's country. The war chief makes his last prophecy. At night he enters his little lodge that has been made by the party of brush and a few blankets thrown over it to make a lodge of it. A little hole is dug in the center and some red earth and water put in [it]. The war lances are taken out and set [with] points up, sometimes in two rows and sometimes in a circle around the medicine lodge.

The war chief enters the lodge and commences his harangue, and calls upon the rocks and earth and many of the departed spirits that have fallen in battle to guide him to where the enemy is the easiest taken and to keep the enemy from being alarmed and [to] keep them asleep until they can approach and get the first fire. By the signs that the war chief makes with his gourd shell with beads in it that make it rattle, and by which rattling and his invoking the spirits, he draws as many of the enemy's spirits to his lodge as he is going to kill of the enemy.

With his incessant rattling and singing, [he] decoys the enemy's spirits into the little puddle of red water [in the hole in the lodge], where the war chief gives them a blow with his rattle and pretends that he has killed them all. The war party are all outside, anxious to hear the result of the charm. After a little the war chief gives a blow on the side of his water hole, then another, and soon, a blow for every scalp they are to take. Sometimes a blow with a groan is heard inside the lodge. This strikes the party with sorrow, for they put great faith in their war chief, and they generally come out about as the war chief tells them, as I have heard many of their war parties relate.

They set out in the dark of the night, after the war chief has got through his ceremonies, going [in] hunt of the enemy. If they find them numerous, they withdraw and go and lay in ambush until morning, and shoot one or two when they go out to hunt, and run [away]. But if they find only a few, they will attack about light and kill all they can, and put off for home. Sometimes they lose a man, sometimes none.

I recollect of an instance where the Sioux went to war and one of the party got killed. It was at Otter Tail Lake. The Sioux came upon a man and woman in a canoe hunting. The Sioux fired upon them and killed the woman dead, but the man was only slightly wounded. There was so many bullet holes through the canoe that it sunk in a few moments. The Chippewa managed to keep his gun dry and the Sioux all plunged into the water to kill the Chippewa. As soon as the Sioux got close enough, the Chippewa fired and killed one dead.

The Sioux in the noise and confusion did not miss their man until they had killed the Chippewa and got to shore and got the scalps of the man and woman. They were about to start for home when one of the party looked round and says, "Where is my brother?" They all spoke up and said they saw him in the water when they made the charge on the enemy. The brother went back and looked in the water and found his brother.

The Chippewa had taken good aim and, no doubt, said he would have a scalp to offset his [own]. The Sioux was shot through the head and was laying in the water about three feet deep. The brother dragged him to shore and they set him up nearby the Chippewa man and woman, and left a quantity of trinkets hanging to his neck. But this did not satisfy the living brother; he made an assault upon the war chief and would have killed him, only that the party interfered and prevented any further bloodshed.

They told the enraged brother he was a fool and told him he had not been invited to come; they all had voluntarily come upon the excursion, and if his brother was killed it was his own lookout. He came for war and got the results of war, and he must put up with what had taken place. The brother finally cooled down and went home with the party without any more trouble amongst themselves. [At] this time I was living at Leaf Lake, a few miles from Otter Tail Lake, and learned the circumstances a few hours after it took place.

Doctoring the sick is performed by all those that belong to the great medicine dance. Both men and women are considered capable of doctoring if they have been initiated into that great dance, but there are a great many of the medicine party that never practice the art of healing the sick. And there are others—fearless, go-ahead creatures—that do nothing else but doctor, and they keep the gourd shell a-going all the time.

Their mode of doctoring is by charming by song without words, merely a chorus of hi, le, li, la, continually for 8 or 10 minutes at a time. Then they stop and rest a moment and the man of the lodge will fill a pipe and give [it to] the doctor to smoke. After smoking, the doctor will commence again, with the same words and tune again, and after he has sang a while, he will commence sucking the parts most affected. He will draw with his mouth as long as he can hold his breath, when he will let go with a stamp on the ground. Gagging and making all sorts of noises, he turns round and takes a little dish with water and some red earth in it which he gargles and whistles and washes out his mouth; [then he] turns and goes at it again and keeps on for half an hour sometimes before he stops for a smoke.

Then he looks at the dish of water to see what he has drawn out by suction, and at the same time determines what the disease is. Sometimes he thinks he has drawn out a quantity of bile; other times he thinks it is some animal that has been sent by some other Indian for revenge for some alleged offense to make them sick. They believe all the medicines have the power of sending different kinds of things by some supernatural power to disturb the peace of another. The doctor has to divine what it is and has to try and drive the animal out [of] the sick person.

Sometimes the doctor will say it is a louse or something of this kind in the body of the sick person. . . . The doctor commences his song as usual, and gets up and walks about and thumps the lodge now and then, and makes all kinds of hideous noises. Sometimes he calls upon the Schun, Schunah, the rays or reflections of the sun. [This] is considered a powerful spirit of the air which they frequently invoke in their doctoring. . . .

After calling for some time, he starts out [of the lodge] and those outside waiting discharge their guns into a bowl of water and the little bark image, and blow them to pieces. The doctor pitches in and goes to sucking and singing over the fragments of what is left. A woman [then] gets upon his back and stands there a moment; then she gets down and leads the doctor by the hair of [his] head back into the lodge where he commences his suctions again. Sometimes they stop and will not doctor any more after the shooting is over.

A woman in her courses must not approach anywhere near this time, for it would spoil all the witchcraft and probably make her sick.

A woman during menstruation cannot approach any lodge where there [are] any war implements or doctors, and her lodge must be made separate from the family. She is not permitted to go into her [family's] lodge until she is well and goes into a pool and washes herself with all her clothes on. And the fire in the family lodge is all removed and a new one built by the striking of a new fire with flint and steel.

[The manuscript ends abruptly at this point. The last two pages were mutilated in a dozen places so that it has not been possible to transcribe them exactly.—*Ed. note.*]

Appendix A

SUPERINTENDENT OF FARMING FOR THE SIOUX

Prescott's recollections make no mention of his activities as superintendent of farming for the Sioux from 1849 through 1856. Although he may have held this position while still official interpreter for Colonel Nathaniel McLean, the Indian agent, it seems more likely that he was interpreter from 1843 to 1849.

From the time when Prescott became the superintendent of farming in 1849, the Mdewakantons, to which band his wife's people belonged, and the Wahpekutes, both lower bands, resided along the lower Minnesota River, about five to twenty miles southwest of Fort Snelling, and along nearby parts of the Mississippi River. They moved from this region in the fall of 1853 to the new reservation about ninety miles to the west-southwest, up the Minnesota River.

It is not clear to what extent Prescott was required to be with his Sioux bands in carrying out his duties as superintendent of farming. At any rate, he seems to have had ample time to carry on a few other activities as well. His main residence from 1843 to 1851 was at Fort Snelling, and after that at Richfield, nearby. Yet he had time to visit Prescott, Wisconsin, from time to time from 1849 to 1852. After 1849 he made a claim near Minnehaha Falls, was active in the Hennepin County Bible Society and the Minnesota Agricultural Society in 1853, and in 1854 built a mill at Richfield of which he was the sole owner at the time of his death in August, 1862.

His activities as superintendent of farming for the Sioux are summarized each year in the reports of the Commissioner of Indian Affairs, 1849–1856. In addition, they are conveniently outlined in the *South Dakota Historical Collections*, volumes 26 and 27, where they are also indexed.

1849—In Charge of Work at Seven Indian Villages

This was a position of importance; and as Prescott began his work in 1849 he had the following men under him, located at seven different villages in the lower Minnesota valley and along the Mississippi

211

River below Fort Snelling: A. Robertson, farmer at Little Crow's village, seven miles below Fort Snelling; John Bush, farmer at Red Wing's village on the west shore of Lake Pepin, where Red Wing, Minnesota, is now located; Oliver Raescott (also spelled Rassicott and Rassisatt), blacksmith at Red Wing's village; M. S. Titus, farmer for the Lake Calhoun band which was now located at Oak Grove, a few miles southwest of Fort Snelling; Hazen P. Mooers, farmer for Black Dog's band, four miles above Mendota; John Mooers, probably a son of the foregoing, farmer for Six's band at Shakopee, about eighteen miles southwest of Fort Snelling on the Minnesota River; Patrick, or Peter, Quinn, farmer for Good Road's band, eight miles from Fort Snelling on the south side of the Minnesota River; Victor Chatel, blacksmith for Good Road's band; and J. Brunel (also spelled Brinnel), farmer for Wabasha's band at Winona, Minnesota, about thirty-five miles below Wabasha and the lower end of Lake Pepin.

Prescott had known a number of these nine men for many years. With the exception of Brunel, who in 1850 "was dismissed for intemperance, and Mr. Francis Lapoint appointed in his place," they all remained with him until 1853, when the Indians were moved to their reservation far up the Minnesota River.

In his first report, that of September 25, 1849, Prescott announced that the Indians were dissatisfied with the removal of the government farmers in 1848 and that the few oxen that remained had been killed, with the result that in 1849 there were no teams to do any plowing when his seven farmers arrived.

At Little Crow's village, 75 acres had been plowed in 1849, 500 yards of temporary fences made, two Indian houses and one storehouse built, 20 tons of hay put up, and 4,875 bushels of corn harvested, though some had been wasted when cholera morbus broke out among the Indians.

At Red Wing's settlement 55 acres had been plowed, 11 houses built to store corn, and 1,650 bushels of corn raised. The Indians had plowed their own corn, and some of the men had even assisted the women in hoeing it!

The former Lake Calhoun band had plowed 45 acres, raised 1,350 bushels of corn, and preserved much of it for future use by harvesting it before it was ripe, boiling the corn, and scraping it into bags where it would keep for several years.

Black Dog's band had plowed 30 acres and raised 900 bushels of corn; a few families also raised vegetables. Six's band had plowed 80 acres and had raised 2,400 bushels of corn, though a considerable amount of it had been wasted. Good Road's band had plowed 45 acres and raised 1,350 bushels of corn. In addition, they had handled logs for nine houses.

Chatel, the blacksmith stationed at Good Road's village, had "handed over, for the five upper bands, from 8th December, 1848, to 30th July, 1849 (nearly eight months), 12 rakes, 575 wrought nails, 57 sets door hinges, 40 sets door-handles, latches, etc., 50 hasps and staples, 73 chains to hang kettles for cooking, 45 half-round adzes, 23 traps, 230 axes of different sizes, 265 fire steels, 50 rat spears, 208 pairs fish spears, 24 pairs stirrups, 16 melting ladles, 63 crooked knives, 199 hoes, 30 tapping-gouges, besides an innumerable quantity for repairing, particularly to guns—many of the new ones requiring repair before they can be used."

The Indians of these seven bands had been issued 625 barrels of flour, 200 barrels of pork, 7,692.5 pounds of lard, and 2,857 bushels of corn. They had picked 200 barrels of cranberries, for which they received $8,000. The agency badly needed a storehouse for provisions, gunpowder, and other supplies.

Prescott had been unable to prevail upon the Indians to send their children to school unless they were boarded and clothed. He believed that a system of manual-training schools, established on Christian principles and requiring daily Bible study, presented the only solution to the problem of educating the Sioux. He felt it was bad policy to congregate them in large villages and proposed that they be given fifty- to one hundred-acre homesteads "in which the individual Indian should have distinct property," and that they be aided in obtaining houses, fences, plows, and the like.

1850—Indifferent Progress

The Mdewakanton Sioux showed indifferent progress in Prescott's report of September 23, 1850. Little Crow's band had plowed sixty-five acres for corn, which yielded about thirty bushels per acre. However, only about a third of the crop had been saved for the winter, for, being short of provisions, the Indians had lived on green corn for two months, thus consuming two-thirds of the crop. During the winter, Robertson, the farmer, had cut rails to fence the cornfield, but a flood swept them away, along with his own garden and fence. For the Indians' horses and his own cattle, he had made from thirty-five to forty tons of hay. He had assisted the chief in building a log house, twenty-two by seventeen feet, for which Nathaniel McLean, the sub-agent, had provided a cookstove. A temporary fence had been built around the cornfield, a pasture provided for the horses, and several small storehouses built.

Red Wing's band had plowed 55 acres, which yielded a full 30 bushels per acre. Five log cabins had been built, 300 rails made to repair a fence, and 400 more made for scaffolding. The farmer had spent much of his time in hauling wood, rails, poles, and 15 tons of hay. During six months the blacksmith had made 902 new articles and repaired 578 others.

At Black Dog's village forty acres had been plowed, yielding thirty bushels per acre. Mooers, the farmer, had cut and hauled twelve hundred rails and six hundred stakes to repair the fence. He had helped to build five log cabins and repaired four others. He had hauled twenty-five loads of poles and forks for scaffolding for drying corn and had stacked forty tons of hay.

Little Six's, the largest band, had lost about half its corn crop in a flood. The Lake Calhoun and Good Road's bands had lost their entire corn crops through the Indians' obstinacy in persisting in planting in the Minnesota valley, which was subject to frequent flooding. Wabasha's band had raised some corn, but not enough for its needs during the winter. However, a new field some distance from the river bottom had been broken up.

Chatel, the blacksmith, had made for the Sioux 2,896 new articles such as muskrat and fish spears, axes, door latches, and fixtures and had repaired 2,360 guns and other articles. He and the smith with Red Wing's band together had made or mended over 8,000 pieces in one year.

Prescott concluded his 1850 report with the following:

The farming has been carried on much the same as last year. I cannot perceive any more industry among them than formerly. In fact, the men appear more inclined to play the gentleman. I have seen several walking about with umbrellas, or ladies' parasols, over their heads, while their wives were hoeing corn under the burning rays of the sun, without any protection. Ask the man why he does not assist to work, the answer generally is, "Will you pay me for it?" One of the farmers furrowed some ground, but some of the Indians forbad him, called him a fool, and told him it was a waste of land and time in making furrows. It is very difficult to get them to thin out their corn when it stands too thick, and they abuse us when we attempt to do so. Scattered as they are, it is almost impossible to make their farming very profitable with only one farmer for a band. The Indians expect him to do most of their work, and are always complaining because he cannot satisfy them all. Nothing permanent or profitable can be done for them until each family has a field, and is protected from the abuses of bad and indolent fellows, who steal half the produce of the farms.

The farmers were all furnished with good new ploughs last spring, and the land was well ploughed. The Indians would have raised much more corn this year than formerly, had it not been for the high water, which destroyed probably one-third of the crop. The Indians are straining to imitate the customs of the white people around them. They will not eat corn unless they are starving, and often sell all their corn for flour and pork or fresh beef. I have known dishes of boiled corn handed to Indian children, when they knocked the dish into the fire and cried for bread. The men, as soon as the annuity provisions are eaten, go about from house to house begging and borrowing flour and pork, and eat but little corn. Six out of the seven bands have been furnished with lumber to make roofs for their houses as an experiment. Some of them, at first, said they would not have any lumber, but now they are all clamorous, and want ten times more than can be purchased. The two cooking-stoves you purchased for two of the chiefs will be used, I think, to advantage.

I cannot suggest any change in the farming. It is expected and hoped that the government will make a treaty to purchase these lands and settle the Indians permanently, when the farming and mechanical operations for all the tribe can be carried on together.

The 100 horses purchased the last spring have more than one-half of them died since they got into the Indians' hands, and I fear there will not be ten of them alive next spring. It was a useless expenditure of $6,000. They could not all get a horse apiece, and those that did not get any are dissatisfied, and every few days a complaint is entered against some one for killing a horse. I suppose they will keep on killing as long as they have a horse left. The rice crop is a total failure this year. There are but few cranberries. These added considerably to their support; but as the government has ordered provisions to be purchased, all the losses and failures will be remedied, and they cannot suffer this winter. The greater part of the corn, I fear, will be sold, as heretofore, as soon as received.

To close my report, I must say the Indians have behaved remarkably well in the temperance cause. Instances of drunkenness are rare. Much praise is due to his Excellency, Governor Ramsey, and yourself, for the earnest temperance advice which has been given them, and all the friends of humanity rejoice at the change in the habits of these Indians.

Prescott's 1850 report to his superior, Nathaniel McLean, was in turn forwarded to McLean's superior, Governor Ramsey, with the remark that "the Indian farmers being so remote from each other (more than 100 miles from what is called the lower farm to the upper) prevents that proper oversight necessary to secure an efficient discharge of the duties of the appointment." Prescott must have had to make periodic visits to the seven bands as he superintended the activities of his farmers.

1851—Indians Heedless of Good Counsel

Prescott's report for 1851 was made about a month after the signing of the 1851 treaties, and it was more discouraging than the reports of the two preceding years. On August 30, 1851, at St. Peter's, he wrote:

SIR:

Another year has nearly passed, since I made my last report of the farming operations among the Sioux Indians. In the past year many events have taken place among the white and red people; the great floods of the west have reached the valley of the Minnesota river; the Indians say the thunder has burst up the fountains, and sent forth great floods of water. The valley of the Minnesota has been overflowed three times in succession since last spring. Tradition gives no account of such an event. Four bands of the Sioux planted in the valley of the Minnesota river; their corn-fields were all swept away; a fifth lost part of their corn-fields. Three villages only have their corn-fields on high land; their corn is good. Our reports, having been called for a month earlier than usual, I have not been able to collect such statistical information as I wished to do, and my report is meagre of our farming operations. One blacksmith has handed in his report of work done for the Indians; this is Mr. V. Chatel. He reports to have made, of different kinds of articles for the Indians, 2,506 pieces, and has repaired for them 1,430 pieces more during the last year. The other smith has not handed in his report of work done for the Sioux but I think has done about two-thirds as much work as Mr. Chatel; which will make in all 6,560 pieces made and repaired by the two smiths. The farmers have planted more land than usual, but their labor, as well as that of the Indians, has been for the floods to wash away. Three bands that have raised some corn will have a yield of about thirty bushels to the acre, including what they waste in gathering; the three villages will have about one hundred and fifty acres of corn, which, rated at thirty bushels per acre, will make 4,500 bushels for three bands. One band have lost about half their crop by high water, and, with the three other bands that have lost their entire crops, no doubt will suffer for food the coming winter.

The ten carts and harness, besides some plough harness have all been issued to the Indians, but they have not made use of them, everyone saying he had an equal right to the carts. The stoves you furnished them, some of them have been used and some not; one chief gave his stove away, and the probability is, that some of the rest will do the same thing. It was to be hoped that the Indians would purchase some provisions with some part of the thirty thousand dollars they received from the government, but I believe a large amount has been laid out in the purchase of old broken-down and worn-out horses. No doubt half or two-thirds of them will die this winter. The Indians were advised by you and other friends to purchase some provisions, but they appear to be heedless to all good counsel, and run into misery when they could avoid it in many instances. The manners and customs of the Indians are yet unchanged; the men love to live in idleness and mischief, and there has been more conjuring and witchcraft going on this summer than I have known for many years. The Indians have received thirty thousand dollars, and in about three weeks we seen them about a begging and borrowing as usual.

Since writing this report, some of the farmers have handed in their reports. They report to have hauled timber for several new buildings, for which lumber has been furnished to cover them; the farmers report to have made from twenty-five to thirty tons of hay each, for the Indian horses; they report, also, that the Indians are very wasteful in gathering their corn so early. They do this, they say, so they can get early to the cranberry swamps. The Indians report that there is a large quantity of cranberries this season.

A treaty has been made, and we long to see it ratified, and the

Indians moved to their new homes, so something permanent and useful may be done for them. In their present places of residence, so scattered about, nothing, in a measure, can be done towards civilizing them. The Indians have been quite temperate until of late; some of them have been drinking whiskey pretty freely; among the drinkers is one of the principal chiefs, [Little Crow].

The commissioners warned them again and again about spending their money for whiskey; also the agent has given the same advice; but money and whiskey are great temptations, and too often too great for them to resist.

1852—Dissatisfaction Among the Indians

In his 1852 report, dated August 20, 1852, at St. Peter's Indian Agency, Prescott wrote that Little Crow's band had a good corn crop, though much was wasted because it was broken while still soft. Some Indians still desired to plant by themselves in order that they might have a variety of vegetables, but they were unable to do so under the prevailing circumstances. Prescott reported:

The habits of the Indian children, pilfering each other's fields, prevent the industrious from making any effort to raise a variety of vegetables. One Indian planted his corn in rows, and plowed it before hoeing; this is the first instance of the kind in this village. I believe about six acres of new ground have been ploughed in addition to the old land, which makes about eighty-five acres of corn for this village this year. . . . The Indians cut poles to fence their fields, and the farmer hauled them, and assisted them to make a temporary fence round their fields; they complain, and say it is of no use to farm without protection of property.

The farmer for Red Wing's band had plowed about seventy acres, the Indians had cultivated it, and the corn looked good. The farmer for Wabasha's band had plowed sixty acres; several of the Indians had planted their corn in rows and had plowed it before hoeing it, and a good crop seemed assured.

At Black Dog's village thirty acres had been plowed and about eight hundred bushels of corn was expected. Mooers had spent much time in hauling wood, provisions, and rails, and was obliged to rebuild all his fence each year. The Indians, too lazy to go for wood, burned a large part of the rails every winter.

At the Lake Calhoun band's village ten acres of old and ten of new land had been plowed. However, their seed corn was bad, and, having been planted on the sod, would not yield well. Cattle had broken down the fence and done much damage to the corn crop. Quinn, at Good Road's village, had plowed twenty acres of new land and, except for the destruction by the cattle, reported conditions similar to those at the Lake Calhoun band's village.

Little Six's band was handicapped with poor seed, and in addition, cattle had broken in. Only twenty acres had been plowed. In summary Prescott wrote:

The high water has prevented the last-named three bands from planting their old fields, and they will be short of corn this winter, and no doubt there will be some suffering among them. The farmers report that in some places the settlers on the late purchase from the Indians have claimed all the hay-ground, and they cannot cut hay for the Indian horses. Some settlers have marked out the Indian farms, and tell the Indians to move off, for the land, they say, belongs to them, since the treaty is ratified. [The treaty of 1851 had been ratified on June 23, 1852.] The Indians, with their farming and their annuities, altogether, have suffered more this year than I have known them to do in a number of years past. The treaty has kept the minds of the Indians constantly agitated, and they talk of nothing else, and their money. Farming and education appear to be of trifling import with them, and, instead of increasing a desire for agriculture and civilization, they are becoming more reckless in gambling and laziness. It is hoped that a change may be effected in this people soon, or their money will be their destruction. The chiefs are at variance with each other, and are striving to see who will be the greatest chief amongst them, though many inducements [are] offered them to get large sums of money from them. This creates dissatisfaction amongst them, and it will be some time before their minds will be at rest, and harmony prevail. The striking out the reservation in the late treaty has set them to complaining about the government; they say they do not want the money—they want a permanent home; and they say the government wants to send them into a boundless prairie to starve them to death; and so long as this state of affairs exists, the Sioux will not improve in agriculture or civilization. . . .

Notwithstanding the Indians are so much in want of mechanical labor, they cannot appreciate the necessity of learning to work for themselves, and never will, I fear, unless our government uses some more efficient means to get manual-labor schools into operation; and I think it will require five years from this time to get the

Indians' minds settled to a condition so that they can be made to
understand which will be the best course to pursue hereafter, on
account of the troubles and difficulties among themselves and the
white people, arising out of the late treaties.

Prescott also reported that one of the blacksmiths had made 1,406
pieces of new work, mainly traps, axes, hoes, rat-spears, and fish-
spears, for the Sioux under him. He had shod 61 horses for the
Indians, and mended or repaired 829 articles, including 228 guns,
224 traps, and 143 axes. This made a total of 2,229 pieces made
and repaired. Chatel, the other blacksmith, had made 3,139 new
articles for the Sioux, had repaired 2,389, including 999 guns, 500
traps, 322 axes and the like, making a grand total for both smiths of
7,757 articles.

1853—Trouble in Moving the Indians

It had been expected and hoped that the Mdewakanton and Wahpekute Sioux around the lower Minnesota and adjacent to the Mississippi would move to their new reservation near the mouth of the
Redwood River at an early date, perhaps no later than the spring or
early summer of 1853. This removal did not, however, take place. In
reporting from "St. Peter's Agency" on September 1, 1853, Prescott
wrote:

> Last spring the farmers were ordered not to plough the old corn-
> fields or build any more houses, but hold themselves in readiness
> to move to the new agency. One of the farmers disobeyed this order
> and ploughed land at one of the old villages, (Wabashaw's), and
> the Indians planted more corn than usual; Wahcotah's band also
> planted six or eight acres. It was foreseen, by the late agent and
> myself, that if they planted as formerly, there must be difficulty in
> getting them to move away to their new homes; and it is now
> found that the disobedience of the above orders has given rise to
> all the trouble in getting the Indians started for the Upper
> Minnesota river. Wabashaw with his band has come up to Crow's
> village, on his way up.
> Four of the farmers were sent in the spring to the new agency,
> and have been employed, with other hands, in erecting a large
> warehouse, blacksmith shop, a cook house, a farmer's house, and
> temporary plank houses to store provisions; they also planted
> about seven acres of corn, on new-ploughed prairie land, but it

proved an entire failure. About one acre of potatoes planted in new ground looks well.

Agent McLean contracted for 600 acres to be broken up, at or near Redwood river; but owing to the *hoof-ail* prevailing extensively among the contractor's cattle, he is not able to complete his contract. It appears he will have about 400 acres opened at different places, convenient for the Indians to plant.

The Wahpahcoota Indians planted some corn contrary to the wishes of the former agent, and consequently the same difficulty has arisen in getting them to move.

The blacksmiths have been employed as usual. One of them has remained with the lower bands during the summer, and is now on his way moving up. The other smith moved to the new agency last spring, and assisted in putting up the new shop, and other buildings, when not employed at his anvil.

The operations of farming and building have been much retarded in consequence of the funds not being placed in the hands of the former agent in sufficient sums to carry out the treaty stipulations for those purposes. The desire to linger near their old haunts, and dislike to abandon the graves of their ancestors, with the fear (real or pretended) that they are destined to starve when separated from their former hunting grounds, have for the present entirely occupied the Indian mind. It must be some time before this feeling is overcome; but I look more seriously on their complaint as to the uncertain tenure of their destined home. If they are to continue looking forward to another removal at the end of three or four years, there must be an end of all hope of their civilization, and their complete and total ruin must be the result.

This report was made to the new Indian Agent, R. G. Murphy, Nathaniel McLean's successor. Murphy, in transmitting the report to his superior, George W. Manypenny, Commissioner of Indian Affairs, wrote:

I beg leave to call your attention to the report of Mr. Prescott . . . particularly to that part which relates to the short period allowed for the Indians to remain on the lands allotted them by President Fillmore. If the five years fixed by him should be dated from the time of the treaties, there are but three years for them to remain. These Indians have intelligence enough to see their situation clearly; and it must be confessed there is but little to encourage them in the endeavor to become agriculturists when they are so shortly to be driven from their fields. The expenditure of so large a sum as

$60,000 of their money on mills, schools, and other improvements, would appear a hardship, if it can be enjoyed only for so short a period.

An amendment to the treaties of 1851 had provided that the President should select for the Sioux new homes other than the reservations along the upper Minnesota. These new homes were to be outside the territory ceded to the United States government in the treaties. The Indians, therefore, were faced with the unsettling prospect of being moved within a short time still farther west, probably into Dakota Territory.

1854—Trouble Among the Tribes

When Prescott submitted his report for 1854, the situation had changed entirely from that of preceding years. Stretching along the upper Minnesota River for about 135 miles was the new Sioux Reservation. The lower bands, the Mdewakantons and the Wahpekutes, which Prescott superintended, inhabited the lower part of the reservation, their governing center being the Lower, or Redwood, Agency, at the mouth of the Redwood River. The upper bands, the Wahpetons and the Sissetons, were farther up the river, and their center was the Upper, or Yellow Medicine, Agency, at the mouth of the river of that name. It was intended that the four bands should remain on their reservation, each in the area allotted to it. The fact that they did not do so was the cause of much trouble.

Mr. A. Robertson, formerly a farmer under Prescott, was now the superintendent of farming for the two upper bands. Aside from this change, Prescott apparently retained all or most of his former farmers and blacksmiths, and also employed other laborers to help with activities at the new site. Prescott probably still maintained his home at Richfield, but must have spent a great deal of time far up the Minnesota from his home.

Prescott wrote his 1854 report from the "Sioux Agency" on October 10, 1854. He stated that 360 acres of land had been placed under contract, presumably for plowing, in the summer of 1853. In the spring of 1854 the fields were all fenced with posts and rails, stretching a length of five or six miles in all. He said further:

> The land has been, most of it, cross-ploughed, and part of it harrowed. I ran the fields off into square acre-lots, and allotted to

small families one acre each, and to large families two and three acres each; but there were not families or Indians enough to plant half the land that was ploughed, the larger half of the Indians preferring to roam about and starve. The Indians at first objected to the new system of farming, wishing to plant in irregular patches all over the fields, and some of them pulled up the stakes that I had stuck for corners, and said they would plant where they pleased. I told them that I was carrying out the orders of the governor and the agent, when they stopped their opposition and went to work. Those that planted have laid up for winter use from ten to thirty bushels of good sound corn per family. The corn was planted in the month of June. Some of the fields would average thirty bushels to the acre, and some not more than fifteen bushels to the acre, the drought having injured some of the crops one-half.

The Indians have planted corn, potatoes, pumpkins, squashes, melons, cucumbers, onions, and beans; but the thievish children stole all, except the corn, before the crops were half grown.

The employes and laborers planted one hundred bushels of potatoes, of which they gathered one wagon-load, the Sisseton and Wahpeton Indians having come down in large numbers (about 3,000) to draw their annuities. They were starving, and in two weeks they stole them nearly all.

The employes and laborers sowed seventy acres in white turnips and rutabagas; the Sissetons and Wahpetons are now living on them, and they have not much else to eat. The turnips and rutabagas were fine and large; but we shall be compelled to pull them before they are fully grown, in order to get some for winter use. There would have been fifteen or twenty thousand bushels, could they have been left until grown.

By order of his excellency Governor Gorman, 160 acres of land has been broken this summer, making in all 520 acres now in readiness for the lower Sioux. The rails are split and posts in readiness to fence the last ploughed fields.

The land in this country is well adapted to the raising of corn. All kinds are raised here except southern dent. The red-cob early dent ripens and brings good crops. The soil is a black sandy loam, and all kinds of northern vegetables come to the greatest perfection; and the Sioux Indians could raise an abundance of food, if they would employ half of their time in farming.

Little Crow's band, most of them, have planted at the agency. Black-dog, Little Six, and the Star, in part, have planted at the agency. Four bands—Wahcoota, Wabashaw, Good Roads, and the Wahpacootas—have not made their appearance at the agency this summer, and are roving about, starving and making great complaints against the government, because they are not fed more; and no doubt there are some white people helping the Indians to complain and be dissatisfied.

His excellency Governor Gorman, superintendent of Indian affairs, with the agent, have used all plausible means to get the Sioux to move to their new homes. Having interpreted in many instances, I know that the governor's and agent's advice and counsel have been wholly for the advancement and improvement of the condition of the Sioux Indians; and his excellency has always urged upon them the necessity of turning their attention to farming and civilization. The governor and agent Murphy have offered them money and agricultural implements, if they would take hold and go to work; but they say that they have sold their lands, and they are going to live on their annuities, and the women to do the work. One Indian bought with his own money a one-horse wagon for $75, and a shovel-plough—the first instance of the kind that I have noticed among the Sioux.

Prescott then listed work done at the Sioux agency and farm during the previous seventeen months, since May 4, 1853. It included 520 acres of land broken; 360 acres fenced with posts and rails; 25,400 rails made; 6,060 posts made; 300 acres of land cross-plowed and part of it harrowed and cultivated; 70 acres sowed in turnips and rutabagas; 12 acres planted in potatoes; 150 tons of hay made the preceding fall; 300 tons of hay made during the past summer; two storehouses 20 by 60 feet with shingle roofs and double floors, and nine other buildings—blacksmith shops, farmers' and laborers' houses, and boarding and cook houses—a total of 11 buildings constructed; and two root-houses and two more farmhouses started. Prescott further reported:

There is no house for the agent, interpreter, and principal farmer, and no office; and the chiefs have no houses yet, as has been promised they should have at their farms, which shows that there is considerable building to be done yet.

There has been but one blacksmith at work this summer, and he has had a hard task to perform, having had all the work of the Indians, and the agricultural implements to repair. This has been too much for him, and he has no doubt injured his health by excessive work. The miserable guns that the Indians draw as annuities, keep the smith half of his time in repairing them; and many of them have to be repaired as soon as they are taken out of the box, before they can be used, and a great many of them burst. In the last five months the smith has made and repaired, of different articles, 987 pieces, 237 of which are guns.

Whilst I am writing this report, a Sisseton went to the smith-shop to get some work done, and stood in the door near, leaning on the muzzle of this gun. The smith drew an axe from the fire that he was welding, laid it on the anvil, and struck it. The sparks flew in every direction; and one spark flew into the pan of the Indian's gun, and it went off and blew the Indian's head to pieces. The relatives have since said they would kill the smith. I sent for the deceased's brother-in-law, and told him it was an accident, and that they must not seek revenge. I gave them two scarlet and two white blankets, and one piece of calico, to bury the dead with; so I think the Indians will be satisfied and let it drop, and be quiet.

There is one important matter I wish to bring before you and his excellency Governor Gorman; that is, the paying of the upper Sioux, in the Medewakanton and Wahpacoota Sioux country. When the Sissetons and Wahpetons come down, they are always in a starving condition, and they plunder the fields of all that they can find, pull down the fences, burn the rails, and run over the fields and tramp down the growing crops, and are as heedless as the animals that feed upon the prairies. The lower Indians feel much grieved at the depredations of the upper Sioux, but can do nothing but make complaint.

The Yellow Medicine, the present location for the farming establishment for the upper Sioux, is as convenient a place for paying the upper Sioux as this agency, and will compel the lower Sisseton and Wahpeton Sioux to leave the Medawakanton part of the reserve, and to keep peace and friendship; and to keep our fields from being plundered annually, and many other depredations from being committed, I would respectfully recommend the payment to the upper Sioux to be made in their own country, or reserve, as both parties have often requested. Hoping that the Sioux will appreciate the good counsels that they have often received from yourself, and his excellency W. A. Gorman, superintendent Indian affairs, and settle down and become a civilized people,

I have the honor to be, your most obedient servant,
Superintendent farming for Sioux

P. PRESCOTT

R. G. Murphy, the Indian agent, in forwarding Prescott's 1854 report to Governor W. A. Gorman, wrote: "The report of Mr. Prescott, superintendent of farming for the Mdewakanton and Wahpekute, shows in detail the works that have been performed for them. . . . these lower bands will have five hundred and twenty acres in a perfect condition, and well fenced, ready for their planting next season." He also expressed the belief that the Indians had raised enough to carry them through the winter without suffering.

The governor, in forwarding the reports to Washington, wrote that Murphy, Prescott, and Robertson had "labored faithfully and incessantly; and it is pleasant to write that all the traders at this agency, and among the Sioux generally, have aided, to the extent of their ability, in keeping the Indians at home, and in encouraging them to devote themselves to agricultural pursuits, as the means best adapted for their happiness and prosperity."

1855—What Makes "The Poor Indian"?

Prescott submitted his report for 1855 on September 10, 1855. Little Six's band had plowed 220 acres; Little Crow's, 80; Black Dog's and Lake Calhoun's, 160; Good Road's, 80; Wahkuti's, 80; Wabashaw's, 80; Wahpekuti's, 100; and families in separate lots, 20. At the agency 40 acres had been plowed for gardens and oats for the horses, making a total of 780 acres under cultivation. Prescott also reported:

Seven bands of the lower Sioux have planted on their reserve this season, that is, the chiefs, but some of these seven bands are still roving among the white settlers, more or less. The Wahpekutis left the agency last fall and have not returned, except the chief with four or five lodges; they did not plant, and only stopped about three weeks, then moved off again.

The Indians have cultivated about 300 acres, the rest lies uncultivated, but the Indians, we hope, will all move to their reserve in the spring and cultivate the most of the land that is ploughed for them; the Indians that have planted, the most of them, have raised nearly enough for their winter supply; some corn was planted on the new ploughed land, but the drought injured the corn so that there has not been so large a yield as was anticipated. The corn that was planted (the most of it) is the small early kind, and does not yield so much per acre as the larger kinds.

Several of the Indians have been industrious in cultivating their corn, and appear desirous to enlarge their fields; some of them have fields ploughed separate from their common field. His Excellency

Governor Gorman, superintendent of Indian affairs, ordered that the Indians should be encouraged in making separate farms, a good and the first step towards civilization, and which will secure to the industrious the fruits of his labor.

The farm for the agency is 40 acres, ploughed last spring; the potatoes are good and large and will yield about 500 bushels; 8 acres of oats will yield about 30 bushels to the acre; the corn and beans are not worth gathering, owing to the drought and hail storms that cut the beans to pieces; 20 acres were sowed in turnips but the seed was old and did not come up well, so there will be a small crop.

There have been 12 log houses put up for the employees and chiefs, but we have no lumber as yet to finish them; the farmers and laborers have been employed in building, making hay, hauling supplies, ploughing, fencing, and various other duties connected with farming.

The saw-mill for the lower Sioux is raised and waiting for the Indians which have not arrived, also the frame for the flouring-mill is now ready to raise; these mills will be of great benefit to the Indians, and advance the business to a speedy completion.

The blacksmiths have been employed in making and repairing such articles as are wanted for farming and hunting; one smith is without a striker; provisions and clothing are so high in this country that the strikers cannot support themselves on a salary of $240 per annum.

The poor Indian is on many a tongue, from north to south and from east to west. I would ask what makes their poverty? Is it debility of body or mind? I should say the latter for the Indian is robust and strong and healthy, and he can chop and plough and plant and hoe corn, if he is so inclined. The women are hardy and strong; they chop wood and carry it half a mile on their backs to warm their children and lazy husbands; the women hoe corn and do all the work about the house or lodge, and yet they are poor, yet not so poor as many white people in the United States. The great trouble with the Indian is in the intellect, which is but a little above that of the dumb brute, and until the mind is improved the Indian will be poor throughout all time, and at whose door will the fault lie? The mind of the Indian must be cultivated as well as the body, or else morality, the great forerunner of civilization, is lost sight of, and all kinds of debauchery remain with the Indians, and often civilization to an Indian is an injury instead of blessing.

This report reflects Prescott's growing conviction that far more should be done for the education of the Indians than was being done.

1856—A Scathing Report

Prescott frankly voiced his concern in his 1856 report. He called this his last report, and so it proved to be. His immediate superior, R. G. Murphy, had been removed from his position, though Prescott apparently fully sympathized with him. It is not clear whether Prescott also had been removed at the time he made his report, or whether he felt that he would be after his critical report was read. Perhaps he desired to resign in any case. At any rate, since it was to be his last report, he wrote freely of some of his long pent-up feelings in regard to the treatment of the Indians on the Minnesota reservations. Certainly he made the report with the best future interests of the Indians in mind.

Thus on September 3, 1856, Prescott wrote:

SIR:

It gives me much pleasure, under existing circumstances, to make my last annual report to you of the farming operations of the Lower Sioux, under your agency for a second term.

Having been in charge of this farming department for the last three and a half years, living with the Sioux and identified with them, I feel it a duty imposed on me to give a plain statement of many particulars relating to my office during that period. I feel that it is important to be known to all persons interested for the Indians.

Estimates and requisitions have annually been made from the Sioux agency office for all the funds due the Sioux by treaty stipulations.

To the honor of the President and Congress, these funds to the full extent have been annually appropriated. And when it was represented a few years ago that an earlier payment of the annuities would be desirable, these appropriations have been since made one year in advance.

Have the officers under the President applied these funds so appropriated in the manner stipulated by the treaties? I can distinctly say, no! The treaties say these funds shall be annually expended, whereas, large amounts have been kept back, and are now in arrear, and that after repeated applications to have them expended. These arrears are not mere petty sums, surplusses or remnants of funds remaining unexpended, but large amounts, thousands and tens of thousands, and in some cases the whole fund appropriated for a special purpose.

It cannot be wondered at that the Indians are dissatisfied and constantly complaining, making the want of faith on the part of the government officers their excuse for misconduct of every kind, and leading them to be at all times inattentive to the expressed wishes of the agent, superintendent and commissioner of Indian affairs. There are always about the Indians people disposed to give them ill advice, and to take advantage of such circumstances as I have pointed out, to render them more and more disinclined to that course of life that has been enjoined them by their Great Father, and towards which they advance rapidly, were it not for the just causes of complaint which I have named, and they often go so far as to accuse the government agent and other employes of the United States government of stealing their moneys. Nay, they have at times asserted the same thing of the President and all the officials under him.

Now, no one has had such opportunity of knowing the real state of affairs here as myself, inasmuch as I have been the medium of communication between the government agent and the Indians for many years, and I have from time to time seen the letters of the Commissioner of Indian Affairs, complaining that more work was not done for the Indians, and shifting all blame from the department on to the shoulders of the agent or the superintendent. This has been very unjust, as far as agent Murphy was concerned, the real blame resting with the department. The evil at this place has arisen principally on the postscript of the letter of instructions to the superintendent of Indian affairs, dated April 19, 1854. By this the superintendent was authorized to dribble out the funds to the agent, clearly intimating that the commissioner did not think him fit to be entrusted with the money, as usual. Remember, at this time the superintendent was not under security, whilst Major Murphy, in addition to a bond in a penalty of $50,000, signed by very responsible sureties, was well known to possess property far more sufficient to meet all his possible liabilities to the government; and now let us see how this new system worked. The expenditures were pressed upon the agent while the funds remained locked up in the hands of the superintendent, and so scantily dealt out by him that the agent was continually laying out his own money, and obliged to withhold vouchers for payment made by him from quarter to quarter, until by repeated visits to St. Paul and great importunity, he could squeeze out some paltry payment on account from the superintendent.

The department is now aware how often Major Murphy has been obliged to retain vouchers for moneys paid him, because he had not sufficient department funds to cover the amounts.

Agent Murphy has been removed, and fault has been found with him for not pushing on the Indian work vigorously, whereas the cause of the delay was the insufficient fund placed at his disposal, and the uncertainty he was always kept in of receiving moneys to meet his liabilities as agent. Laborers were employed, and after working a month or two had to be discharged for want of funds to pay their wages and buy provisions, &c. Under the treaty of 1851, one of the most prominent stipulations was, that schools were to be established, for which $6,000 annually was appropriated. Up to this moment we are without schools, and any preparation for them has been expressly prohibited by the Commissioner of Indian Affairs.

All the friends of the Indians had looked to the present administration with confidence that the business of education would be prosecuted with vigor; but they have looked in vain, and this, the most important step for the Indian's present, as well as eternal, welfare, is utterly neglected. And this is not the worst: the fund of 1837 is still in arrear, to which five years of the 1851 treaty is added, making an accumulation of $60,000 of education money belonging to the Lower Sioux alone, to tempt the cupidity of those who look upon it as their interest to retain the Indian in his present state of barbarism.

Instead of the propriety of conduct that might be taught and enforced under a school system, our Sabbaths are now occupied by war songs and dances, horse races, ball play, and other Indian immoralities, whilst the Indians are dissatisfied that this important part of the treaty is neglected.

Last year we, at length, got our saw-mill at work. The consequence has been that our buildings have made some progress this summer; but our agricultural operations have dragged on heavily, for want of sufficient supplies of money. A large portion of this year's work has been done on credit, and some of the employes have five months' pay due them, and this whilst thousands of dollars of the Indian money lies in the hands of some officer of the Indian department.

In my report of last year, I gave an account of land ploughed or broken for the Lower Sioux by contract and our Indian teams. This year new breaking has been added, as follows: by contract, 102 acres; and by agency teams, 144 acres—together 246 acres—which, added to last year's account of 780 acres, makes a total of 1,026 acres now under plough.

Lumber has been hauled, and roofs put upon nine houses for Indians who have separated themselves from the community system.

Three hundred tons of hay have been cut for the cattle and horses.

Three large roof houses have been built; two hundred and thirty acres of land fenced for the Indian farms; one hundred and twelve acres of land sowed in wheat. Forty acres of the land ploughed by the agency teams have been fenced and sowed in rutabaga, turnips, and oats; but the oats were late, and will yield no crop, whilst the turnips, on which we relied partly for winter feed of cattle, are nearly all taken off by the Indians. Every effort has been made to stop their depredations, but to no purpose. They say the money is theirs, the farms and all the products, and they will help themselves to anything they see growing.

Other forty acres, planted early in corn and oats, were destroyed by the hail-storm.

One house, thirty by twenty, has been finished and painted for superintendent of farming; one other house, of same size, prepared for a school-house. The physician's house has been repaired and partly painted. A carpenter's shop, blacksmith's house, store house, and a dwelling house for the chief, Wabashaw, have been erected, and are now in course of finishing.

The saw-mill has been improved and put in complete operation, but the water is low. The Indians are clamorous for lumber, and cannot be supplied fast enough. The grist mill will be ready to run in a few days.

I again repeat, that much of this summer's work has been done on credit. This cannot be continued, and the laborers must be discharged and the work stopped unless a different system is commenced.

The blacksmith's department has been carried on by one smith only, without an assistant, most of the summer, owing to the allowed salary being insufficient. We have now a second smith and an assistant, on trial for one month, to determine whether they can live on the present salary.

As usual, I have to report that there is no dwelling house for the agent, no office, no council house, and no interpreter's house.

The Indian crops are short; and some, having no corn at all, will be obliged to leave the reserve to subsist during the winter.

As to the good conduct of the Indians I cannot boast. We have had more trouble with them the past three or four years than I have known in thirty-four years that I have lived with them.

Scythes were supplied to about twenty, to cut hay for their horses; but some of them broke or sold their scythes, leaving their horses to hunt food for themselves in the winter. For those that made hay, I have had the agency teams assist in hauling.

I will now proceed to state, in corroboration of my report, the amounts due, since the commencement of Major Murphy's last term, for agricultural, civilization, and school purposes, under the treaties of 1837 and 1851, and the amounts placed in their hands, and expended.

Prescott's report then illustrated in detail the point he was trying to make. He showed that under the treaties of 1837 and 1851, $163,500.00, much of it intended for education, remained unspent. Subtracting the amount paid to agent Murphy from the second quarter of 1853 through the second quarter of 1856, $63,953.59, left a balance of $99,536.41 in the Indian fund. This, Prescott contended, should have been advanced each year to fulfill the terms of the treaties.

He pointed out that $4,700.00 had been charged against the money payable to the Indians, whereas it should have been charged against the federal government. Another $10,000 had been spent for horses for the Indians when Nathaniel McLean began his term as agent in 1849. These sums, amounting to $14,700.00, if subtracted from the balance of $99,536.41 remaining with the Indian fund would reduce that balance to $84,836.41.

Prescott then proceeded to itemize how Murphy had spent the $63,953.59 placed in his hands as agent. $13,510.00 had been spent at the Redwood Agency for houses and warehouses, breaking 240 acres, fencing, road making, bridging, farmers' pay, smiths' salaries, tools, etc. A sum of $53,833.00 had been spent at the agency eight miles below Redwood and at the mills on the Redwood River for similar work as well as for lumber, a physician's salary, medicines, horses, oxen, harness, wagons, farming implements, a saw mill, a flour mill, hauling, and the like. This totaled $67,343.00, some $3,389.41 in excess of the amount allotted.

Prescott ended his report: "I trust this unpleasant detail will be sufficiently apologized for by my anxiety for the welfare of the Indians, and my feeling that it is my imperative duty not to withhold the truth."

Then he added this postcript:

It is generally believed by the people of this Territory that most of the improvements here, such as building roads, bridges, fences, &c., have been done by the United States government. This is not the fact; all the work here, and even carrying the mail from Fort Ridgely to Yellow Medicine, a distance of forty-eight miles, has been done with Indian moneys.

Prescott's scathing report was sent to his superior, Richard G. Murphy, the Indian agent, who supported his complaints that the Bureau of Indian Affairs in Washington was not fulfilling its treaty obligations. Murphy made his annual report on September 24, 1856, three weeks after Prescott submitted his report. It was addressed to Francis Huebschmann, superintendent of Indian affairs of the Northern Superintendency, which included all of Minnesota and Wisconsin and some adjacent areas.

Murphy supported Prescott's report and stressed many of the points in it. "I have begun to despair of the civilization of these Indians," he wrote. "Certainly it will never occur from any act of the United States government unless a different system is pursued. No promise, and surely no threat, on the part of the government by government officers, must ever be made without being performed to the utmost extent."

Huebschmann did not entirely support Murphy's and Prescott's reports. He wrote to his own superior, George W. Manypenny, Commissioner of Indian Affairs, in part as follows:

Large sums of money have been expended for improvements for these bands, but if the object is to teach the Indians to be their own farmers the result is not satisfactory. Most all the work done, except the planting of corn done by the women, has been performed by white employes, and it seems that it even had not been seriously thought of to employ Indians. I found a spirit of lassitude prevailing at the agency, and was disposed to hold the writer of the annual farm report no less responsible for it than others.

He went on to explain the delay in payments which had been authorized under the treaties. Huebschmann was pitting his six

months of knowledge of and experience with the Sioux against
Prescott's thirty-six years of experience with them.

When Prescott's 1856 report reached Manypenny, the Commissioner was highly indignant. On November 20, 1856, he wrote to
Huebschmann at Milwaukee:

Sir:

An examination of the annual report of P. Prescott . . . dated
September 3, 1856, and addressed to Major Murphy, late agent,
has led me to believe that one of the greatest obstacles in the way
of domesticating those Indians has been the employment of Mr.
Prescott in the very important position he has occupied with the
tribe. His report bears unmistakable evidence that he has enter-
tained and harbored very erroneous views; and that imparting
them to the Indians, as he doubtless has done, it is not surprising
that they have been constantly dissatisfied, and hence have been
difficult to be controlled or managed.

Without admitting the correctness of or reviewing the account
current which Mr. Prescott parades in his report, as superintendent
of farming, and in which he treats of matters altogether foreign to
his duties, and in relation to which he cannot be presumed to be
accurately informed, and without adverting to his volunteer
defence of the removed agent, it may be observed that in view of
the fact that agent Murphy had, according to his own showing in
his annual report, dated September 24, 1856, paid out and
expended for these Indians the large sum of $562,000 in three and
a half years, and the very meagre account of lands ploughed and
fenced and other improvements which the superintendent of
farming exhibits, it is a matter of congratulation that a considerable amount of funds for objects of education, improvement, and
other useful ends has been retained in the treasury, and may now,
it is hoped, be expended under more favorable auspices.

Mr. Prescott speaks of this report being his last one; to this
there can certainly be no objection. And it is to be regretted that the
temper and spirit manifested by him in it had not been disclosed
at an earlier day, and his official connexion with the Sioux Indians
been thus severed long since.

In the selection of a successor to this superintendent of farming,
you will admonish agent Flandrau to exercise great care and
caution, to the end that the services of a man suitable in every
respect for a post of such great responsibility may be obtained.

I do not deem it necessary to go into any defence of my action
in the premises. . . .

From the foregoing it will be seen that Manypenny admitted the truth of Prescott's complaint that large sums of money intended for educational and agricultural purposes had been arbitrarily withheld in violation of treaty terms.

Before the 1857 reports were made a number of changes had taken place. Manypenny was replaced by James W. Denver. Whether Prescott's report played any part in the change is impossible to say. Murphy's position was taken over by Charles E. Flandrau, and James Magner took Prescott's place as "Farmer for Lower Sioux."

It is interesting that Denver recommended what Prescott had been urging for several years. On November 30, 1857, Denver wrote:

Manual labor schools should be established, where they can learn how to conduct properly their agricultural pursuits, and especially where the boys could be educated as farmers, and the girls in housewifery and the dairy; and where also there could be imparted to both the rudiments of a plain and useful education. Mechanics' shops should also be established where necessary, and where as many of the boys as possible should be placed and trained to a knowledge of the mechanic arts suited to the condition and wants of their people. It is, if possible, more important that the Indian should be taught to till the soil, and to labor in the mechanical shops, than to have even a common school education.

The adult Indians should be encouraged to cultivate the lands assigned to them, each to have the exclusive control, under the tribal right of his own possessions, and of the products of his own labor. . . .

The Sioux were still complaining about not receiving funds due them long after Prescott's 1856 report was made. Their discontent is commonly given as a major cause of the Sioux Uprising of August, 1862, in which Prescott and some five hundred other white people lost their lives.

In March, 1857, Mr. Flandrau, the new agent for the Sioux, and Philander Prescott, as an experienced guide and interpreter, accompanied Captain Bernard E. Bee of Company D, 10th Infantry, from Fort Ridgely, with a company of forty-eight men. They went in search of Inkpaduta's renegade band of Wahpekute Sioux, who had murdered thirty-two white settlers at Spirit Lake and six more at Springfield, now Jackson, Minnesota, and had carried off four young white women as captives.

Hindered by a heavy snow which made travel impossible except under the most extreme hardships, Flandrau and Prescott turned back to their responsibilities at the Lower Agency. The soldiers pushed on, but were unsuccessful in their search for the culprits, who fled westward into South Dakota with their white captives.

This troubled season was accompanied by many councils with the Indians at which the services of an experienced translator must have been required. Although no mention is made of Prescott in this connection, it appears likely that he assisted in at least some of them.

Appendix B

CHRONOLOGY OF THE UPPER MISSISSIPPI

1654–
1660
Radisson and Groseilliers, French traders, make two journeys into the "upper country," possibly Minnesota, and demonstrate possibilities of a remunerative fur trade.

1673
Marquette and Jolliet reach the mouth of the Wisconsin River and discover the great Mississippi River.

1679
Daniel Greysolon, Sieur du Luth (DuLhut) plants the banner of France in the vicinity of Duluth and in the principal village of the Sioux tribe near Mille Lacs.

1680
Father Louis Hennepin and companions explore the upper Mississippi River area and discover and name the Falls of St. Anthony.

1682
Robert Cavalier de La Salle takes formal possession, in the name of the King of France, of the territory drained by the Mississippi and its tributaries.

1689
At Fort St. Antoine, near the foot of Lake Pepin, Nicholas Perrot, who reached the upper Mississippi several years before, lays formal claim to all the upper river for France.

1695
Pierre Charles le Sueur builds a fort on Prairie Island above Red Wing.

1700
Le Sueur establishes Fort L'Huillier on the Blue Earth River near present-day Mankato.

1727
Jesuits establish Fort Beauharnois at Frontenac on Lake Pepin and open the first mission in Minnesota.

1731
Sieur de la Verendrye and party begin exploring the waterways on the northern border and extend operations far northwest into Canada. One of the many forts erected along this route is St. Charles, on the Lake of the Woods, within the present area of Minnesota.

237

1754 The French and Indian War breaks out, affecting settlements in the Detroit area.

1756 France and England formally declare war.
Frontenac post, the last French fort on the upper Mississippi, is abandoned.

1760 On September 8 the French surrender to the English at Montreal, thus marking the decline of French power in North America.
On November 29 Major Robert Rogers receives the surrender of Detroit, after taking the Great Lakes fortifications.

1761 On September 28 the British occupy Fort Michilimackinac, destined to become a great fur center.

1762 The King of France, by a secret pact, cedes New Orleans island and all French land west of the Mississippi River to Spain, although that nation makes no attempt to occupy or explore the upper river country.

1763 France cedes to Great Britain the Minnesota country east of the Mississippi River. British traders take over the fur trade.

1766– Jonathan Carver, exploring for the British, ascends the St.
1767 Peter's (Minnesota) River.

1783 The land east of the Mississippi River to the Great Lakes is ceded by Great Britain to the newly established United States.

1784 The Northwest Company secures control of the Minnesota fur trade.

1794 The Northwest Company builds a post on Sandy Lake.
The British government refuses to make a commercial treaty or to give up the forts in the western territory of the United States through which its agents still wield great influence over the Indians, but Chief Justice John Jay negotiates a treaty which settles the difficulties for about twelve years.

1795 Spain claims exclusive rights to the Mississippi River, thus causing much trouble until a treaty is made providing for common navigation.

1796 The Laws of the Ordinance of 1787 are extended over the

Northwest Territory, including the northeastern third of Minnesota, east of the Mississippi River.

1800 By the Treaty of San Ildefonso, Spain cedes Louisiana Territory to France.

1801 Philander Prescott is born in Phelpstown, New York.

1803 By the Louisiana Purchase from France, the United States gains ownership of a vast region west of the Mississippi River, including western Minnesota.

President Jefferson asks Congress for $2,000 for an expedition to expand the Indian trade.

1805 Lieutenant Zebulon Montgomery Pike leads an expedition of twenty men to the upper reaches of the Mississippi. He obtains grants of land from the Sioux Indians on which to establish military posts at the mouths of the St. Peter's (Minnesota) and St. Croix rivers.

Pike instructs the Chippewas to keep peace with the Sioux, to give up their British flags and emblems, to pay their debts to the traders, and to stop the use of liquor.

Since there is no immediate follow-up of civil or military authority on the part of the United States government, affairs on the upper Mississippi remained the same. The Northwest Company continued to rule the fur industry in the territory west of Lake Superior.

1807 The Hudson's Bay Company and the Northwest Company continue their rivalry for supremacy in the fur trade.

1808 John Jacob Astor obtains a charter for the American Fur Company from the state of New York.

Although there are no longer British troops south of the Canadian boundary, the laws of the United States do not exclude British traders from the country about the Great Lakes and the headwaters of the Mississippi.

1812 British military occupation is re-established on the upper Mississippi. Indians of the Minnesota region join the British side in the war.

Lord Selkirk establishes a colony of Irish and Scots at the present site of Winnipeg, Manitoba, in the lower Red River Valley.

1813   Commodore Oliver H. Perry wins the Battle of Lake Erie.
        The British evacuate Detroit.

1815   By the Treaty of Ghent, February 17, Great Britain gives up
        all claim to trade south of the Canadian border. The last
        British garrison on the upper Mississippi evacuates Prairie
        du Chien.

1816   An act of Congress, April 29, excludes foreigners from
        participating in the fur trade of the United States except in
        subordinate capacities under American traders.
        The Northwest Company is forced to give up its interests on
        American soil as the American Fur Company takes over.
        To protect American interests, Fort Crawford is built at
        Prairie du Chien and Fort Howard near the mouth of the
        Fox River at Green Bay, Wisconsin.

1817   Major Stephen H. Long locates sites for future military
        posts. He reports the upper country swarming with *voyageurs*
        and the Indians still loyal to Britain.

1818   A section·in the Illinois enabling act makes part of the Old
        Northwest Territory north of that state a part of the territory
        of Michigan. When the county of Crawford, Michigan, is
        established, the part of Minnesota lying east of the Missis-
        sippi comes under Michigan's authority and the area in
        theory is so designated for seventeen years.

1819   U.S. troops under Lieut. Col. Henry Leavenworth reach the
        confluence of the Minnesota and Mississippi rivers and, on
        the site of Mendota, establish a cantonment known as Camp
        New Hope in August.
        Lawrence Taliaferro begins his service as Indian agent.
        Philander Prescott leaves his home in Phelpstown, New
        York, resides at Detroit for a time, and joins his brother
        Zachariah as sutler's employees at Camp New Hope in the
        winter of 1819–1820.

1820   The troops move across the Mississippi to Camp Cold Water,
        beside a large spring just north of the Minnesota's mouth.
        Col. Leavenworth is succeeded by Col. Josiah Snelling, who
        soon punishes the Indians for murder.

On September 10, Fort St. Anthony is begun on the bluffs overlooking both rivers.

Governor Lewis Cass of Michigan Territory visits Camp Cold Water and attempts mediation between the Sioux and Chippewas.

1821 A sawmill is started by troops on the west bank of the Falls of St. Anthony.

Five Swiss families from the Selkirk colony seek refuge and start farming near Fort Anthony.

The British Crown forces the Northwest Company and the Hudson's Bay Company to merge.

Congress abolishes the U.S. factories for trading with the Indians, leaving the American Fur Company free to fight its battles with private traders.

The American Fur Company establishes three posts near Lake of the Woods in competition with the Hudson's Bay Company.

1822 The Columbia Fur Company organizes with headquarters at Lake Traverse and posts in Minnesota, northern Iowa, and on the Missouri River.

1823 The *Virginia*, the first steamboat to navigate the Mississippi from St. Louis to the mouth of the Minnesota River, reaches Fort Anthony.

Major Stephen H. Long and party explore the Minnesota River and Red River valleys.

A grist and flour mill starts operating near the sawmill of St. Anthony Falls.

An Italian, Giacomo C. Beltrami, explores near the source of the Mississippi River.

1824 Under the act of Congress, May 26, Major Lawrence Taliaferro, Indian Agent, makes seven locations of Indian trading posts on the waters of the upper Mississippi.

1825 Fort St. Anthony's name is officially changed to Fort Snelling.

At a grand council in Prairie du Chien, the Sioux and Chippewas agree upon a dividing boundary to prevent future bloodshed.

About this time the U.S. government decides on removal of Indians to reservations as a definite policy.

1826   The Red River overflows, causing many of the colonists in the Selkirk settlement to seek refuge at Fort Snelling the following year.

1827   The Columbia Fur Company combines with the American Fur Company.

1829   The Sioux farming colony, called Eatonville, begins at Lake Calhoun.

1832   Henry R. Schoolcraft locates the source of the Mississippi in a lake which he names Itasca, July 13.
       Philander Prescott and Joseph Laframboise go to the Big Sioux River in eastern South Dakota to spend the following winter.

1833   The first Protestant mission among Minnesota Indians west of the Mississippi River is established at Leech Lake by the Reverend W. T. Boutwell.

1834   The Pond brothers, missionaries to the Sioux, arrive at Fort Snelling and during the summer build a cabin on Lake Calhoun.
       Henry H. Sibley, agent of the American Fur Company, establishes a trading post at Mendota near Fort Snelling.
       An act of Congress forbids introduction of liquor into Indian country but the law is habitually disregarded.
       The Indian Intercourse Act forbids white men, except traders with authorized licenses, from entering reservations.

1835   Philander Prescott is interpreter for troops with the Sioux-Chippewa boundary survey party headed by Major J. L. Bean.
       The Lac qui Parle mission is founded by the Reverend T. S. Williamson, M.D.
       A Presbyterian church, the first for white people in Minnesota, is organized at Fort Snelling.
       George Catlin, famous painter of Indian subjects, and George W. Featherstonhaugh, geologist, visit the area.

1836   Joseph N. Nicollet, after making scientific explorations of the upper Mississippi, announces at Fort Snelling that the source of the river is a *rivulet* feeding Lake Itasca.

Wisconsin Territory is organized. The eastern part of Minnesota, considered a part of Crawford County, Michigan, now becomes a part of Crawford County, Wisconsin.

Major Lawrence Taliaferro, Indian Agent at Fort Snelling, is ordered to organize a delegation of Sioux Indians to take to Washington.

1837   The Chippewa Indians cede to Wisconsin Territory their timber lands on the St. Croix and its tributaries. The Sioux cede to the United States their lands east of the Mississippi. By such cessions the United States obtains possession of the triangle between the Mississippi and St. Croix rivers, as well as a part of northern Wisconsin.

1838   Official notice of the ratification of the Treaty of 1837 is received at Fort Snelling.

With the establishment of squatters' claims, the twin cities of Minneapolis and St. Paul have their beginnings.

Joseph N. Nicollet and John Charles Fremont explore southwestern Minnesota.

1839   Pillager Chippewas murder Neka (the Beaver), a Sioux, near the mission at Lake Harriet.

Amos J. Bruce succeeds Major Lawrence Taliaferro as U.S. Indian Agent at Fort Snelling.

1840   Settlers expelled from the military reservation of Fort Snelling start the village called the Pig's Eye, which later becomes St. Paul.

1842   The Battle of Kaposia takes place between the Chippewas and the Sioux.

1846–   Treaties are negotiated with the Winnebagos; but when the
1847   time comes for removal of the Indians to a new reservation, they are reluctant to go.

1848   May 29, Wisconsin becomes the thirtieth state, but without jurisdiction over the part of its territory in the Minnesota region.

October 20, Henry H. Sibley, of Mendota, is elected delegate to Congress from that part of the Wisconsin Territory not included in the new state.

The Winnebagos finally move to a new location.

1849   On March 3, Minnesota Territory is created by Congress. It comprises an area of 166,000 square miles, with the Mississippi River flowing through its center. White population is 4,000. From the spring of 1840 on, the all-absorbing interest of the white men of the territory has been the acquisition of the lands occupied by the Sioux Indians lying between the Mississippi River and the Big Sioux.

April 28, the *Minnesota Pioneer*, the first newspaper to be printed in Minnesota, begins publication.

June 1, Governor Alexander Ramsey declares the Territory organized.

September 3, the first Territorial Legislature convenes at St. Paul and adjourns November 1.

November 15, the Minnesota Historical Society, the oldest cultural institution in the state, is organized, with Governor Ramsey as president.

1850   Hole-in-the-Day and two Chippewa companions kill a Sioux. Three hundred Indian warriors hold a council at Fort Snelling.

Henry M. Rice receives contract from the Commissioner of Indian Affairs to remove the Winnebagos to a reservation in northern Minnesota.

Steamboat excursions on the Minnesota River give much publicity to the excellent quality of the Minnesota valley.

The census records 6,077 white inhabitants.

1851   Eight thousand Indians assemble and agree to treaties at Traverse des Sioux and Mendota, by which they cede their lands west of the Mississippi to the U.S. government.

1852   The treaties of 1851 are ratified.

The military reservation at Fort Snelling is greatly reduced and new boundaries defined by Congress. Minneapolis is laid out on former reservation grounds. Congress orders that the St. Peter's River be designated officially as the Minnesota River.

1853 "Suland" is nearly empty of Indians, as they are removed to their reservation in the upper Minnesota valley.
A great tide of immigration to the Sioux cession begins.
Minnesota Territorial Agricultural Society is founded.

1854 Minnesota Territory is legally opened to settlement.
The Richfield Mills are built by Prescott, Moffet, and Pettijohn.
Fort Ridgely is built on the Minnesota River.

1855 Great pine regions about the headwaters of the Mississippi are opened for purchase as fast as surveys can be made.

1857 As the result of a population boom, Minnesota now has a population of 150,037.
The Minnesota Constitutional Convention adopts a constitution and elects state officials.
Secretary of War Floyd sells Fort Snelling.
The Spirit Lake massacre disturbs the frontier.
A financial panic strikes the country, delaying settlement.

1858 On May 11 Minnesota becomes thirty-second state.

1859 Alexander Ramsey is elected governor.

1861 With the beginning of the Civil War, many of the troops are ordered away from Fort Snelling to engage in the War.

1862 The Sioux Uprising takes place in Minnesota, beginning on August 17. Philander Prescott, a friend of the Sioux for more than forty years, is one of the first to be killed. The lives of more than five hundred settlers are taken by the Indians.

Appendix C

THE PRESCOTT FAMILY

Joel Prescott, the son of David and Abigail Wright Prescott, was born on June 20, 1759, in Groton, Massachusetts. At the beginning of the Revolution he was a young lad and remained at home to help his father while his older brothers went into the army. A kinsman, Colonel Prescott, performed distinguished service at Bunker Hill.[1]

For a time in 1788, Dr. Joel Prescott lived in Geneva, Ontario County, New York, as the town's first physician. The next year he moved to Phelps, then called Vienna, in the same county, near Oneida Lake. The Doctor was one of the earliest pioneers of that place. Most of the settlers in Ontario County had come from New England, though some came from Maryland, bringing slaves with them.

In 1790, Dr. Prescott bought a one hundred–acre farm one mile west of Oaks Corners, a small settlement about four miles southeast of Phelps village. There he took his bride, Lucy Reed, the daughter of Seth Reed whom he had married at Phelps, New York, on September 8, 1793.

At the first Phelps town meeting held in 1796, Dr. Prescott was elected one of the assessors. He was also an early supervisor and for several years chairman of the Board of Supervisors of Ontario County. In addition, he was the town's first school commissioner.

Dr. and Mrs. Prescott's children were: Imley, born in 1794; Zachariah Wright, born in 1796; John Reed, born in 1798; Philander, born September 17, 1801; Phidelia, born in 1803; Sophia, born in 1806; and two other children, who died in infancy.

About 1807 a nephew of Dr. Prescott, who bore the same name as

[1] According to Francis B. Heitman, *Historical Register and Dictionary of the U.S. Army* (Washington: G.P.O., 1903): "Colonel William Prescott (Mass.), was Colonel of a Massachusetts Regiment, 19th May to December 1775. He was Colonel of the 7th Continental Infantry. Also, Benjamin Prescott, Massachusetts, was a Private in Lexington Alarm, April 1775; Lieutenant of Prescott's Massachusetts Regiment, May, 1775; killed at Bunker Hill, 17th June 1775."

his uncle, went to Phelps to read and study medicine with the Doctor. He married Clarissa Stearns, the daughter of Joel Stearns.

After a lingering illness from "dropsy in the abdomen," the Doctor died on October 5, 1811, in Phelps, leaving his family in rather poor circumstances. The nephew succeeded to his uncle's medical practice. Some time after the Doctor's death Lucy Reed Prescott remarried but died of consumption in 1818.

Imley, who was a quartermaster in the War of 1812, married Maria Cross in 1816. John died in 1817. Phidelia married Owen Edmonston and later moved to Kentucky. She died in 1843.

Zachariah Wright Prescott served as a clerk to Louis Devotion, sutler for the United States troops at Detroit and Fort Snelling from 1819 to 1822; worked for the Powells in St. Louis; and from 1825 to 1827 represented the Columbia Fur Company at Fort Confederation on the upper branches of the Des Moines River, in Humboldt County, Iowa. Part of that time he was trading with the Yankton Sioux. Zachariah returned to Vienna, New York, and married Panthea Merry. According to Mrs. Ralph O. Stratton, secretary and curator of the Ontario County Historical Society of Canandaigua, New York, "he invented and had in operation in his store in Phelps a telegraph line long before Morse's invention, but with his death in 1851 the impractical scheme was thought so visionary it was dropped." His widow married Owen Edmonston, whose first wife, Phidelia Prescott, had died in 1843.

Sophia married Porter Hawkes and later, James B. Darrow. Her descendants were still living in Geneva, New York, as late as 1939.

Left an orphan at seventeen, Philander Prescott had difficulty in finding work at home, so he decided to accept the invitation of his brother Zachariah to join him in Detroit. When an uncle, Nathan Reed, refused to loan him money for the trip, Philander set out with only a few dollars and walked the entire distance from Phelps to Buffalo, where he boarded a steamboat. Shortly after Philander reached Detroit, his brother had to leave with troops to go to the mouth of the Minnesota River. Mr. Devotion hired Philander to help move a shipment of goods, making it possible for him to follow Zachariah and join him late in 1819 or in early January, 1820, at Camp New Hope, the forerunner of Fort Snelling.

Since details of Prescott's experiences between 1820 and 1857 as a sutler's assistant, Indian trader, riverman, interpreter, innkeeper, and supervisor of Indian farmers are given in his recollections and government reports, they will not be repeated here.

In 1823 Prescott was married in the Indian fashion to Spirit-in-the-Moon, the daughter of a Sioux chief. She was a faithful wife and homemaker. Although the Prescotts had nine children, only two—Hiram and Lucy—are mentioned by name in Prescott's writings. The oldest son, William, born in 1824, died at the Choctaw Academy in the winter of 1835. Lucy, born in 1828, married Eli Pettijohn in 1850. Harriet, born in 1829, died in 1833. Hiram, born in 1832, married Lavinia Hamilton in 1857. Caroline, born in 1836, died the next year. Lawrence Taliaferro, born in 1838, performed notable service in the Civil War. Married and the father of two children, he died in 1869. Julia, born in 1841, was married to John C. Tyler in 1869. Sophia, born in 1844, married Emsily Jackson Hamilton in 1867. They had one child. Mary Elizabeth Whitehouse, born in 1846, died in 1848.

Sorrow over the death of his oldest boy, William in 1835, and difficulties with his Indian mother-in-law may have temporarily embittered Prescott to the point of deciding to abandon his Indian wife and children. Although he gives not the slightest hint of this in his own recollections, the fact that the details of 1835 and 1836 seem especially confused or lacking may confirm the following statement by John H. Stevens, who knew Prescott well and had lived in his home during 1849–1850:

Prescott became dissatisfied with his northwestern possessions. He had never married the Indian woman except in the Indian fashion; that is, he gave a pony and some goods for her to her parents. It did not seem difficult or cruel to abandon her. Other traders left their wives and children—why should not he? She was abundantly able to care for herself, his and her children, for their wants were few; and she had well-to-do relatives—Indians, of course, but Indians are fond of their kith and kin. He had made some money; he would sell his interests and make more; then he would leave all and go south to Texas or some other place, and start anew without incumbrances—wife, child, or chick. He made his way down the Mississippi, traversed Texas and Louisiana, visited the Choctaw, Creek and Chickasaw Indians, but found poor prospects for starting a new business in the lower country. He spent two or three years in hunting and traveling. It is probable that, discouraged, once in a while he indulged in fire-water to a greater extent than was for his good.

While Mr. Prescott was near the headwaters of the Sabine river, he visited a religious protracted-meeting, which was attended pretty much by Crackers. He became, through the influence of the preacher, a changed man. Although several thousand miles away from the Dakota wife and children that he had abandoned—who were wandering with the mother's tribe over the plains—he determined to return to them at once, and do what he should have done at first—marry the woman according to the rules of Christianity. After a long journey he landed at the St. Peter agency, where he found that the mother of his children was away beyond the coteaus in the buffalo range of the Missouri valley. With his pack on his back he started in search of her. It was midsummer when he found her. Poor Indian woman that she was, she was overjoyed to see him, but could not understand why he would not live with her any more as his wife, until after a long journey should be made to find a regularly ordained minister of the gospel, and they should be married in the same manner as the white folks. After urging, coaxing and praying, he persuaded her to leave her people and, with her children, the broad prairies were crossed, the home of a missionary was found, the solemn marriage rites were performed, and at the same time and by the same holy ordinance his children were made legitimate.

Mr. Prescott has often spoken to me of the great privation and suffering that attended this (to him) sacred pilgrimage. That Indian woman was an excellent housekeeper, fond of her domestic duties, an affectionate wife, and a good mother. It could not well be otherwise when we consider that she had a noble, Christian husband. Her hospitable house was always full of people. It was the only roof at Fort Snelling that afforded a stopping-place for travelers and strangers.[2]

Whether Stevens' account is accurate in all details is not certain, but it has been repeated by two or three other writers.

According to Presbyterian church history records, Prescott did join the church at Lake Harriet on June 18, 1837; and under a provision in the treaty made with the Sioux that year, Spirit-in-the-Moon and Prescott were remarried by the Reverend Samuel W. Pond, a missionary. Mrs. Prescott was baptized, and her name was changed to Mary from Nag-he-no-Wenah (Spirit-in-the-Moon).

In the Autumn of 1837, Prescott's family lived with him in his

[2] *Personal Recollections of Minnesota and Its People and Early History of Minneapolis* (Minneapolis: Tribune Co., 1890), pp. 43–44.

winter quarters across from Traverse des Sioux, near St. Peter's, but apparently returned to their small house at Lake Harriet for the winter. Presumably the family was also with Prescott when he guarded his claims near the townsite of future Prescott, Wisconsin. In addition to a little farm there, Prescott had a wood lot and sold wood to steamboats.

In 1843 he became a government interpreter for the Sioux. This position entitled him to housing at Fort Snelling; and for about ten years thereafter the Prescotts maintained a home in the stone government building near the entrance to Fort Snelling, next to the Indian Agent. Their hospitality was enjoyed by many visitors, as there was no hotel at the Fort. Daniel Stanchfield, a lumberman, stated that he was a guest there in 1847 before starting on his exploring trip. On July 5, 1848, about three hundred of the principal men of the Winnebagos and Sioux assembled at Prescott's home for a great council, which ended amicably.

In 1849 Philander Prescott endeavored to stake a claim on Minnehaha Creek near the Falls; but since the land was on the reservation, he could not take possession.

On December 26, 1849, a meeting of the members of the First Presbyterian Church was called by a committee of the Presbytery of Dakota. It was held at Fort Snelling in the home of Philander Prescott, who was clerk of the session for thirteen years.

In 1851, after considerable delay in the acceptance of papers in Washington because of claim jumpers, Prescott obtained title to two hundred acres of land at Prescott, Wisconsin.

Great anxiety in the Fort Snelling area resulted from the law passed by Congress in 1852 which reduced the size of the Fort Snelling reservation, because it contained no provision for the relief of the settlers on the land. In order to protect their claims, the long-time residents, including Prescott and John H. Stevens, organized a claim association with a five-member executive committee. The committee, which met every Saturday, adopted strict rules against claim jumpers. According to Stevens, "only in one instance was the association called upon to resort to severe measures. A cat-o-nine-tails laid on the bare back of the trespasser on a claim down toward the Minnehaha had the desired effect."

On New Year's night, 1850, Lucy Prescott, twenty-two years old, was married to Eli Pettijohn, thirty-one, a native of Ohio. Lucy had been "sent abroad," probably "back east," for an education. According to the Reverend E. D. Neill, she attended "a boarding school of some celebrity."

John Stevens, who knew the Prescotts well, wrote of Lucy:

> She was like a bird about the old stone building, singing and making everyone happy. I never wondered that her father so fondly loved her.

> A young man of excellent character from Illinois [sic] was employed around the missionary grounds and the Indian farms. He was a Christian man; she was a Christian girl . . . one evening just at the close of the old year and the beginning of the new, there was a large gathering at the old weather-beaten homestead. There were officers of high rank in the army, in full uniform, with their wives; officers holding high trusts in civil positions, with their wives and daughters; gentlemen, with their ladies, in full evening costume; and men and women whose fathers were white and mothers were red; Dakota relatives and friends of the bride in their blankets—making in all about as curious an assembly, as unique a gathering, as ever attended a wedding feast, and one that, as Rev. Mr. Neill (who officiated on the occasion) says, "could only be seen on the outposts of civilization."

AT THE MARRIAGE FEAST

> A varied feast followed the wedding ceremony—one which pleased the white people, and delighted the red guests. The father was seemingly the happiest man in the territory that night— scarcely excepting the groom. What a shadow of the memory of the past was thrown over the father of the bride that eventful evening! None of us could persuade the mother to appear in the parlor during the marriage ceremony, but immediately afterwards she waited on the guests, and was doubtless as pleased as was her husband that her daughter was wedded to a white Christian. The bride's Indian uncles, aunts, and cousins were present, wrapped in their blankets, and viewed the ceremony with seemingly cold, weary, and stolid countenances, through the parlor doors.[3]

General Richard W. Johnson, who arrived at Fort Snelling on October 4, 1849, described the same event:

> As the winter closed in around us in 1849, shutting out all visitors, life in the garrison became very monotonous; but one

[3] *Ibid.*, pp. 45–46.

little event, outside of the regular routine, occurred to vary the sameness of our every-day life. Just outside of the walls of the fort resided Mr. Philander Prescott, connected with the Indian Department as interpreter. His wife was a full-blooded Sioux, by whom he had one or more children. One was a pretty maiden, reasonably well educated. Invitations were extended to the officers and their wives to attend her marriage to Mr. Eli Pettijohn. The ceremony was to take place at eight o'clock in the evening of January 1, 1850. Promptly at the appointed time, I was on hand, taking with me the young lady who afterward became my wife.

Such an assemblage as I met at Mr. Prescott's I never saw before nor since. There was the dignified, venerable Loomis; the elegantly dressed officers, their wives, and daughters; civilized Indians, and Indians not civilized; elaborately dressed women, and women scantily attired. The bride and groom shone out by their elegant and tasteful adornments. She was pretty, as all brides are; and he was happy, as all grooms should be. At the conclusion of the ceremony a sumptuous repast was served; and all departed after wishing the bridal party a happy voyage over the sea of life, and with the wish that every day might bring such a pleasant occasion.[4]

The Reverend E. D. Neill, the Presbyterian minister who performed the ceremony, said, in part:

Among the guests present were the officers of the garrison in full uniform, with their wives, the United States Agent for the Dahkotahs, and family, the bois brules of the neighbourhood, the Indian relatives of the mother. The mother did not make her appearance, but, as the minister proceeded with the ceremony, the Dahkotah relatives gathered in the hall and looked in through the door.

The marriage feast was worthy of the occasion. In consequence of the numbers, the officers and those of European extraction partook first; then the bois brules of Ojibway and Dahkotah descent; and finally, the native Americans, who did ample justice to the plentiful supply spread before them.[5]

Eli Pettijohn became a man of some importance in Minnesota politics. He was one of the two hundred or so men who organized

[4] "Fort Snelling from Its Foundation to the Present Time," *Minnesota Historical Collections*, VIII (1895–1898), 343–435.

[5] *The History of Minnesota from the Earliest French Explorations to the Present Time* (Minneapolis: Minn. Hist. Co., 1882), pp. 523–524.

the Republican party of the territory, March 29 and 30, 1855, and was chosen one of the six vice-presidents of the group. In 1850, he was installed as an elder in the First Presbyterian Church in Minnesota, of which both he and his wife were members. He served in that capacity until 1865.

Pettijohn was associated briefly with his father-in-law and Willis G. Moffett in a milling enterprise. He and his wife later moved to California, where he became a breakfast food manufacturer. The Pettijohns later returned to Minnesota to reside.

Prescott, along with his friend John H. Stevens, was one of ten incorporators named when the Minnesota Agricultural Society was incorporated by an act of the legislature on February 20, 1853. Later in the same year, on September 18, the Hennepin County Bible Society was organized, the first of its kind in Hennepin County. Prescott was one of the fourteen local agents, four of whom were ministers.

In 1854 Prescott, in partnership with Willis G. Moffett and Eli Pettijohn, erected a mill at the mouth of the Minnehaha stream. A post office named Harmony was established at the mill, and the little town that grew up there was first called Richland, and later Richfield. At the time of his death, Prescott was the sole owner of the turbine-wheel mill, which had four runs of stone and a capacity of twenty barrels in ten hours. Prescott's home in Richfield was located near his mill, at what is now 4440 Snelling Avenue in Minneapolis.

On August 17, 1862, Indian unrest came to a head when the Sioux wiped out a settlement of white settlers at Acton township. Philander Prescott, who was serving as interpreter at the Lower, or Redwood, Agency on the Minnesota River when word reached him of the tragedy, was warned to flee for his life. Although he was unwell, he fled on foot toward Fort Ridgely, and had nearly reached the fort when he was met by some Indians of his acquaintance. According to the Reverend Samuel Pond, "They appeared friendly and after conversing with him a minute, passed on as if they did not intend to molest him, but turned and shot him in the back.... Even his murderers seem to have been ashamed to have him know that they intended to kill him for they did not attack him in front, although he was unarmed, feeble, and defenceless." [6]

[6] "The Dakotas or Sioux in Minnesota as They Were in 1834," *Minnesota Historical Collections*, XII (1908), 338.

John H. Stevens gave the following account:

Early on this fatal Monday morning (August 18, 1862) Mr. Prescott and Rev. J. D. Hinman learned from Little Crow that the storm of savage wrath was gathering, and that their only safety was in instant flight. Mrs. Hinman was, fortunately, at Faribault. The white-haired interpreter, Philander Prescott, nearly seventy years of age, hastily left his house soon after his meeting with Little Crow, and fled toward Ridgely. The other members of his family remained behind, knowing that their relations to the tribe would save them. Mr. Prescott had gone several miles along the west bank of the Minnesota river when he was overtaken, his murderers came and talked with him. He reasoned with them, saying: "I am an old man; I have lived with you now forty-five years, almost half a century. My wife and children are among you, of your own blood; I have never done you any harm, and have been your true friend in all your troubles; why should you wish to kill me?" Their reply was: "We would save your life if we could, but the WHITE MAN MUST DIE; we cannot spare your life; our orders are to kill all white men; we cannot spare you." It is said upon the authority of the Indians that he was shot while talking with them and looking calmly into their eyes. Mr. Prescott was the true, tried, and faithful friend of the Indian, and had labored long in their interest. His benevolence to the red-men kept him ever poor. Mr. Hinman escaped to Fort Ridgely.[7]

Mrs. Prescott and the children who had been with Prescott at the Redwood Agency were taken prisoner during the Uprising and placed in a camp of captive women. Despite the threats of Little Crow, they escaped from the camp and were not followed.

Mrs. Prescott died in 1867 at the home of her daughter, Mrs. Eli Pettijohn, in Shakopee, Minnesota.

[7] *Personal Recollections of Minnesota*, pp. 364–365.

Appendix D

PHILANDER PRESCOTT'S WRITINGS

Alexander Ramsey, the first governor of the new Territory of Minnesota from April 2, 1849, until May 15, 1853, and later elected the state's second governor in 1860, was thoroughly aware of the necessity and importance of having the history of Minnesota preserved by those who had helped to make it. Ramsey was president of the Minnesota Historical Society from 1849 to 1863, and again from 1891 until 1903. About 1860, the Governor asked Philander Prescott to write his recollections, knowing that he had seen the state develop from a wilderness.

Although Prescott had had little formal education and his spelling, punctuation, and paragraphing were faulty, his recording of events and his measurement of men were excellent. He filled 208 pages in longhand with recollections of his personal experiences while participating in important happenings in the Territory prior to 1852. At that date his manuscript breaks off abruptly, leaving untold the details of the events of the last ten years of his life.

Fortunately, however, details of Prescott's activities as a teacher and superintendent of farming for the Sioux on their reservations and in their villages (1849–1856) are published in the *Annual Reports of the Commissioner of Indian Affairs* in Washington, D.C. These reports help to explain the dissatisfaction which was building up in the Sioux which led to the Sioux Uprising of 1862 in which Prescott was one of the earliest victims.

Miraculously during the destruction which accompanied the Uprising, Prescott's manuscript was saved. A letter from Eli Pettijohn, Prescott's son-in-law, written on September 12, 1875, to the Minnesota Historical Society stated that the manuscript was in his wife's hands and could be consulted at any time. In 1893, Mrs. Pettijohn gave the manuscript to the Society. At that time Alexander Ramsey was president of the Minnesota Historical Society, and it seems most likely that he was instrumental in obtaining the manuscript.

255

In 1894 a small part of the manuscript was published under the title, "Autobiography and Reminiscences of Philander Prescott," dated Minnehaha, Minnesota, February 18, 1861, in the *Minnesota Historical Collections* (Volume VI). This, however, carries Prescott's story up to only about 1830. The 208-page manuscript written by Prescott is being published here complete for the first time.

Prescott's annual reports as Superintendent of Indian Farming to the Commissioner of Indian Affairs have been summarized and indexed in the *South Dakota Historical Collections* (Volumes XXVI and XXVII) by Will G. Robinson.

Prescott wrote much about the Sioux and contributed three valuable articles on their history, customs, and religion to Henry R. Schoolcraft's *Information Respecting the History, Condition and Prospects of the Indian Tribes of the United States* (6 vols.; Philadelphia: Lippincott, Grambo, 1851–1857). Schoolcraft, who evidently relied greatly on his statements, described Prescott as being "allied to the Sioux tribe; of whom he records the customs and traditions, speaks their language fluently, and has lived many years among them in various situations and positions. His means of personal observation have, therefore, been ample; he is, moreover, a man of entire integrity of character, and unimpeachable veracity. A plain man, without pretence to education, he records simply what he has seen and heard [Vol. II, p. 168]."

Bibliography

MAGAZINES AND NEWSPAPERS

"Accessions," *Minnesota History Bulletin*, Vol. IV, Nos. 1–2 (February–May 1921), 65–75.

"Alexander Faribault," *Minnesota History*, Vol. VIII, No. 2 (June 1927), 177–180.

BAIRD, ELIZABETH THERESA. "Indian Customs and Early Recollections," *Wisconsin Historical Collections*, IX (1880–1882), 303–326.

BAIRD, HENRY S. "Recollections of the Early History of Northern Wisconsin," *Wisconsin Historical Collections*, IV (1857–1858), 197–251.

BLAKELY, RUSSELL. "History of the Discovery of the Mississippi River and the Advent of Commerce in Minnesota," *Minnesota Historical Collections*, VIII (1895–1898), 303–418.

CHILDS, COL. EBENEZER. "Recollections of Wisconsin Since 1820," *Wisconsin Historical Collections*, IV (1857–1858), 153–195.

DE LA RONDE, JOHN T. "Personal Narrative," *Wisconsin Historical Collections*, VII (1873–1876), 344–365.

"A Description of Northern Minnesota by a Fur-Trader in 1807" (ed. Grace Lee Nute), *Minnesota History Bulletin*, Vol. V, No. 1 (February 1923), 28–39.

"The Diary of Martin McLeod" (ed. Grace Lee Nute), *Minnesota History Bulletin*, Vol. IV, No. 7–8 (August–November 1922), 351–439.

"Early Days at Fort Snelling," *Minnesota Historical Collections*, I (1850–1856), 420–438.

FOLSOM, WILLIAM H. C. "History of Lumbering in the St. Croix Valley, with Biographic Sketches," *Minnesota Historical Collections*, IX (1898–1900), 291–324.

"The French Regime in Wisconsin—II" (ed. Reuben Gold Thwaites), *Wisconsin Historical Collections*, XVII (1906), 1–518.

"The Fur-Trade in Wisconsin, 1812–1825" (ed. Reuben Gold Thwaites), *Wisconsin Historical Collections*, XX (1911), 1–395.

GUNN, GEORGE HENRY. "Peter Garrioch at St. Peter's, 1837," *Minnesota History*, Vol. XX, No. 2 (June 1939), 119–128.

"Henry Mower Rice," *Minnesota Historical Collections*, IX (1898–1900), 654–658.

HUGHES, THOMAS. "History of Steamboating on the Mississippi River," *Minnesota Historical Collections*, Vol. X, Pt. 1 (1905), 131–163.

HUGHES, THOMAS. "The Treaty of Traverse des Sioux in 1851," *Minnesota Historical Collections*, Vol. X, Pt. 1 (1905), 101–129.

JENKS, WILLIAM L. "Fort Gratiot and Its Builder, General Charles Gratiot," *Michigan History*, Vol. IV, No. 1 (January 1920), 141–155.

JOHNSON, GEN. RICHARD W. "Fort Snelling from Its Foundation to the Present Time," *Minnesota Historical Collections*, VIII (1895–1898), 427–448.

"Life and Public Services of Hon. Willis A. Gorman," *Minnesota Historical Collections*, III (1870–1880), 314–332.

LOCKWOOD, JAMES H. "Early Times and Events in Wisconsin," *Wisconsin Historical Collections*, II (1855), 98–196.

MASTICS, AL. "Walk-in-the-Water," *Inland Seas*, X (Fall 1954).

"Minnesota Biographies," *Minnesota Historical Collections*, XIV (1912), 1–892.

"Minnesota Geographic Names," *Minnesota Historical Collections*, XVII (1920), 1–654.

Minnesotian, July 10, 1852.

"Narrative of Morgan L. Martin," *Wisconsin Historical Collections*, XI (1888), 393–394.

NEILL, E. D. "Occurrences in and Around Fort Snelling, from 1819 to 1840," *Minnesota Historical Collections*, II (1860–1867), 102–142.

"News and Comments," *Minnesota History*, Vol. IX, No. 2 (June 1928), 193.

NUTE, GRACE LEE. "Posts in the Minnesota Fur-Trading Area, 1660–1855," *Minnesota History*, Vol. XI, No. 4 (December 1930), 353–385.

PARKER, DONALD D. "Early Explorations and Fur Trading in South Dakota," *South Dakota Historical Collections*, XXV (1950), 1–211.

PATCHIN, SYDNEY A. "The Development of Banking in Minnesota," *Minnesota History Bulletin*, Vol. II, No. 3 (August 1917), 111–168.

PETERSEN, WILLIAM J. "Captain Joseph Throckmorton," *Palimpsest*, Vol. X, No. (April 1929), 129–144.

"Pike's Explorations in Minnesota, 1805–6," *Minnesota Historical Collections*, I (1850–1856), 368–416.

POND, SAMUEL W. "The Dakotas or Sioux in Minnesota as They Were in 1834," *Minnesota Historical Collections*, XII (1908), 319–501.

———. "Indian Warfare in Minnesota," *Minnesota Historical Collections*, III (1870–1880), 129–138.

———. "Two Missionaries in the Sioux Country: The Narrative of Samuel W. Pond" (ed. Theodore C. Blegen), *Minnesota History*, Vol. XXI, No. 2 (June 1940), 158–175.

PRESCOTT, PHILANDER. "Autobiography and Reminiscences of Philander Prescott," *Minnesota Historical Collections*, Vol. VI, Pt. 1 (1894), 475–491.

PRITCHETT, JOHN PERRY. "Some Red River Fur-Trade Activities," *Minnesota History Bulletin*, Vol. V, No. 6 (May 1924), 401–423.

"Records of Fort Tecumseh," *South Dakota Historical Collections*, IX (1918), 93–239.

"Relations with Western Canada," *Minnesota History Bulletin*, Vol. II, No. 1 (February 1917), 19–23.

"Reviews of Books," *Minnesota History Bulletin*, Vol. II, No. 2 (May 1917), 85–88.

RHOADS, JAMES B. "The Fort Snelling Area in 1835," *Minnesota History*, Vol. XXXV, No. 1 (March 1956), 22–29.

RIGGS, STEPHEN R. "Dakota Portraits" (ed. Willoughby M. Babcock, Jr.), *Minnesota History Bulletin*, Vol. II, No. 8 (November 1918), 481–568.

———. "Protestant Missions in the Northwest," *Minnesota Historical Collections*, VI (1894), 117–188.

ROBINSON, DOANE. "A History of the Sioux Indians," *South Dakota Historical Collections*, II (1904), 1–508.

ROBINSON, WILL G. "Digest of Reports of the Commission of Indian Affairs," *South Dakota Historical Collections*, XXVI (1952), 456–533; XXVII (1954), 160–515.

"Running the Gantlet: A Thrilling Incident of Early Days at Fort Snelling," *Minnesota Historical Collections*, I (1850–1856), 439–456.

St. Paul *Chronicle and Register*, April 6, 1850.

SIBLEY, HENRY H. "Memoir of Jean Baptiste Faribault," *Minnesota Historical Collections*, III (1870–1880), 168–179.

———. "Reminiscences; Historical and Personal," *Minnesota Historical Collections*, I (1850–1856), 457–485.

———. "Reminiscences of the Early Days of Minnesota," *Minnesota Historical Collections*, III (1870–1880), 242–282.

STEVENSON, C. STANLEY. "Expeditions into Dakota," *South Dakota Historical Collections*, IX (1918), 347–375.

TANNER, EDWARD. "Wisconsin in 1818," *Wisconsin Historical Collections*, VIII (1877–1879), 287–292.

WOODALL, ALLEN E. "William Joseph Snelling and the Early Northwest," *Minnesota History*, Vol. X, No. 4 (December 1929), 367–385.

BOOKS

BILLINGTON, RAY ALLEN, and JAMES B. HEDGES. *Westward Expansion: A History of the American Frontier.* 2d ed. New York: Macmillan, 1960.

CHITTENDEN, HIRAM M. *The American Fur Trade of the Far West: A History of the Pioneer Trading Posts and Early Fur Companies of the Missouri Valley and the Rocky Mountains and the Overland Commerce with Santa Fe.* 3 vols. New York: Harper, 1902.

CLARK, THOMAS D. *Frontier America*. New York: Charles Scribner's Sons, 1959.

EASTMAN, MARY HENDERSON. *Dahcotah; of Life and Legends of the Sioux Around Fort Snelling*. New York, 1849.

FARMER, SILAS. *History of Detroit and Michigan*. New York: Farmer and Company, 1884.

FOLWELL, WILLIAM WATTS. *A History of Minnesota*. 4 vols. St. Paul: Minnesota Historical Society, 1921–1930.

GOODWIN, CARDINAL LEONIDAS. *The Trans-Mississippi West (1803–1853): A History of Its Acquisition and Settlement*. New York: D. Appleton and Co., 1922.

HANSEN, MARCUS L. *Old Fort Snelling, 1819–1858*. Iowa City: Iowa State Historical Society, 1918.

HEITMAN, FRANCIS B. *Historical Register and Dictionary of the U.S. Army, from Its Organization Sept. 29, 1789, to March 2, 1903*. Washington: G.P.O., 1903.

HODGE, FREDERICK WEBB (ed.). *Handbook of American Indians North of Mexico*. 2 vols. New York: Pageant Books, 1959.

KEATING, WILLIAM HYPOLITUS. *Narrative of an Expedition to the Source of St. Peter's River, Lake Winnepeek, Lake of the Woods, &c, Performed in the Year 1823, by Order of the Hon. J. C. Calhoun, Secretary of War, Under the Command of Stephen H. Long, Major, USTE, Comp. from the Notes of Major Long, Messrs. Say, Keating, and Calhoun, by William H. Keating*. 2 vols. Philadelphia: H. C. Carey and I. Lea, 1824.

MARSHALL, REV. ALBERT B. *History of the First Presbyterian Church of Minneapolis, Minnesota, 1835–1910*. Minneapolis: Minn. Printing Co., 1910.

Minnesota: A State Guide. WPA; 2d pr., New York: Hastings House, 1947.

NEILL, EDWARD DUFFIELD. 4 vols. *History of Hennepin County and the City of Minneapolis*. Minneapolis: North Star Pub. Co., 1881.

———. *The History of Minnesota from the Earliest French Explorations to the Present Time*. 4th ed. Minneapolis: Minn. Hist. Co., 1882.

PARKER, DONALD D. *Lac Qui Parle, Its Missionaries, Traders and Indians*. Privately pub., 1964.

PEAKE, ORA BROOKS. *A History of the United States Indian Factory System, 1795–1822*. Denver: Sage Books, 1954.

RIDLEY, HELEN POST. *When Phelps Was Young*. Phelps, New York: Echo Press, 1939.

RIGGS, STEPHEN RETURN. *Mary and I: Forty Years with the Sioux*. Introd. by Rev. S. C. Bartlett. Boston: Congregational Sunday-School and Publishing Society, 1888.

RUSSELL, CHARLES EDWARD. *A-Raftin' on the Mississip'*. New York: Century Co., *Ca.* 1928.

SCANLAN, PETER LAWRENCE. *Prairie du Chien: French, British, American.* Privately pub., 1937.

SCHOOLCRAFT, HENRY R. *Information Respecting the History, Condition and Prospects of the Indian Tribes of the United States: Collected and Prepared Under the Direction of the Bureau of Indian Affairs, Per Act of Congress of March 3d, 1847.* 6 vols. Philadelphia: Lippincott, Grambo, 1851–1857.

————. *Narrative Journal of Travels Through the Northwestern Regions of the United States Extending from Detroit Through the Great Chain of American Lakes to the Sources of the Mississippi River in the Year 1820.* Ed. by Mentor L. Williams. East Lansing: Michigan State College Press, 1953.

SNELLING, WILLIAM JOSEPH. *Tales of the Northwest.* Ed. by John T. Flanagan. Minneapolis: University of Minnesota Press, 1936.

STEVENS, JOHN H. *Personal Recollections of Minnesota and Its People and Early History of Minneapolis.* Minneapolis: Tribune Co., 1890.

UPHAM, WARREN, *et al. Minnesota in Three Centuries, 1655–1908.* 4 vols. Mankato: Minnesota Free Press, 1908.

VAN CLEVE, CHARLOTTE OUISCONSIN. *"Three Score Years and Ten": Life-Long Memories of Fort Snelling, and Other Parts of the West.* Minneapolis: Harrison and Smith, 1888.

WINCHELL, NEWTON H. *The Aborigines of Minnesota.* St. Paul: Minnesota Historical Society, 1911.

DOCUMENTS

AMERICAN STATE PAPERS, Important Documents and Dispatches which accompanied the message of the President of the United States of America, to both Houses of Congress, on the third of April 1798, Respecting the Differences between America and France, including instructions to the American envoy, and their entire correspondence with the Executive directory of France, together with the President's message to Congress on 19th March, 1798. United States Department of State.

U.S. COMMISSIONER OF INDIAN AFFAIRS. *Annual Report of the Commissioner of Indian Affairs to the Secretary of the Interior.* Washington: G.P.O., 1849, 1850, 1851, 1852, 1853, 1854, 1855, 1856, 1863, and 1866.

Acknowledgments

I would like to thank the Minnesota Historical Society for permission to publish Philander Prescott's recollections. I would also like to express my appreciation to the following: Mrs. Ralph O. Stratton of the Ontario County, New York, Historical Society; Benton H. Wilcox, librarian, State Historical Society of Wisconsin; Clyde C. Walton, state historian, Illinois State Historical Library; the Detroit Public Library; and the South Dakota State University Library.

DONALD DEAN PARKER

Index